D0944957

[illegible] [illegible] Garland 10/86

AN OLD PROVENÇAL PRIMER

AN OLD PROVENÇAL PRIMER

Nathaniel B. Smith
Thomas G. Bergin

GARLAND PUBLISHING, INC. • NEW YORK & LONDON
1984

PC
3223
.S65
1984

© 1984 Nathaniel B. Smith and Thomas G. Bergin
All rights reserved

Library of Congress Cataloging in Publication Data

Smith, Nathaniel B.
An Old Provençal primer.

Bibliography: p.
Includes index.
1. Provençal language—Grammar. I. Bergin, Thomas Goddard, 1904– . II. Title.
PC3223.S65 1984 449'.82421 83-48469
ISBN 0-8240-9030-6 (alk. paper)

GREENWOOD LIBRARY
LONGWOOD UNIVERSITY
REDFORD & RACE STREET
FARMVILLE, VA 23909

Cover design by Larry Walczak

Printed on acid-free, 250-year-life paper
Manufactured in the United States of America

For
ALL THE PLIMPTONS
with thanks for their patience
for many summers
NBS

To the memory of
BENJAMIN PARSONS BOURLAND
of Western Reserve University
master and friend
TGB

LONGWOOD LIBRARY
1000510646

CONTENTS

PREFACE

Today a medieval Romance idiom can, without evoking surprise, be treated as a synchronic linguistic entity of its own, not merely as a stage in the diachronic movement from Classical Latin toward the modern period. As much as for its origins and history and for the precocious and brilliant poetry which made it revered through the courts of Europe, the rich and harmonious language of the troubadours deserves study in its own right. Motives for studying Old Provençal are hence both linguistic and literary.

This grammar book is meant for students and scholars who wish to learn to read the troubadours' poetry, or to become familiar with the characteristics of this language for nonliterary purposes, or to consult a thorough reference grammar in order, for example, to determine whether a certain textual reading is grammatically usual or possible, or to compare features of Provençal to those of related languages. No such work can be termed "complete"; yet our aim has been to include more material (except on historical phonology) than our predecessors. Unless otherwise stated, our remarks concern the standard idiom of the "classical" lyric and narrative, more particularly of the late twelfth-century troubadours, with occasional observations involving other periods, dialectal features, and documents or charters. We have aimed to give the latest results of specialized research as well as summaries of well-known areas, and we have tried to bear in mind the differing linguistic preparations of the student, the general Romanist, and the Provençal specialist. Important concepts and terms are explained as needed, and grammatical discussions are comprehensive enough to avoid sending the reader constantly to other works. Today, the troubadours are more widely studied and their songs are more frequently heard in concerts and on recordings in English-speaking countries than ever before; therefore, a particular concern has been to portray pronunciation accurately and fully.

While raising pertinent and sometimes even controversial questions, we have not endeavored to answer them all; but we do describe almost all forms and most syntactical constructions that one is likely to encounter, along with the principles and linguistic framework which will facilitate the reader's own analyses in new situations. We have given frequent illustrative examples, always translated; but we intend no implication that exceptions and counter-examples cannot on occasion be found.

Rather than taking Latin as our starting point, as has been the usual practice in Provençal grammars, we give a synchronic description of the language of the troubadours. We have arranged our chapters in the order we recommend for class use, starting with pronunciation, then moving to the declinable parts of speech, the more complicated verb system, and finally general syntax. We have avoided footnotes, but give a fairly detailed bibliography keyed to the text for further study of specific points.

It is preferable that language and literature be studied concurrently. A grammar book becomes more meaningful when it confirms students' own insights or answers questions they have already posed. With nothing more than an understanding of the case system and some experience in another Romance Language, the beginner can read interesting texts. For such a program involving grammar and literature, two quarters or semesters will no doubt be required.

Our reading selections are in prose or in narrative verse, which are easier for the beginner than is the troubadours' poetry. However, since the troubadours are the usual focus of attention for Provençal studies and since regular references to the troubadours will stimulate the student's literary sensitivity, all illustrative quotations are from T.G. Bergin et al., *Anthology of the Provençal Troubadours*, 2nd ed., 2 vols. (New Haven: Yale University Press, 1973), to which all poem and line numbers refer. There is, however, no need to consult the *Anthology*, since quotations give sufficient context for linguistic purposes. We regard such illustrations as medieval artifacts revealing authentic Old Provençal constructions, without feeling bound to consider manuscript filiation in order to determine "correct" readings.

This book had its genesis in a series of handouts prepared by T.G. Bergin for his many Old Provençal classes over the years and then gathered together by him in 1973–74. This and much other material was reworked and expanded by N.B. Smith in 1977–83, in consultation with his former teacher, who also assumed primary responsibility for the readings and glossary.

We wish to express our gratitude to our own students, particularly to several of T.G. Bergin's former students for using his original materials in their own classes and encouraging his project, and to Maria Simonelli for offering suggestions at an early stage. The cohesiveness and linguistic accuracy of our work have profited very greatly over the past six years from the detailed and patient advice of M. Roy Harris, Frede Jensen, and Suzanne Fleischman. In addition, Diana T. Mériz, Thomas R. Hart, Elizabeth Wilson, and Raleigh Morgan, Jr., have been so kind as to comment on specific parts and aspects of the *Primer.* We are also grateful to Harry Williams, F.R.P. Akehurst, and Frank Chambers, who have used portions of our *Primer* in their classes and have given us pedagogically helpful advice which led, most notably, to the elimination of almost all the historical material that we had originally planned to include. We wish to thank all of these generous colleagues while disculpating them for responsibility for any errors and oversights that may remain.

We are also indebted to the faithful skills of Martha B. Smith, who typed most of the manuscript more than once, and to Connie McCall of Mulberry Studios, Cambridge, Mass., who painstakingly produced the final typescript. The Graduate School of Boston University kindly provided partial financing of the final typing. It was a pleasure to work with Gary Kuris, Senior Editor, Garland Publishing, Inc.; and although this volume is not formally part of the Garland Library of Medieval Literature, which is edited by James J. Wilhelm, we would also like to thank this former student of T.G. Bergin's, as well as Garland's vice-president Ralph Carlson, for their encouragement and support.

Boston, Massachusetts N.B.S.
Madison, Connecticut T.G.B.

NORMALIZED OP SPELLING

Where variant spellings coexist, in our discussions we shall adopt the following normalized system, which represents a compromise between historical principles, clarity, and the manuscripts' actual graphies.

b = /b/ (*balp* 'stammering')

c = /k/ except before *e* and *i* (*can* 'when,' not *quan*), including the result of CL *ca* (*castęl* 'castle,' not *chastel*)

ç = /s/ before *e* and *i*, when derived from *c* + *e* or *i* and when initial (*cima* 'top') or nonfinal after a consonant (*mercẹ* 'mercy')

ç = (*c* with cedilla) is not used

ch = /č/ (*fruch* 'fruit'); *ch* from *ct* or *c't* is used in preference to *it* (*fach* 'done,' not *fait*)

d = /d/ (*dǫt* 'dowry'); -*d*- is kept even where it can fall dialectally (*vida* 'life,' not *via*)

e = the usual result of tonic CL *ĕ* even where the diphthongized variant *ie* also exists (*vęlh* 'old,' not *vielh*)

g = /g/ before *a*, *o*, *u*, or a consonant (*gan* 'glove,' not *guan*), including the result of CL *ga* (*gauzir* 'to enjoy,' not *jauzir*); -*g*- is kept even where it can fall dialectally (*amiga* 'friend,' f., not *amia; regina* 'queen,' not *reïna*)

g = /ğ/ before *e* and *i* (*getar* 'to throw,' not *jetar*), even where some dialects have /i̯/ (*máger* 'greater,' not *máier*); for the result of *g'd* and *g't*, /ğ/ is used in preference to *id* (*fregẹt* 'cool,' not *freidet*); see also *tg*

gu = /g/ only before *e* and *i* (*guęrra* 'war')

h is not used except in *ch, lh, nh*

i = the vowel /i/ (*crit* 'cry')

= the semivowel /i̯/ (*paire* 'father,' *verai̯/a* 'true')

-is = final /i̯s/ or /-i̯s̮/, even where some dialects have /-i̯s̮/ represented in the spelling (thus we write *crẹis* 'grows,' not *creish*)

iss = intervocalic /i̯s/ derived from *ps* (*caissa* 'box), *sc* + *e* or *i* (*náisser* 'to be born'), *x* (*laissar* 'to leave'), /cty/ (*faissọn* 'manner'), /ssy/ (*baissar* 'to lower'), /sty/ (*angọissa* 'anguish'), or /sky/ (*faissa* 'band'). *Iss* is used even though some dialects have /i̯s̮/

iz = /i̯z/ derived from /nsy/ (*maizọn* 'house') or /sy/ (*baizar* 'to kiss'), even though some dialects have /i̯z̮/

j = /ğ/ before *a, o,* and *u* (*jọrn* 'day,' not *iorn* as in the manuscripts). *J* is used even where some dialects have /i̯/ (thus, we write *majọr* 'greater,' not *maior*). For the result of *g'd* and *g't* /ğ/ is preferred to *id* (*frejura* 'cold,' not *freidura; cujar* 'to believe,' not *cuidar*. See also *tj* k is not used

l = /l/ (*alba* 'dawn,' *abril* 'April'), even where many dialects have /u̯/; *ll* is not used

lh = /l̮/ (*filh* 'son')

m = /m/ (*semblar* 'to seem'), even where *n* is possible

n = /n/ (*nǫu* 'new')
  = /ŋ/ before /k/ and /g/ (*oncle* 'uncle')

-ṇ = unstable *n* (always so shown by us, though usually not to be pronounced; see 4.14)

nh = /n̮/ (*vinha* 'vine')

o = the usual result of tonic CL *ŏ* even where diphthongized variants also exist (*fǫlha* 'leaf,' not *fuęlha* or *fuǫlha*)

p = /p/ (*ǫrp* 'blind')

qu = /k/ before *e* or *i* (*qui* 'who,' not *qi* or *ki*; *can* 'when,' not *quan*)

r = /rr/ when initial (*rǫsa* 'rose')
  = /r/ when not initial (*cara* 'face,' *onọr* 'honor,' *tọr* 'tower')

rr = intervocalic /rr/ (*tęrra* 'earth')

s = nonintervocalic /s/ when not *c* or *-tz* (*sen* 'he feels;' *forsar* 'to force'; *amans* 'lover,' nom. sg.; *dọls* 'sweet')
  = intervocalic /s/ only after prefixes (*desús* 'above')
  = intervocalic /z/ elsewhere, i.e., when derived from intervocalic *s* and *ns* that were not before yod (*rǫsa* 'rose'), probably also by syntactical phonetics before a word beginning in a vowel (*las amairitz* 'the lovers,' f.); see also *iz*

s = nonintervocalic /z/ only by regressive assimilation, when *s* is etymological (*isla* 'island')

ss = intervocalic /s/ (*lassa* 'weary,' f.; *plassa* 'place'); see also *iss*

t = /t/ (*nut* 'naked')

tg = /ǧ/ before *e* and *i*, when derived from a group beginning in *t* or *d* (*mȩtge* 'doctor')

tj = /ǧ/ before *a*, *o*, *u*, when derived from a group beginning in *t* or *d* (*jutjar* 'to judge')

tz = final /-ts/ after a vowel or *r*, when derived from *c* + *i* or *e* (*patz* 'peace,' *partz* 'he tolerates'), from *c* + yod (*bratz* 'arm'), from *qu* + yod (*latz* 'snare'), from *t* + yod (*catz* 'he hunts,' *tȩrtz* 'third'), from *t* + *s* (*vendȩtz* 'you sell,' *vendutz* 'sold,' *partz* 'parts'), from *d* + -*s* (*nutz* 'naked,' *descǫrtz* 'discords;), or from *rg* or *r'g* before *e* or *i* (*sọrtz* 'he raises')

u = vocalic /ü/ (*mur* 'wall')
  = semivocalic /ü̯/ (*fuȩlha* 'leaf')
  = semivocalic /u̯/ (*mǫu* 'moves'; *mȩua* 'mine,' f.)

ui is retained even where it can reduce to *u* (*tuit* 'all,' m. nom. pl., not *tut*)

v = /v/ (*vida* 'life,' not *uida* as in the manuscripts); intervocalic -*v*- is kept even where it can fall dialectally (thus we write *Provensa*, not *Proensa*)

x is not used (*doncs* 'then,' not *doncx*)

y is not used (but note that in phonetic notation it represents Vulgar Latin yod) z = intervocalic /z/ if not spelled *s*. The chief sources for this /z/ are intervocalic -*d*- (*lauzar* 'to advise'), intervocalic *c* + *e* or *i* (*plazer* 'to please'), and intervocalic /ty/ (*prezar* 'to esteem'); we also use -*z*- in *s*/*z* preterits. See also *iz*

z = nonintervocalic *z* when not *s* (*zęl* 'zeal,' *quinze* 'fifteen'); see also -*tz*

We adopt the shorter form of groups of consonants which can become simplified or which can receive intercalated glide consonants, thus *tems* 'time' (not *temps*) and *domna* 'lady' (not *dompna*). Similarly we do not show superfluous etymological consonants, so write *semana* 'week' (not *setmana*). We write compounds like *midons* 'milady' and *jamais* 'ever' as one word.

Exceptions to all the foregoing conventions occur in quotations from literary texts, in tables, in lists of forms, in descriptions of variant or dialectal spellings, and for other special reasons.

Insofar as possible, we have followed the system of normalization proposed for the Corpus des Troubadours project (see our bibliography).

Unless otherwise specified, we cite declinable words in the oblique singular case, and adjectives in the masculine.

For the usual pronunciations of OP spellings, see 3.2 and 4.2.

ABBREVIATIONS, SYMBOLS, AND OTHER CONVENTIONS

A) Abbreviations

adj. = adjective
ant. = anterior
art. = article
CL = Classical Latin
cond. = conditional (A, 1 sg. in -*ria*; B, in -*ra*)
f. = feminine
fut. = future
impf. = imperfect
impv. = imperative
ind. = indicative
inf. = infinitive
m. = masculine
mf. = m. and f.
nom. = nominative, subject case
obl. = oblique, object case
OP = Old Provençal
part. = participle
pl. = plural (1 pl. = first person plural, etc.)
plupf. = pluperfect
pres. = present
pret. = preterit

pron. = pronoun
sg. = singular (1 sg. = first person singular)
subj. = subjunctive
vr. = reflexive (or other pronominal) verb

B) Symbols

·x (raised dot) = enclitic contraction (2.7)

x' (apostrophe) = proclitic contraction (2.7) and other elisions (2.8)

ẍ (dieresis) = a vowel in hiatus where it might otherwise be mistaken for a semivowel (see 3.10)

/ / = phonetic symbols are so enclosed; we will here use a broad phonetic notation, between the extremes of narrow phonetic notation and phonemic notation (for symbols representing individual sounds, see 3.2 and 4.2)

x̃ = a nasalized vowel

ẋ = 1) unstable *n*, 4.14 (always indicated in italics and charts)

2) closed *e* or *o* (usually indicated once per section for each word or root in italics or in charts, but not in quotations; not used if quality is unknown, ambiguous, or intermediate, but always indicated in phonemic notation or where it falls on a tonic syllable that would otherwise need to be shown with *x̂*, as described below; *ẋ* is normally not shown in unstressed vowels or before nasal consonants, where *e* and *o* are automatically closed, with a few exceptions before *n* and *nh*; and *ẋ* is not shown in the very frequent

infinitives ending in -*ẹr* and nouns and adjectives in suffixal -*ọr*, -*adọr*, -*edọr*, -*idọr*)

3) posterior *a* (shown only for special purposes)

x̦ = an open vowel (indicated as for *x̣*)

(x) = 1) an unstable consonant (other than *ṇ*) which may fall in certain circumstances (shown only for special purposes)

2) any letter, phoneme, prefix, or other element whose presence is optional or dialectal in a given word

3) a prefix in a compound whose simple form is less common

x́ = a tonic vowel (always indicated in phonetic notation, but shown in OP words only when relevant to the discussion at hand or when stress deviates from the rules given in 2.5; however, the tonic vowel will not be shown as *x́* when shown by the diacritical marks *x̣* and *x̦*)

x̀ = a secondarily stressed vowel (indicated only when relevant to the discussion; see 2.4)

x̭ = semivocalic (indicated always in phonemic notation, but in actual spellings only when relevant to the discussion at hand)

x͡y = two adjoining vowels normally in hiatus, but exceptionally considered as forming one syllable

x̮ = a completely or partially palatalized consonant

x-	= absolutely initial in the word (*i*- = initial *i*)
-x-	= intervocalic (-*s*- = intervocalic *s*)
-x	= absolutely final in the word (-*s* = final *s*)
∅	= zero ending (i.e., no inflection); or, a dropped sound or letter
-	= 1) division between syllables; *tra-ïr* 'to betray' 2) division between a prefix and a root whose simple form does not exist: *au-cire* 'to kill'
/	= division between a base form and an added inflection or suffix: *franc/a* 'noble,' m. and f. sg.; *alcan(t)/ẹt* 'some; a little'
<	= (is) derived from
>	= becomes, is the source of
+	= preceding, added to
*	= after a verb, shows that the paradigm is given among the special verbs in chapter 11 (only used in chapter 10)
~	= in alternation with, in contrast to
=	= is the same as, equals, represents

C) Other Conventions

Quotations from the *Anthology* of Bergin *et al.* are identified by poem number and line number, separated by a colon (thus, 1:1-7). Such quotations are reproduced exactly, except that we have used the raised dot where some texts have a period, hyphen, or colon; moreover, we begin all full lines of poetry with a capital letter, and omit the additional spacing that is used to show internal rhymes.

Sections of this *Primer* are identified by chapter and section, separated by periods (e.g., 5.3 or 5.4.1); subsections are shown, e.g., as 12.8,A or 12.8,A1.

All quotations from the *Anthology*, along with other real or imagined quotations illustrating points under consideration, are given in double quotation marks. But we italicize words and expressions that are cited or listed, as well as single-word quotations that belong to a list of italicized terms.

We give, enclosed in single quotation marks, translations of all Provençal words and quotations, but only once per section for each, and often excepting the commonest terms such as articles, some prepositions, and a few verbs.

Tables give forms in their order of frequency, insofar as possible; forms following a semicolon or in parentheses are infrequent.

In the exercises, the reader need not supply diacritical marks unless specifically asked to do so, even though for the sake of completeness we often supply them in our answers.

1
THE HISTORY AND CHARACTER OF OLD PROVENÇAL

Occitan, or Provençal, is the indigenous language of roughly the southern third of France. It is today spoken or understood by several million persons, mostly in rural or mountainous areas, including some valleys on the Italian side of the Alps. Since the fifteenth century, Occitan has been gradually losing ground in favor of French. But until then it was the sole maternal language of the entire native population. Aside from its intrinsic linguistic interest and beauty, it is widely known and studied for its rich contributions to literature.

This language was variously and concurrently identified in the Middle Ages, first as *lenga romana* or simply *roman* in the sense of 'vernacular'; as *lemosin* from about 1200 and *pro(v)ensal* from about 1280, after the name of the areas called Limousin and Provence; and from 1290 as *lenga d'oc*, from the affirmative particle *ǫc* in contrast to French *oïl* (*oui*) and Italian *sì*. The term Provençal, predominant from the sixteenth century on and particularly in the nineteenth-century literary revival, has generally been retained to designate the language of the troubadours. The usual pronunciation is /pRǫvãsál/ as in French, though some American scholars prefer the anglicized pronunciation /prəvę́ntsəl/. Neither of these, however, represents the native pronunciation, which is medieval standard /prọvẹntsál/ > /pruvẹnsál/ and modern /pruvẹnsál/ in central Languedoc, /pruvẹ̃ŋsáu̯/ in Provence proper, etc.

As the name of today's language, "Occitan" now prevails among scholars. This is not, as sometimes alleged, a recent neologism, but rather is first attested around 1300 under the form *occitanus*, a crossing of *oc* and *aquitanus* "Aquitanian." We will here use the following terminology and chronology for the stages of the language:

to ca. 500	Vulgar Latin
ca. 500 to ca. 800	Gallo-Romance
ca. 800 to ca. 1000	Early Provençal
ca. 1000 to ca. 1350	Old Provençal (OP)
ca. 1350 to ca. 1550	Middle Occitan
ca. 1550 to present	Modern Occitan

Reasons for the linguistic individuality of Occitan are multiple. The prehistoric populations such as Ligurians, Iberians, and Celts constituted a unique substratum influencing the development of Latin, which was introduced when the Roman conquest began in 122 B.C. Romanization lasted longer and was more intensive in southern Gaul than in the North, though the Gaulish language may have survived as late as the fifth century, while Basque, centered in the northwestern Pyrenees, remains today.

"Vulgar Latin" is a somewhat misleading term traditionally designating the Latin spoken in most of the declining Roman Empire. Never a unified phenomenon even in Italy, Vulgar Latin took on slightly differing characteristics in each province. Then--during the period usually called Gallo-Romance for the territories corresponding more or less to today's France--the North of Gaul, under the influence of a strong Germanic superstratum, diverged linguistically more and more from the South, and both moved farther away from Latin. By the end of the eighth century, we can refer to a Provençal language whose speakers, unless they had special training, probably understood neither Latin nor French. "Early Provençal" refers to the preliterary period, during which still only Latin was written. A significant turning point is marked by the Council of Tours, which in 813 recognized that Latin was no longer understood by the masses and proclaimed that sermons should be translated "into the rustic Roman or German tongues." No doubt, the ninth and tenth centuries produced Provençal religious works, such as hymns and liturgical dramas, which were not written down.

Then, heralded by isolated vernacular works inserted into some late tenth-century Latin oaths of fidelity, and a bilingual *alba*, the OP period began with the *Boeci* (a fragmentary translation of Boethius' *De Consolatione* and the oldest known rhymed poetry in a Romance Language) and the life of *Sancta Fides*, preserved in manuscripts probably of the first and second thirds of the eleventh century, respectively. Some religious poems from St. Martial of Limoges date from the same century; seven of the eight surviving literary manuscripts before 1200 are religious in nature. French has earlier texts, but of all the Romance Languages OP has the most documents--charters, deeds, oaths, etc.--before 1200, including one from 1102 and sixteen others from before about 1120. Provençal seems to have enjoyed a head start of about a century over its sister languages as regards official use of the vernacular for administrative and legal purposes. This is probably because its municipal institutions were developed early, its commercial interchanges were active, and its feudal structures relatively weak.

The eleventh- and twelfth-century manuscripts, whether literary or utilitarian, show some traits of different dialects: Limousin, Auvergnat, Provençal, Alpine Provençal, Languedocian, and the particularly individualistic Gascon. However, Latinizing habits, regional scribal schools whose practices often influenced adjoining dialect areas, and flourishing interregional trade and communications tended to counteract the forces favoring dialectal divergence. A koine--a unified "standard" language--may have existed for administrative purposes (pro: Bec, *Langue occitane*, pp. 73-76; contra: Grafström, *Morphologie*, pp. 171-172).

For literary purposes, such a koine was certainly used by the troubadours and was well understood in court circles from about 1100 on, at a time when French literature retained a marked dialectal fragmentation. Unfortunately, the troubadours' poetry has not come down to us in the most reliable of texts.

After or during a period of oral transmission, the intervention of several generations of scribes transformed to some extent the troubadours' own spellings, certain words and grammatical constructions, and even whole lines. Some of these variations go back as far as the troubadours themselves, who apparently often issued different versions of their own texts. The poems now survive in fewer than a hundred often fragmentary medieval *chansonniers* or anthologies compiled from the mid thirteenth century onward, four-fifths of them copied in Italy, Catalonia, or northern France. Furthermore, we have music for only about one-tenth of the songs, and even then the rhythmic values are not indicated.

At the least, the syllable count of each line and the rhymes among lines indicate the troubadours' own linguistic practices. And these features betray only a small number of dialectal traits, such as a few Poitevinisms in William IX. The existing medieval OP grammars--Raimon Vidal de Besalu's *Razos de trobar*, ca. 1200, Uc Faidit's *Donatz Proensals*, ca. 1240, and several others--show a high degree of linguistic standardization. It is significant that these are all written for Catalans or Italians, hence for foreigners. A Provençal grammar for natives was not felt to be needed till Guilhem Molinier composed the *Leys d'amors* in the 1330's; by then, the prestige of the literary koine had deteriorated to the extent that these precepts, intended for poets competing in an annual contest in Toulouse, were based on the idiom of that city. The triumph of dialectalisms in that manual and in literature, along with their rapid extension in the spoken tongue, marked the transition to the Middle Occitan period.

OP, like most languages, comprised several sociolinguistic levels of usage, which might be schematized as follows:

	local	*regional*	*supra-regional*	*standardized*
spontaneous	sub-dialects	dialects	trade, religion, etc.	
formal		documents	non-lyric literature: administrative koine?	literary koine

It is within this type of complex framework that we speak of "popular" words, those which have followed normal phonetic evolution, usually on the local or regional level; and "learnèd" words, whose evolution has been slowed down by Latinizing analogies or which have been directly borrowed from Latin or Greek. Even in the troubadours, few words can be considered learnèd; and the clerical influence is far less strong on OP than on Old French. Still, the formal language is certainly more conservative--more held back by learnèd models--than the spontaneous spoken idiom, and the troubadours' koine is a relatively sophisticated class idiom which might well have been hard to follow for the twelfth-century peasant.

In the present work, the unqualified term "OP" will designate the troubadours' koine. Through their originality and style, their varied genres and types of versification, their ideal of perfect rhyme and of linguistic exactitude, their classical conception of poetry as a craft, and their exaltation of *fin' amors* ('courtly love'), they made OP the first Romance Language to be codified in grammar books and the first to be "exported" into foreign areas: Catalan lyric poets wrote in OP from 1150 on, and some north Italian ones from about 1200 on.

The geographical basis of this koine has been a subject of controversy. The acceptance of contrasting features, as in *chan* or *can* 'song' and *fach* or *fait* 'done,' makes localization difficult. Earlier scholars believed in the primacy of Poitou, which produced William IX, or of the Limousin, homeland of many troubadours and source of the term *lemosin* for the language. However, Poitevin, already then a transitional dialect soon to fall into the French orbit, and Limousin, which shows important divergences from the troubadours' texts, are linguistically unsuitable for this role. Recent investigations by Pfister and Rohr have bolstered the opinion of Jeanroy (*Poésie lyrique*, I, 46) and others, pointing to a more central geographical basis, namely Languedoc. It now seems probable that the territory bounded approximately by the major cities of Toulouse, Cahors, Rodez, Montpellier, Béziers, and Narbonne, the source of a majority of the early documents and much of the literary tradition, also provided the base of the troubadours' koine and of an administrative koine if there was one.

The exact relation of OP to the other Romance Languages has been much debated. With Old French it shares the two-case system, the general loss of final vowels except -*a*, and the shift of *u* from /u/ to /ü/. OP lies between French and the other Romance Languages with respect to preservation of proparoxytons, reduction of other unstressed syllables, and weakening of intervocalic consonants. It has less diphthongization of tonic /ę/ and /ǫ/ than French, Spanish, or Italian, but more than Catalan. Its vocabulary, like that of Catalan and Italian, largely reflects the traditional Romance stock and lacks most of the numerous Germanic and Arabic loan words taken in respectively by French and Spanish.

Traditionally, Occitan has been considered part of a Gallo-Romance group along with French, Franco-Provençal, and Rheto-Romance; Gascon is also included by those who term it a separate language rather than an Occitan dialect. However, many far-reaching deviations set French quite far apart from the other three idioms. By its general phonological and lexical conservatism, Occitan is much closer to the Mediterranean languages, in particular to Catalan, which adjoins it along a line slightly east of the southeastern Pyrenees. From the characterization of Catalan as a "bridge-language" between Gallo-Romance and Ibero-Romance, it was only a short step to propose an "Occitano-Romance" family, itself a bridge between the other two. Occitano-Romance, according to P. Bec (*Langue occitane*, p. 53; *Manuel*, pp. 2-3), includes Catalan, Occitan, and Gascon. The affinity of these three idioms, very strong in the Middle Ages, has since then been somewhat weakened by Castilian and French hegemony. Still,

Occitan and Catalan today are to a striking degree mutually comprehensible, while Occitan and French, or Catalan and Castilian, are not.

2
OP PRONUNCIATION AND ORTHOGRAPHY: GENERAL

2.1 Phonetics, Phonology, and Phonemes

The sounds produced by the voice can be classified in three types. In vowels, air passes without obstruction through the buccal cavity. In semivowels, parts of the lower and the upper portions of the buccal cavity almost touch, producing a vocalic sound of reduced clarity incapable of forming an independent syllable. (We will use the adjective "vocalic" to refer to both vowels and semivowels.) In consonants, parts of the top and bottom of the buccal cavity either touch or are so close as to produce a sound of rushing, hissing, or the like.

In nasalized vowels and nasal consonants, the airstream in part resonates in the nasal cavities and flows out through the nose; all other sounds are known as "oral."

Phonology is the study of sounds in relation to their function in a given language. A phoneme is a sound or group of sounds having a distinctive function. In OP, *amar* 'to love' and *anar* 'to go' are separate words, forming a minimal pair distinguished only by the difference between *m* and *n*; hence, *m* and *n* are different phonemes in OP. Allophones, variants of a single phoneme, are found in complementary distribution as dictated by their context. For example, OP /ŋ/ and /n/ are allophones: /ŋ/ occurs before /g/ and /k/ (*angle* 'corner,' *anc* 'ever') and /n/ everywhere else.

We will be indicating OP pronunciation by using a broad phonetic notation, with symbols enclosed between slash marks.

2.2 Evidence for OP Pronunciation

The pronunciation represented by the manuscript spellings can generally be quite well determined from the following types of evidence:

1) variations and evolution in spelling; e.g., when *se*, *si*,begin to replace *ce*, *ci*, we know that /ts/ > /s/;

2) comparison to Classical, Vulgar, and Medieval Latin;

3) the form of OP names and words in Latin and other documents;

4) comparison to other Romance Languages;

5) OP rhymes, as well as assonances in some of the earlier works;

6) the metrics of OP verse;

7) rhyme dictionaries and grammars written in the OP period;

8) spellings using non-OP conventions (e.g., *ci* and *gl* for *ch* and *lh* in OP texts copied in Italy) or non-Latin letters;

9) the form in which OP words are borrowed by other languages and vice versa;

10) subsequent development into modern Occitan.

Nevertheless, problems in interpreting OP spelling arise from the following factors:

1) Although the troubadours composed in an artificially unified literary language, traces of individual dialects and earlier chronological stages persist, so that some words may have two or more possible forms corresponding to different pronunciations, e.g., *nǫch*, *nǫit*, *nuęch*, *nuęit*, etc. 'night.'

2) A troubadour's own spelling or pronunciation may be deformed by successive scribes.

3) No truly consistent orthographic system existed; even within one dialect or manuscript, a single sound may be represented in various ways (e.g., *senhor*, *seignor*, etc. 'lord') and several sounds may be represented by one spelling (e.g., *c* as /ts/ > /s/ and as /k/).

4) Troubadour manuscripts, unlike some early non-troubadour writings, lack diacritical marks showing where tonic stress falls.

5) Pronunciation evolves somewhat during the OP period, while spelling in general does not.

Fortunately for the reader of this *Primer*, the sounds of OP almost all exist in English, and letters are spoken "as they look" far more than in many modern languages. The only frequent silent letter is *h*.

2.3 Spelling Conventions

In OP the letters *k* and *w* are rare, except for *ki* and *ke* occasionally replacing *qui* and *que* 'who, whom' and a few oddities like *dukęssa* (26:37) for *duquessa* 'duchess.' *X* is almost always, and *z* usually, final in the word. *Y* is often but not consistently used, with the value if *i*, where the single vertical stroke of *i* might have been hard to distinguish from surrounding letters, or in final position. Similarly, *j* and *v* are mere orthographical variants of *i* and *u*. The only diacritical marks employed in OP were the cedilla in ç (originally *cz*) representing /ts/ > /s/ before *a*, *o*, *u* or when final; and the acute accent marking tonic stress.

Punctuation in OP manuscripts is generally restricted to a dot separating verses of poetry or, in prose, clauses or sentences. A slash mark is occasionally used where today we would put a comma or a hyphen. Words are often run together, particularly where short words like articles and prepositions are concerned. Medieval scribes used certain abbreviations, such as q^{i} = *qui* 'who'; q̄ = *que* 'that'; ꝑ = *per* 'for'; and ml't = *molt* 'much.' The superscript bar represents *m* or *n*: nō = *noṇ* 'not,' mēbrāsa = *membransa* 'memory.'

There are two basic types of edition. Diplomatic editions use various typographic symbols to approximate the exact graphic conventions of a single manuscript, while critical editions resolve abbreviations, use modern punctuation and separate most run-together words. Most critical editions reserve *j* and *v* for consonantal sounds and use *i* and *u* only for vowels and semivowels. For conventions regarding hiatus and elision, see 2.6-7. Critical editions also generally take into account the "reliability" of various manuscripts, choose one "base manuscript," and make emendations or choose readings from other manuscripts as felt appropriate to arrive at a version thought to be closer to a lost "original" or "archetype."

2.4 Stress

There are three degrees of stress or intensity, that is, the expiratory force--often with lengthened duration--with which vowels are pronounced:

1) The tonic vowel, the most prominent in a word, carries the principal stress, which we mark as needed with an acute accent. Words comprise three classes, according to which syllable has the principal stress: oxytons are stressed on the final syllable (*a-míc* 'friend,' m.), paroxytons on the penultimate (next-to-last) syllable (*a-mí-ga* 'friend,' f.), and proparoxytons on the antepenultimate (*lá-gre-ma* 'tear'). For adverbs in *-men(t)*, cf. 3.4.

2) A secondary stress, which can be indicated by the grave accent, affects the initial syllable in a word (*càn-tár* 'to sing') and/or a syllable that would be tonic if it were not part of a longer word (thus, *-zi* in *vè-zì-ne-tát* 'neighborhood'). In addition, prefixes carry their own secondary stress (*rè-clà-már* 'to invoke').

3) Other vowels are atonic, with no stress at all; these can be intertonic, like *-ne* in *vèzìnetát*, or penultimate or final like *-gre-* and *-ma* in *lágrema*.

The term "stressed" indicates tonic syllables; and "unstressed," all others. Pretonic syllables precede the tonic syllable, posttonic ones follow it, and intertonic syllables come between a secondary and a tonic stress.

Some early nontroubadour manuscripts use the acute accent to show tonic stress, the stronger element in a diphthong, or a vowel in hiatus; otherwise, the modern reader must rely on linguistic analysis to determine these characteristics.

OP stress is a distinctive feature, that is, it can distinguish two words that are otherwise identical (ignoring any differences in vowel quality that are due precisely to the differing stress). Thus we find *cántan* 'they sing' ~ *cantán* 'singing'; *partirá*, 3 sg. future ~ *partíra*, 1 and 3 sg. conditional B, from *partir* 'to leave'; *vías* 'ways' ~ *viás* (*viatz*) 'quickly'; and *quęri*, 1 sg. present indicative (alternate form) ~ *querí*, 1 and 3 sg. preterit, from *quęrre* 'to seek.'

2.5 OP Stress: Specific Rules

A) Words ending in a vowel, a vowel plus *s*, or a flectional -*n* are stressed on the penultimate syllable: *fílha* 'daughter,' *cánta* 'he sings,' *cantaría* 'he would sing,' *máire* 'mother,' *empęri* 'empire'; *fílhas* 'daughters,' *cántas* 'you sing'; *áman*, *ámoṇ* 'they love,' *cantávan* 'they were singing,' *cantęron* 'they sang.'

Exceptions:

1) The 2 and 3 sg. and 3 pl. of the future in all verbs and the 1 and 3 sg. of the preterite in I-verbs are stressed on the final syllable: *cantará* 'he will sing,' *vendrás* 'you will sell,' *partirán* 'they will leave'; *partí* 'I left, he left.'

2) A few words are stressed on a final syllable that ends in a vowel or a vowel plus *s* and that was

originally a monosyllabic word or root: *aquí* 'here,' *açǫ́* 'that,' *desvá* 'vanishes,' *desús* 'above.'

3) A few other words end in a stressed vowel or vowel plus *s*: *mercẹ́* 'mercy,' *Jaufrẹ́* (a proper name), *cortẹ́s* 'courteous,' and words with the suffixes *-ẹ́s*, *-ás*, *-ís*.

4) The large number of oxytons ending in unstable *n* have a final stressed vowel when the *-n* is not shown: *certá* 'certain,' *sovẹ́* 'he remembers,' etc.

5) Such learnèd proparoxytons as *lágrema* 'tear,' *mónegue* 'monk,' and *glę́zia* 'church' preserve their original stress. (Further development also yields paroxytonic variants: *larme*, *mongue*, *gl̨eiza*.)

B) Words ending in a consonant (other than flectional *n* or postvocalic *s*) or in a diphthong or triphthong are stressed on the final syllable: *amíc* 'friend,' *cavál* 'horse,' *amám* 'we love,' *cantę́s* (1 and 3 sg. imperfect subjunctive of *cantar*), *amọ́r* 'love,' *amátz* 'you love,' *verái* 'true,' *cant(i)ę́i* 'I sang.' This group includes words ending in stable *n* before an unstable *-t*, whether or not the *t* is shown, thus *cantán(t)*, *cantán* 'singing' and all other present participles; *fermamén(t)*, *fermamén* 'firmly' and all adverbs with this suffix; and some other words like *sovén(t)*, *sovén* 'often.' It also includes the many oxytons ending in unstable *n* when the *n* is shown: *albespín̩* 'hawthorn,' *razón̩* 'reason,' *Marcabrún̩* (proper name), etc.

Exceptions:

1) A number of words ending in *-er* stress the penult:

mǫ́lher 'woman' (nom. sg.), *Rǫ́zer* 'Rhone,' *sénher* 'lord' (nom. sg.), *sǫ́zer* 'father-in-law,' and infinitives such as *plánher* 'to lament' and *vǫ́lver* 'to turn.'

2) So too a few words ending in unstable nonflectional *n* or a few other consonants; *jọ́veṇ* 'young,' *frẹ́vol* 'weak,' *ávol* 'vile,' *apǫ́stol* 'pope,' *catǫ́lic* 'Catholic,' *prînce(p)* 'prince.'

C) We shall use the acute accent from now on to indicate stress only for the exceptions listed above. Thus we will write *cantas* but 2 sg. future *cantarás*; we write *certaṇ* but *certá*; *soveṇ* 'he remembers' and *soven* 'often' are both oxytons; *aman* and *amoṇ* 'they love' are paroxytons because their *-n* is flectional, but *aman* 'loving' is an oxyton because present participles have an underlying unstable *-t*.

Whenever the tonic vowel is an *e* or *o*, however, the two subscripts, which show vowel quality at the same time, will suffice to indicate the stressed vowel. Thus, we write not *cortẹ́s* but simply *cortẹs*.

OP stress almost always falls on the same syllable as in the equivalent word of other Romance Languages, since the Latin stress pattern is largely continued.

2.6 *Syllabification*

An OP syllable normally consists of a monophthong (i.e., a single vowel sound), a diphthong, or a triphthong, preceded, when not initial in a word, by a consonant or group of consonants, thus *ra-ma* 'branch,' *pai-re* 'father,' *grieu-men* 'gravely.' Such syllables ending in a "free" vowel sound are called "open." Digraphs representing one sound naturally also allow the preceding syllable to remain open: *fa-chu-ra* 'form,' *pla-ssa* 'place,' *ma-lha* 'mail.' Similarly, the groups *b, d, f, g, k, p, t,* or *v* plus *l* or *r* are syllable-initial: *fẹ-ble* 'weak,' *ma-gre* 'thin.' On the other hand, a vowel is "blocked" and the syllable is said to be "closed" before other pairs of consonants, in which case the first consonant goes with the first syllable and the second with the second syllable, thus *em-pe-ra-dor* 'emperor,' *con-tra-da* 'country,' *sir-ven-tẹs* (a genre). If there are three consonants, the middle one goes with the third if they can form a syllable-initial group (*ọl-tra* 'beyond'), otherwise with the first (*sanc-nar* 'to bleed'). If a final syllable ends in a consonant, it is also, perforce, closed.

When two adjoining vowels form two syllables rather than a diphthong, most editions use a dieresis (3.10), thus *traïr* 'to betray' ~ *trair(e)* 'to draw.' To show such cases of hiatus, the manuscripts sometimes insert a silent *h*, as in *trahir*.

2.7 Proclitics and Enclitics

Clitics are unstressed words, generally monosyllables, which the speech rhythm attaches as proclitics to the following word or as enclitics to the preceding word. In direct contact with a vowel (but usually not after a semivowel), clitics normally lose their syllabic status, their own vowel being reduced to a semivowel or else elided.

Contracted proclitics are followed by an apostrophe ("l'amors" 'love' for "la amors"), while contracted enclitics are preceded by a raised dot or sometimes a hyphen ("no·l sap" 'he does not know it' for "no lo sap"). Between two vowels, clitics are preferably attached to the word to which they are the most closely related grammatically, thus "ma domna m'am" 'my lady loves me,' but "Di·m en Richart" 'Tell Sir Richard for me' (76:50). However, editorial practice varies and we find, e.g., "ma domna·m am." Elision in enjambment between two lines is rare (e.g., 107:13-14).

Clitics include articles, personal and neuter pronouns, the conjunction and pronoun *que*, possessive adjectives, prepositions, conjunctions, and a few other words such as the titles *En*, *N'*, *·N* 'Lord' and *Na*, *N'* 'Lady' (which can be considered "personal articles").

2.8 Metrical Scansion

OP verse is metrically structured according to the number of syllables per line, which the troubadours counted with utmost care. Lines of ten syllables dominate in the epic and lines of eight in narrative, while the lyric prefers seven, eight, and ten but admits from one to fourteen. The number of syllables can vary from one line to the next, but since the form and melody (excepting probably musical rhythm) are identical in all stanzas of almost all genres, the number of syllables must be the same in corresponding lines of different stanzas. If in a given line the number of syllables is not clear, one may refer to the lines in the same position in other stanzas. Tornadas (shorter metrical segments at the end of the poem) have the same meter and rhymes as the last part of the last stanza.

Different manuscripts often give differing numbers of syllables for the same line of a poem. The modern editor generally chooses a reading having the syllable count required by the poem's form, and will emend the line if no manuscript is satisfactory, under the assumption that deviation is due to scribes, not to the troubadour. The manner of transmission actually makes it impossible to know whether the troubadours themselves occasionally took liberties with the syllable count. The place of the cesura (a pause within a line) can vary, particularly in shorter lines, but the divisions 4/6 and 6/6 are usual.

Final unstressed -*a* or -*e* is normally elided before a word beginning with a vowel, unless a pause or line end intervenes. Manuscripts generally omit an elided vowel, whose place editions indicate by an apostrophe, e.g., with 3 sg. -*a* elided: "Mas lo mieus chans comens' aissi" 'But my song begins thus' (25:5). Even if the vowel remains written out, it generally has no phonetic value and does not form a diphthong with the following vowel.

However, if needed metrically, a vowel in this situation remains syllabic, thus forming hiatus. Inconsistency can occur even within one poem or different renditions of one line; for example, "E·l pair'adusia l'essermen" 'And his father brought the kindling' (26:10) has elision of *paire*, but -*e* counts as a syllable in "En son paire ac bon sirven" 'In his father, there was a good servant' (26:7).

Tonic vowels are not elided: "Lai on anc dol non ac ni aurá íra" 'There where pain never was nor will sadness be' (75:40). Apheresis--the elision of initial vowels--is rare: "so·s tresors" 'it is a treasure' (69:39), "Si 'naissi m'aucis" 'If you kill me thus' (57:28), "m'a 'nvazida" 'he has attacked me' (17:34). In order to avoid hiatus, a few words optionally have a final dental consonant: *e(t)*, *ez*, *ed* 'and,' *a(d)*, *az* 'to,' *ǫ(z)*, *od* 'or,' *que(z)*, *qued* 'that,' all probably pronounced with /z/. Thus, we usually find "e leis" 'and her' but often "ez ieu" 'and I.'

In describing metrical form, one does not count the "feminine" syllables that follow the last stressed vowel in a line. Hence, a heptasyllable can actually contain eight syllables, though still described as seven or, to be more precise, 7+, as in "Farai chansoneta nueva" 'I will make a new song' (5:1).

2.9 Rhyme

For the troubadours, the art of rhyming is a challenge which confers more prestige as the rhymes become rarer and harder to find. Generally the epic is composed in stanzas of variable length, the narrative in rhymed couplets, and the lyric in stanzas of fixed length within a given poem. Lyric stanzas, generally from five to seven per poem, are frequently identical to each other (*cọblas unissonans*); occasionally, rhymes change every two stanzas (*coblas dọblas*) or in other more imaginative permutations.

The troubadours' rhymes demand identity of at least the first of the following, with increasing richness the more elements are added:

1) tonic vowels: *latî / s'aisî* (7:3-5)

2) pretonic semivowels or consonants: *nuęva / pluęva* (5:1-2), *brisa / prisa* (12:7-9)

3) consonants or semivowels after the tonic vowel: *covinen / sen* (2:1-2), *au / chevau* (3:4-6), *natz / iratz* (3:7-8)

4) feminine vowel endings: *duptansa / comensansa* (12:1-2)

5) rarely, consonants following a posttonic vowel: *siscles / giscles* (43:5-6)

Troubadour rhymes are almost always perfect. Occasionally, dialectal variants like -*au* for -*al* or most notably -*ai̯a* for -*aja* are exploited; and rhymes between *ę* and *ẹ* or *ǫ* and *ọ* do occur, especially in Catalan troubadours, as in *lęis* 'her' rhymed with *lẹis* 'laws.' It is, however, hard to distinguish between acceptable dialectal variation, poetic license, and error. Clear-cut poetic license, such as *iọves* (136:29) rhymed with words in -*ẹs*, is rare.

In schematizing metrical form, masculine (oxytonic) rhymes are represented by small letters and feminine (paroxytonic) rhymes by capitals, italics, letters plus apostrophes, or prime letters. Thus the first stanza of No. 5 can be expressed as A7+ A7+ A7+ b7 A7+ b8 and the second as C7+ C7+ C7+ b7 C7+ b8. In assonance, used in some early narrative and epic poems, the tonic vowels, and posttonic ones if any, are the same, but the following, intervening or preceding consonants need not be.

Chapter 2: Exercises

(In these and all exercises, the literary quotations contain spellings that do not necessarily conform to our system of normalization.)

A. (2.5) By citing the equivalent word in another Romance Language or Latin, indicate the OP tonic stress

1. doussa 'sweet' (f. sg.)
2. estoria 'history'
3. sozer 'father-in-law'
4. cortes 'courtly'

B. By following the rules given in 2.5, indicate the stressed vowels

1. jo canti, tu cantas, el canta, nos cantam, vos cantatz, ilh cantan (pres. ind. of *cantar*, with alternative form in 1 sg.)
2. Guilhem Comte de Peiteus, Bernart de Ventadorn, Raïmbaut d'Aurenga, Folquet de Marselha, Lanfranc Cigala, Cerveriṇ de Girona (all troubadours)
3. alba, cansoṇ, dansa, descort, pastorela, tensoṇ (poetic genres)

C. (2.7-8) In the following lines, cross out the vowels which should normally be elided, and state the resulting number of syllables

1. Mas aitan fera estranheza ha longuamen
2. Que si el lo tenia un an que ieu lo tengues mais de cen
3. Que ieu anc no lo agui en poder
4. En cest sonet coinde e leri

D. (2.8) Assuming elision wherever possible, even though not reflected in the spelling, how many syllables do the following lines contain?

1. Tant fina amors cum cella qu'el cor m'intra
2. E·m fon hom ma terra e la m'art
3. De tal guisa que no·m puoscha aiudar

3

VOWELS AND SEMIVOWELS

3.1 The OP Vocalic System: Technical Description

OP vocalic sounds can be described according to the following factors:

A) Aperture, the degree to which the tongue approaches the top of the mouth

1) Semivowels lie between consonants and high vowels

2) Vowels come in four degrees:

a) High: the mouth is relatively closed, the tongue relatively raised

b) Mid-high: between high and low, but nearer high

c) Mid-low: between mid-high and low

d) Low: the mouth is relatively open, the tongue flat

B) Point of articulation

1) Front (anterior, palatal): the tongue is raised in the middle to approach the palate

2) Back (posterior, velar): the tongue is raised at the back to approach the velum

C) Position of the lips:

1) Rounded (labialized)

2) Non-rounded

These characteristics are illustrated by the following "vowel trapezoid," which should be imagined superimposed onto a cross-section of a head facing left:

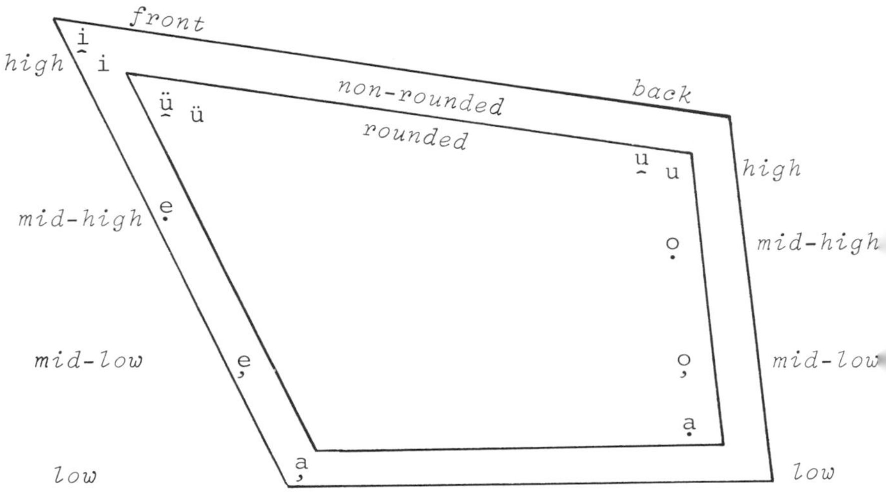

3.2 The Usual Pronunciation of Spelling for Vowels and Semivowels

Here are the most frequent correspondences of written symbols to actual sounds for late twelfth-century vowels and semivowels:

y = /i̯/: jǫy 'joy'
i = /i̯/: joi 'joy'
= /i/: filh 'son'
e = /ẹ/ (closed *e*): beṇ 'well,' sẹr 'evening'
= /ę/ (open *e*): fęr 'iron'
a = /ą/ (anterior *a*): mą 'my' (f. sg.)
= /ạ/ (posterior *a*): mạṇ 'hand'

o	=	/ǫ/	(open *o*): pǫrt 'port'
	=	/ọ/	(closed *o*): bọṇ 'good,' fọrca 'fork'
u	=	/u/	cubrir 'cover,' dunc 'then'
	=	/u̯/	viu 'alive'
	=	/ü/	pur 'pure'
	=	/ü̯/	füec 'fire'

These OP sounds are capable of distinguishing minimal pairs and are hence phonemic, except for /ü̯/ (see 3.8). The vowels are "pure," lacking the *y* or *w* glide that often follows English vowels. The OP literary language probably lacks perceptibly nasalized vowels. The distinction between /ę/ and /ẹ/ and between /ǫ/ and /ọ/ is one of aperture; however, the distinction between /ą/ and /ạ/ is one of position: /ą/ has the tongue raised toward the palate and /ạ/ toward the velum.

We will use the two subscript marks to indicate the quality of stressed *e* and *o*, subject to the restrictions shown for x̣ in section B of our list of "Abbreviations, Symbols, and Other Conventions."

3.3 Stressed Vowels

Tonic *a* is most often anterior /ą/, but is posterior /ạ/ when

1) before unstable -*ṇ* or -*ṇs*: *Tolzạṇ* 'Toulousain," *mạṇs* 'hands';

2) probably, or often, or in some dialects, when tonic and final, in which position -*a* often rhymes with -*ạṇ*: *va* 'goes,' *cantarà* 'he will sing,' *está* 'is' (such rhymes confirm that *a* before *n* is not nasalized, at least in the literary tongue);

3) perhaps in the endings -*ana*, -*anc* (and -*anca?*);

the medieval grammarians give, e.g., *grạna* 'grain,' *fraṇcs* 'noble' (nom. sg.);

4) possibly, at least in some dialects, before *m* and stable *n*: *an* 'year,' *can(t)* 'song,' *fam* 'hunger,' *esperansa* 'hope' (but probably not before *nh*).

The two *a*'s distinguish minimal pairs, but probably only involving -*ns*: *gras* 'fat' ~ *grạṇs* 'grain' (nom. sg.); *nąs* 'nose' ~ *nạṇs* 'dwarf' (nom. sg.). Rhymes of -*ạṇs* with -*ąs* and -*an(t)*s are rare and improper.

Tonic *e* can be *ę* or *ẹ*, with minimal pairs such as *sęr* 'servant' and *sẹr* 'evening' or *pęl* 'skin' and *pẹl* 'hair'; *e* is closed before *n*, *m*, and probably *nh*, whether final or not.

The vowel /i/ is represented by *i* or rarely *y* when these either are not next to a vowel (*ira* 'anger,' *amic* 'friend,' *viṇ* 'wine') or are next to a vowel with hiatus (*via* 'way,' *reïna* 'queen.')

The use of *y* by scribes is quite capricious (2.3); most dictionaries and glossaries list words with initial *y* under *i*-. Final -*i* and -*iṇ* rhyme, as do -*is*, and -*iṇs*. For *i* pronounced /i̯/ and /ǧ/, see 3.7-8 and 4.11

Tonic *o* is open or closed, with some common homographs such as *cọr* 'when' ~ *cǫr(s)* 'heart' ~ *cǫrs* 'body' ~ *cọrs* 'course.' *O* is closed in the common suffix -*ọr* and before *n* and *m*, except in -*ǫ́ni*: *bọṇ* 'good,' *dọmna* 'lady,' but *demǫni* 'demon.' Tonic *o* closes before *nh* in some dialects but not others; so that in the troubadours we find, e.g., *lǫnh*, *luęnh*, *lọnh* 'far.' /Ǫ/ and /ọ/ do not rhyme, but -*ọ* and -*ọṇ* do. Not earlier than the thirteenth century, tonic /ọ/ closes to /u/, generally with no orthographic change: *amor* / amọr / > /amur/.

U is a vowel when either not next to a vowel (*luna* 'moon,' *uṇ* 'one') or next to a vowel in hiatus (*traüt* 'tribute'). For *u* representing the semivowels /u̯/ and /ü̯/ see 3.6 and 3.8; as /v/, 4.9. The vowel *u* (occasionally even when < /ọ/) evolves in OP from /u/ to /ü/. The quite obscure chronology of this change depended on dialect and phonetic environment, and various motivations have been suggested. At least by the time that stressed /ọ/ became /u/, /u/ must have moved toward or to /ü/, since /u/ < /ọ/ and /ü/ < /u/ are held separate in the rhyme. The pronunciation /ü/ is to be recommended for reading aloud.

3.4 Unstressed Vowels

The unstressed vowels *i* and *u* are pronounced as when tonic: *ivern* 'winter,' *testimǫni* 'witness,' *viatge* 'voyage'; *usar* 'to use,' *continu* 'continuous,' *tuar* 'to kill.' Unstressed *a* and *e* are pronounced /ạ/ and /ẹ/: *lunạ* 'moon,' *ẹgal* 'equal.' Unstressed *o* is /ọ/, which probably by the twelfth century closes further to /u/: /vọlẹr/ > /vulẹr/, still usually written *voler*; /dọlọr > /dulọr/, usually spelled *dolor*. However, the spelling *u* for /u/ < /ọ/ is not rare, especially when prenasal (*sun* for *son* 'his,' *voluntat* for *volontat* 'will') or pretonic, where metaphony may be a factor and *u* may even represent /ü/ replacing /u/ (*fulia* for *folia* 'madness,' *cubrir* for *cobrir* 'to cover').

Adverbs ending in *-men(t)* pose a particular problem. Since the feminine adjective that forms the first element of the adverb also exists as an independent word and since virtually any adjective can be adverbialized in this way, one may assume that speakers were conscious of the adverb's compound nature. Hence, in the adverb one would treat the adjectival element as if it retains tonic stress and would pronounce, e.g., *bęlamen* 'beautifully' or *fǫrtmen* 'strongly,' with the /ę/ and /ǫ/ not closing to /ẹ/ and /ọ/.

3.5 Diphthongs: General

A diphthong will here be defined as a vocalic group made up of a vowel and a semivowel, though not necessarily in that order. The vowel has stronger stress and is more open; the semivowel has weaker stress and is more closed. We will call a diphthong "closing" if the vowel precedes the semivowel, and "opening" if the semivowel precedes the vowel.

OP has most of the closing diphthongs permitted by its vocalic system, but fewer opening diphthongs:

vowel + /u/	*+ /i/*	*/u/, /ü/ + vowel*	*/i/ +*
au̯	ai̯		(i̯a)
ęu̯	ęi̯	u̯ę́ > ü̯ę́	i̯ę́
ẹu̯	ẹi̯		
iu̯			
ǫu̯	ǫu̯	u̯ǫ́ > ü̯ǫ́	
ọu̯	ọi̯		
	üi̯		

Only exceptionally (3.10) can other combinations of vocalic phonemes represent diphthongs, or can unstressed syllables contain opening diphthongs other than *ia*.

3.6 The Letter u *as the Semivowels /u̯/ and /ü̯/*

Besides representing the vowels /u/, /ü/ (3.3-4) and the consonant /v/ (4.9), the letter *u* also stands for the semivowels /u̯/ and /ü̯/.

In *qu* and *gu*, the *u* is a silent sign indicating the pronunciations /k/, /g/, not /č/, /ǧ/, before *e* and *i*: *quitar* 'to leave,' *guidar* 'to guide' (but Gascon has /ku̯/, /gu̯/). A superfluous *u* is frequent before *a*: *lengua*, *lenga* 'tongue'; *quan*, *can* 'when.' However, *orguǫlh*, *orguęlh* (or *orgǫlh*) 'pride' has an opening diphthong. Diphthongal *u* is occasionally spelled *o* (3.10).

As the second element in closing diphthongs, *u* is pronounced /u̯/, not /ü̯/; *au̯r* 'gold,' *gręu̯* 'heavy', *bẹu̯re* 'to drink,' *viu̯* 'alive,' *mǫu̯re* 'to move,' *rọu̯re* 'oak.' The /u̯/ can also be spelled with *l* before certain consonants (4.13). During the thirteenth century, *iu* generally received a glide *e* to form the triphthong *ięu* (3.11). *Ou* can simplify to *o* (or /ọ/ >/u/): *dossamen* < *dọu̯ssamen* < *dọlsamen* 'sweetly') or can dissimiliate to, or at least alternate with, *oi* (*rọi̯re*, *rọu̯re* 'oak'). Pretonic *eu* can become *au*: *leu̯part*, *lau̯part* 'leopard.' And *au* can become *ai*: *au̯sens*, *ai̯sens* 'absinth.'

For *u* in opening diphthongs, see 3.8.

3.7 The Letters i *and* y *as the Semivowel /i̯/*

The manuscripts' *i* can be pronounced as the vowel /i/ (3.3-4), the consonant /ǧ/ (4.11, and the semivowel /i̯/. *Y* can represent all these except /ǧ/.

For intervocalic *i*, most dialects seem to prefer /ǧ/, with /i̯/ in some northern areas; the literary language allows both pronunciations. An acceptable practice is to pronounce *-i-* in general as /ǧ/, but as /i̯/ in the following situations: 1) when the *i* is in a root which elsewhere has /i̯/: *joiọs* 'joyous,' of the family of *jǫi* 'joy'; *reial* 'royal,' related to *rẹi* 'king' with /i̯/ (*reg*, possibly /reč/, is very rare); *veraia* 'true' (f.), with /i̯/ as in m. *verai*; 2) in the suffix *-ięr*: *desiięr* 'desire,' *boięr* 'cow-herd,' *renoięr* 'usurer'); and 3) in the rhyme, where the troubadours seem to prefer the pronunciation /i̯/, which affords more rhymes and seems more harmonious than /ǧ/; for example, though *aia*, the 3 sg. present subjective of *aver*, can in theory be /aǧa/, it almost always occurs in series of rhymes with words like *gaia* and *veraia*, which can end only in /-ai̯a/. In addition, the pronunciation of *-aia*, *-eia*, *-oia*, and *-uia* with /i̯/ is supported, in many verb paradigms, by the presence of final *i* /-i̯/ in several categories.

Some editors, when faced with the manuscripts' intervocalic *i*, retain *i*; but others print *j* wherever they feel the pronunciation should be /ǧ/.

Closing diphthongs ending in /i̯/ are very frequent, as in *paire* 'father,' *pęitz* 'worse,' *pẹis* 'fish,' *pǫis* 'then,' *conọisser* 'to know,' *duire* 'to lead.' Final postvocalic *-i* is normally pronounced /i̯/; and some editors permit *j* to represent /i̯/, thus *dej*

(42:61) for *dẹi* 'I should.' (However, postvocalic *-i* or *-j* may also represent /č/; see 4.11,B.) Diphthongs ending in /i̯/ are subject to alteration in some words, with *ei* > *ai*, *eu*, *e*, *i*; and *ai* > *a*, *i*, *ei*, *i*; and *ui* > *u*. The first of these changes often monophthongizes an initial syllable, as in *meitat*, *mitat* 'half' and *reisidar*, *residar* 'to awaken.' On the other hand, final *ẹ* can dialectally diphthongize to *ẹi*, thus the personal pronouns *mẹ* and *tẹ* can become *mei* and *tei*, and we also find, e.g., *mercẹy* 'mercy' (14:37).

For /i̯/ in opening diphthongs and final *-ia*, see 3.8 and 3.10; for the probable non-pronunciation of *i* before /č/ and /n̯/, see 4.11,B and 4.14.

3.8 Opening Diphthongs from Diphthongization of Tonic Vowels

The opening diphthongs *i̯ę* and *u̯ǫ* > *u̯ę* can optionally replace tonic /ę/ and /ǫ/ before certain immediately following sounds. In the chart below, parentheses around a word indicate only occasional or dialectal diphthongization; and square brackets show diphthongization probably due to analogy rather than regular phonological development. Only one form is given for each word, even though non-diphthongized forms, and often other diphthongized forms, also exist.

following sound		*examples of OP diphthongization*	
spelling	*pronunciation*	*/ę́/ > /i̯ę́/*	*/ǫ́/ > /u̯ǫ́/, /u̯ę́/, /üǫ́/, /üę́/*
1) palatals			
-ch, -(i)g	/č/	li̯ęg 'bed'	nu̯ęg 'night'
ge, gi, j	/ǧ/	pi̯ę́jer 'worse'	plu̯ęja 'rain'
lh, (i)ll	/l̯/	vi̯ęlh 'old'	fu̯ǫlha 'leaf'
nh	/n̯/	---	(lu̯ęnh 'far')
(i)r	/r/	fi̯ę(i̯)ra 'fair'	mu̯ęr 'I die'
(i)s(s)	/s/	i̯ęi̯s 'goes out'	pu̯ǫi̯s 'then'
(i)s, (i)z	/z/	gli̯ę(i̯)za 'church'	pru̯ęsme 'fellow man'
(i)t	/t/	pi̯ę(i̯)tz 'chest'	nu̯ǫi̯t 'night'
i, y	/i̯/	mi̯ęi̯ 'my' (nom. pl.)	pu̯ǫi̯ 'hill'
2) labials			
b	/b/	---	[cu̯ębre 'I cover]
f	/f/	---	[su̯ęfre 'I suffer]
p	/p/	---	[tru̯ęp 'I find]
v	/v/	---	[nu̯ęva 'new' (f.sg.)]
u	/u̯/	(li̯ęu̯ 'light)	nu̯ǫu̯ 'new'
3) velars			
c	/k/	[si̯ęc 'he follows']	(fu̯ǫc 'fire)
g	/g/	[li̯ęgon 'they read']	(su̯ęgre 'father-in-law')

Diphthongization of tonic /ę/ and /ǫ/ is not regularly indicated in the older texts. Even in the troubadours it remains optional; or, it may be that the simple vowel *e* or *o* is still used to represent what is by then in fact a diphthong. In that case, the manuscripts' *vęlh* 'old' and *vǫlh* 'I want' should perhaps be pronounced as if diphthongized; but one probably does best to pronounce only the diphthongs actually written. Diphthongization of /ǫ́/ seems to be earlier and more widespread than that of /ę́/, and it occurs in more numerous phonological environments.

In the troubadours' usage, *(i̯)r*, *(i̯)s(s)*, *(i̯)z*, and *(i̯)t* had probably lost the palatalization of the consonant which earlier had caused the preceding /ę́/ or /ǫ́/ to diphthongize.

A few words have diphthongization in circumstances other than those described above, whether by analogy (*nięr* 'black,' *fięr* 'he strikes,' *puęsc* 'I can') or by Poitevin influence (*pluęva* 'it may rain' in 5:2).

Phonetically, OP has four opening diphthongs starting with a labial semivowel: /u̯ǫ/, /u̯ę/, /ü̯ǫ/, /ü̯ę/. But phonemically they are interchangeable with each other and with their source /ǫ́/. For example, *folha* /fǫ́l̮a/ 'leaf' exists also as *fuolha* /fu̯ǫ́l̮a/ ~ /fü̯ǫ́l̮a/ and *fuelha* /fu̯ę́l̮a/ ~ /fü̯ę́l̮a/. Though these different forms may originally have had some dialectal basis, the troubadours and scribes use them indifferently even within a single text. In this case, one might expect the more advanced form *uę* to be the one that corresponded to the author's or at least the scribe's own pronunciation; but the modern reader may as well pronounce *uę* and *uǫ* as written, even where inconsistency within one text results. In these diphthongs the semivowel *u* remained /u̯/ in some dialects but apparently became /ü̯/ in most; since the situation is so unclear, there is no objection to following the phonetic line of least resistance and pronouncing /u̯/ before the back vowel and /ü̯/ before the front vowel, thus /u̯ǫ/ but /ü̯ę/.

Certain words have preferred forms, i.e., *jǫc* 'game,' rarely *juęc*, and never with *uǫ*; *nǫu* 'nine,' with *nuǫu* and *nuęu* corresponding only to *nǫu* 'new.' Another possible result of this evolution is reduction to the vowel *u* pronounced /ü/, thus *luc* (or *lǫc*, *luǫc*, *luęc*) 'place.' However, a *u* in such cases may at times be a spelling for the diphthong *uǫ* or *uę*.

The very common suffix *-ęr/a* or *-ęi̯r/a* also frequently diphthongizes to *-i̯ęr/a* (or less often, *-i̯ęi̯r/a*).

3.9 Vocalic Alternation

Vocalic alternation (apophony) can occur in differently stressed forms of one word or root. It is most prominent when *ę* and *ǫ* become diphthongized under the stress, thus *vuǫlh*, *vuęlh* (or *vǫlh*) 'I want' ~ *vǫlém* > /vulẹ́m/ 'we want' and *vięlh* (or *vęlh*) ~ vẹlhẹ́za 'old age.' Sometimes, one or the other form is generalized; for example, the analogy of *lęva* 'he raises' imposes non-diphthongized *lęu* 'I raise,' with the result that diphthongized *lięu* can only be a variant of the adjective *lęu* 'light.'

Vocalic alternation also occurs where tonic /a̧/, /ȩ/, /o̧/ correspond to unstressed /ạ/, /ẹ/, /ọ/; for this and other types of vocalic alternation in verbs, see 10.13.

3.10 Hiatus

Other than in adjoining words in the phrase (2.8), the main OP combinations of vowels in hiatus (2.6) fall into the following groups:

1) *i* plus *a*, *e*, *o*; either element can be stressed or both unstressed: thus, the 1 and 3 sg. imperfect indicative and conditional A ending has -*ía*, while *viatz* 'quickly' has -*iá*- and -*ia*- is unstressed in *cambiamen* 'change';

2) *u* (preferably pronounced /ü/) plus *a*, *e*, *i*, *o*; for example, *tua* 'your' (f. sg.), *manual* 'by hand,' *continuamen* 'continuously';

3) *a*, *e*, or *o* plus *i* or *u*, with the second or neither element stressed, thus *obeïr* 'to obey,' *obeïmen* 'obedience,' *reüza* 'pushes back,' *a reüzoṇs* 'backwards';

4) *a*, *e*, or *o* plus *a*, *e*, or *o*, usually with stress on the second or neither element; *leoṇ* 'lion,' *creatura* 'creature,' etc., *aa* and *ee* can also occur, as in *traazoṇ* 'treason' or *cobeẹza* 'cupidity.'

For indicating hiatus, editorial practice varies. It seems superfluous to use the dieresis on groups other than those that can form diphthongs (3.5); thus, *io*, *ua*, and combinations of *a*, *e* and *o* with each other or themselves need no dieresis. Also, it is unnecessary to indicate hiatus before an unstressed verb ending, as in *tuen* 'they kill,' or in the normally dissyllabic imperfect and conditional markers *-ia, -ias, -iam, -iatz, -ian, -ioṇ (-ien)*, or in words like *grácia* 'grace' (see below). With such words, where metrics so demand, one can indicate the less usual diphthongal status as in *grácȋa*.

On the whole, OP keeps cases of diphthongs and hiatus separate with remarkable consistency. However, for metrical reasons the troubadours occasionally exploit the possibility of syneresis, the reduction of hiatus to a diphthong. Thus, *violar* 'to play the vielle' (a stringed instrument) can be pronounced /viu̯-lár/ as well as /vi-u-lár/; *paor* 'fear,' normally /pa-ọ́r/, can be counted as one syllable (/pa͡ọr/? /páur/?). The ending *-íọṇ*, is occasionally reduced to one syllable; and other diphthongs arise in later or dialectal usage.

Syllabification and stress are not changed in the rare cases when *o* replaces *u* in diphthongs (*paraola* for *paraula* 'word') or in hiatus (*pęrdoa* for *pęrdua* 'loss,' *manoal* for *manual* 'by hand,' *soau* for *suau* 'gentle'); like other unstressed *o*'s, these are probably pronounced as if written *u*, although pronunciations with /a͡o/ or /oa/ cannot be ruled out.

In addition, posttonic or intertonic *ia* is often counted as monosyllabic, as in *glǫ́ria* 'glory' pronounced /glǫ́-ri̯a/ alongside /glǫ́-ri-a/, or in *sa-via-mén* for *sa-vi-a-mén* 'wisely.' Another solution for this apparently troublesome group was to shift the stress away from the antepenultimate syllable, thus *gra-cȋ-a* for *grá-ci-a*. Even the stressed *i* in final *-ȋa* shows a tendency increasing after the twelfth century, to reduce to /i̯/, whether in the verbal ending, which can become /-i̯á/, or in dissyllables like *sia* 'let it be' and *dia* 'day,' which can come to be pronounced /si̯á/ and /di̯á/ in place of /sía/ and /día/. Words like *cam-bi-ar* 'to change' or *cam-bi-a-men* 'change' generally maintain syllabic *i* because it can be tonic in forms like 3 sg. present indicative *cam-bí-a*; however, reduction to *cam-bi̯ar*, *cám-bia*, etc., can also occur, especially in the later period.

3.11 Triphthongs

The triphthong--a group of three vocalic sounds belonging to one syllable--is quite common in OP, in the following combinations:

i̯ęi̯: *lięit* 'bed';
i̯ęu̯: *lięu* 'light';
u̯ǫi̯, *u̯ęi̯*: *nuǫit*, *nuęit* 'night';
u̯ǫu̯, *u̯ęu̯*: *buǫu*, *buęu* 'ox.'

Since triphthongs arise from an opening diphthong plus a semivowel, they have a full vowel as their central element and are optional, coexisting with diphthongs, as in *lęit*, *lęu*, *nǫit*, *bǫu*. One can pronounce the first element *u* as /ü/ before *e* and as /u̯/ before *o*, as in the diphthongs *ue* and *uo* (3.8). Just as *e* and *o* may stand for /i̯ę/ and /u̯ǫ/ (3.8), so it is possible that spellings like *leit*, *leu*, *noit* and *bou* can represent triphthongs; but it is simpler to pronounce such words as written.

All other combinations of three vocalic elements represent two syllables, for example, *su-au* 'gentle.' Some triphthongs tend to simplify by dropping one element, as in *cuęir* 'leather' > *cuer*, *puęis* 'then' >

pues, and especially before enclitics: *ięu* 'I' + *lo* 'it' > *ię·l*, *cantięi* 'I sang' + *lo* > *cantię·l*. With the first semivowel dropped, we find *uǫi* > *oi*: *muǫir* 'I die' > *moir*. On the other hand, the triphthong *ieu* may arise, particularly after the twelfth century, from intercalation of a glide element in *iu*, thus producing *vięure* (138:15) for *viure* 'to live,' *vięu* (181:48) for *viu* 'he lives,' *pieuzela* (181:58) for *piuzęla* 'maiden,' and *qui·eus* for *qui* 'who' plus *vos*, *·us* 'you.'

Chapter 3: Exercises

A. Transcribe these manuscript spellings in the same broad phonetic notation we have been using; indicate the preferred pronunciation, including tonic stress (2.4-5) and the quality of *e* and *o* (whether stressed or not)

1. guan 'glove'
2. orguolh 'pride'
3. nadaus 'Christmas'
4. dous 'sweet'
5. fuoc 'fire'
6. truep 'I find'
7. agui 'I had'
8. poiar 'to mount'
9. maior 'greater'
10. sui 'I am'
11. caitiu 'captive'
12. malvais 'bad'
13. lieys 'her'
14. ueit 'eight'
15. muou 'he moves'
16. vaquiera 'cow-herd'

B. Divide into syllables and indicate tonic stress (see also 2.4-6)

1. cadiera 'chair'
2. toalhola 'handkerchief'
3. suau 'gentle'
4. escien 'knowledge'
5. fiansa 'confidence'
6. paraola 'word'
7. jauzionda 'joyful' (f.)
8. campolieit 'tent'

C. Based on chapter 3 and sections 2.7-8, mark with apostrophes or diereses those vowels that should normally be elided (this will not always be as in the *Anthology*); and state the number of syllables in each line (if two lines in sequence are given, they have equal syllable count)

1. Papiols, sias tan cochos, / Di me en Richart que el es leos
2. Autre escondich vos farai plus sobrier
3. Et enueia me, per Saint Salvaire, / En bona cort avols violaire
4. En Elias, si ieu midonz soan
5. Ben ferm liatz per maistria, / Car mal liars es gran follia

4
CONSONANTS

4.1 Consonants: General

Consonants can be described according to two factors:

1) The point of articulation, that is, the point in the buccal cavity where the air flow is most constricted. This point is described, from front to back, by the following adjectives, corresponding to a preponderant role of the indicated speech organs:

bilabial: both lips
labiodental: the upper teeth and lower lip
dental: the upper and lower teeth
alveolar: the alveolar ridge
palatal: the (hard) palate
velar: the soft palate

2) The mode of constriction:

occlusive: the airstream stops momentarily
fricative: a hissing or rushing noise
affricative: an occlusive plus a fricative
liquid: *l* and *r* sounds
nasal: air resonates in the nasal cavity

In addition, the first three modes produce pairs of consonants, voiced (that is, with vibration of the vocal cords) and unvoiced. Other consonants are unvoiced only in certain positions. The term "sibilant" designates dental and palatal fricatives and affricatives.

4.2 Phonetic Symbols for Consonants

mode of constriction	*point of articulation*					
	bilabial	*labiodental*	*dental*	*alveolar*	*palatal*	*velar*
occlusive						
unvoiced	/p/		/t/			/k/
voiced	/b/		/d/			/g/
affricative						
unvoiced			/ts/		/č/	
voiced			/dz/		/ǧ/	
fricative						
unvoiced		/f/	/s/		/s̮/	
voiced		/v/	/z/		/z̮/	
liquid						
trill				/r/,/rr/		
lateral				/l/	/l̮/	/ƚ/
nasal	/m/		/n/		/n̮/	/ŋ/

4.3 Usual Pronunciation of OP Spellings Representing Consonants

Only the most frequent spellings and pronunciations for late twelfth-century Provençal are given; for further details and variations see the following sections.

b = /b/
c = /k/ before *a*, *o*, *u*, or a consonant, or final
 = /s/ before *e* or *i*
ç = /s/
ch = /č/

d = /d/
f = /f/
g = /g/ before *a*, *o*, *u*, or a consonant
= /ǧ/ before *e* or *i*
-(*i*)*g* = /č/ (final)
gn = /n̮/
gu = /g/ (used before *e* or *i*, sometimes *a* and *o*)
-*gz* = /č/ (final)
h = /∅/ (initial, intervocalic)
-(*i*)*h* = /č/ (final)
j = /ǧ/ (spelled *i* in the manuscripts)
l = /l/
ill = /l̮/ (the *i* is unpronounced unless syllabic)
lh = /l̮/ (often as *ilh* with unpronounced *i*)
ll = /l/ or /l̮/ according to the word (if not *ill*)
m = /m/
n = /n/
= /ŋ/ before *c* and *g*
= /ɱ/ before *b* and *v*
nh = /n̮/
p = /p/
qu = /k/ (used before *e* and *i*, sometimes *a* and *o*)
r = /rr/ (initial)
= (r) (non-initial)
rr = /rr/
s = /s/ in any position
= /z/ (intervocalic)
ss = /s/ (intervocalic)
t = /t/
tg, *tj* = /ǧ/
-*tz* = /ts/ (final)

v = /v/ (spelled *u* in the manuscripts)
x = /ks/ (final, often in *-cx*)
z = /z/ intervocalic
= /ts/ (final, especially in *-tz*)

4.4 Generalities on OP Consonants

Final occlusives and fricatives are devoiced; hence, *-b*, *-d*, *-g*, *-z*, *-v* should be pronounced as if spelled with the more usual *-p*, *-t*, *-c* (or *ch*), *-s*, *-f*. Devoicing also occurs before final *-s* or *-z*.

A phenomenon which can have the contrary effect is syntactical phonetics, through which a sound adapts to an adjoining sound in another word. In particular, single final unvoiced consonants probably often become voiced before a following vowel in a closely related word (*las alas* 'the wings' /laz álas/) and perhaps also before a voiced consonant (*las domnas* 'the ladies' /laz dọmnas/?). Such voicing seems to be indicated by occasional spellings like "ez blanca" 'is white' (5:13). Through syntactical phonetics, final *-p*, *-t*, *-c*, *-s*, and *-f* can hence become pronounced as *b*, *d*, *g*, *z*, *v*.

Doubled consonants are generally pronounced as if single and hence are usually ignored in alphabetizing words, thus *apprendre* = *aprendre* 'to learn.' The most common needlessly doubled consonants are *f*, *m*, *n*, *p*, and *t*. In the remainder of this chapter and book, doubled consonants will be mentioned only where they have distinctive values, notably in *cc*, *ss*, *rr*, and *ll*.

Many words contain "glide consonants," that is, *b*, *p*, *d*, or *t* inserted to facilitate the transition between two other consonants. The most frequent such cases of epenthesis are the following:

	+l	*+n*	*+t*	*+s*
l+			ldr	lts
m+	mbl	mpn	mbr	mps
n+	ndl		ndr	nts
s+			str, sdr	

Often the glide consonant is optional, as in *dom(p)na* 'lady' or *vescom(p)s* 'viscount' (nom. sg.); in such cases it may be lightly pronounced, if at all. But in other words or combinations the glide consonant is obligatory or virtually so: *cambra* 'room,' *ęstre* 'to be.'

4.5 Etymological Consonants and the Letter h

The classical Provençal spelling system is quite economical; functionless letters are rare. Some etymological consonants are, however, introduced, particularly after the twelfth century, such as the *c* in *auctor* 'witness' or the *pt* in *septmana* for *semana* 'week'; but such letters were probably not pronounced.

The only frequent silent letter is *h*, which can reflect either etymology (*hǫra* or *ora* 'hour') or mere caprice (*habandonar* for *abandonar* 'to abandon'); it can also be introduced to mark hiatus (2.6). In initial position, manuscripts often add *h* to show that a following *u* is not a *v*, as in *huęlh* for *uelh* 'eye,' which could otherwise be read as *vęlh* 'old.' Initial *h* is customarily disregarded in alphabetizing words.

H by itself has its own phonetic value only in *-(i)h* representing /č/ (4.11) or /s̮/ (4.10,E) and in Gascon initial *h-* derived from *f-*. *H* is also employed in the diagraphs *ch*, *lh*, *nh*, and dialectal *sh* to show palatalization.

4.6 /p/ and /b/: Bilabial Occlusives

The sound /p/ is represented by

p: *patz* 'peace,' *aprendre* 'to learn,' *trǫp* '(too) much';

-b: *ǫrb* 'blind' (or *orp*);

b in *-bs* (and *-bz*): *obs* 'need' (or *ops*).

The sound /b/ is spelled with *b* (except *-b*, *-bs*, *-bz*): *bęl* 'beautiful,' *abelir* 'to please'; also, the preposition *ab* 'with' seems to retain /b/.

4.7 /t/ and /d/: Dental Occlusives

The sound /t/ is represented by

t: *tensoṇ* (a genre), *atendre* 'to wait,' *fat* 'foolish';

-d: *vẹrd* 'green' (more often *vert*);

d in *-ds*, *-dz*: *nuds*, *nudz* 'naked' (nom. sg.; more often *nutz*);

th in a few learnèd words: *thesaur* 'treasure' (105:22).

The sound /d/ is spelled *d* (except in *-d*, *-ds*, *-dz*): *dar* 'to give,' *pęrdre* 'to lose.' Intervocalic *-d-* falls dialectically, particularly between *i* and *a*, thus furnishing a convenient rhyme: *gui(d)a* 'guide,' *cri(d)a* 'he cries,' *vi(d)a* 'life,' etc. For *-d-* alternating with *-z-*, see 4.10.

Final -*nt* usually loses its unstable *t*, which we indicate by -*(t)* when we wish to show a word's underlying form. In some other circumstances -*t* can also fall: *cru(t)* 'raw,' *drẹi(t)* 'right,' *esgar(t)* 'glance,' *fǫr(t)* 'very.'

4.8 /k/ and /g/: Velar Occlusives

The sound 'k' is represented by

c except before *e* or *i*: *cǫc* 'cook,' *acǫrt* 'agreement';

qu: *qui* 'who,' *lanquan* 'when' (with silent *u*);

q without *u* rarely: *qi* for *qui*;

k rarely: *ki* for *qui*, *kalenda* 'first day of the month';

-*g*: *larg* 'big' (more often *larc*)

g in -*gs* (and probably -*gz*): *longs*, *longz* 'long' (nom. sg.; usually *loncs*, *loncz*);

ch rarely, in learnèd words or by Italian influence: *archangel* 'archangel,' *christian* 'Christian' (more often *crestiaṇ*);

x = /ks/: *fuęx* 'fires' (or -*cs*, -*cx*, -*cz*).

The manuscripts use *qu* chiefly where Latin has *qu*, but even there we often find *c*: *can* or *quan* 'when'; *catre* or *quatre* 'four.' When final or before -*s*, *c* can drop dialectally in certain words: *ami(c)* 'friend,' *sirventẹs(c)*, 'sirventes,' *blan(c)s* 'white' (nom. sg.), etc. For *ch*, -*g*, -*gx*, -*gz* representing /č/, see 4.11,B; for *x* as /s̮/, see 4.10,E.

The sound /g/ is spelled

g (except -*g*, -*gs*, -*gz*, *ge*, *gi*, and *gy*): *gran* 'big,' *aiga* 'water';

gu: *guẹrra* 'war' (with silent *u*);

gh rarely, by Italian influence: *preghar* for *pregar* 'to pray';

x = probably /gz/ in the learnèd prefix *ex*- plus vowel: *exemple* for *eissemple* 'example.'

In theory, *gu* is reserved for indicating hard /g/ before *e*, *i*, or *y*; but we do find spellings like *guant* for *gant* 'glove' or *gerra* /gẹ́rra/ for *guerra*. The ending -*iga* has a dialectal variant -*ia* which is often exploited in the rhyme, as in *ami(g)a* 'friend' (f.). For /k/ and /g/ alternating with /č/ and /ǧ/, see 4.11.

4.9 /f/ and /v/: Labialized Fricatives

The sound /f/ is represented by

f in all positions: *faire* 'to do,' *afaire* 'affair,' *sẹrf* 'servant' (or *ser*);

ph (learnèd): *philosophia* 'philosophy';

-*v*: *salv* 'safe' (more often *sal*, *salf*).

And /v/ is spelled *v* (except final): *venir* 'to come.'

The manuscript symbol *u* usually is consonantal when initial, intervocalic, or final after another consonant. However, according to its origin, the manuscripts' initial or intervocalic *u* can also represent /ü̯/ or /u̯/ (*uẹlh* 'eye'; *miẹua* 'mine,' f. sg.; see 3.8 and 3.11); postvocalic final *u* is occasionally consonantal (*lav* 'I wash'); and post-consonantal final -*u* also exists (*continu* 'continuous').

Many words in -*v*- with adjoining *o* or *u* have alternate forms with Ø: *Pro(v)ensa* 'Provence,' *pa(v)ọr* 'fear,' etc.

4.10 /s/, /ts/, /z/: Dental Fricatives and Affricatives

A) The manuscripts represent the sound /s/, with considerable inconsistency, by the following symbols:

s in any position: *saint* 'holy,' *pasar* 'to pass,' *cansoṇ* 'song,' *pas* 'step';

ss (normally only intervocalic): *passar* 'to pass';

c before *e*, *i*, or *y*: *cen* 'hundred';

ç before *a*, *o*, *u*: *cançọṇ* 'song,' *faça* 'face'; the manuscripts sometimes omit the cedilla;

-*z*: *drapz* 'cloth' (nom. sg.), *fuecz* 'fires,' *áutrez* 'other' (obl. pl., 39:2); all these more normally have -*s*;

z for *ç*: *canzoṇ*, *valensa* 'worth';

sc (learnèd or hypercorrect): *escien(t)* 'knowledge';

x = /ks/: see 4.8;

cc = /ks/ before *e*, *i* or *y*: *occiden(t)* 'west.'

B) The affricative /ts/ is represented by

-*tz*: *patz* 'peace,' *parlatz* 'you speak,' *tẹrtz* 'third,' *antz* 'before';

-*ts*: in the same words as -*tz*;

-*z* in the same words as -*tz*, or as in the examples given in 5.6 and 7.4;

-(*i*)*gz*, -(*i*)*chs*, -(*i*)*hs*: *fagz*, etc. 'done' (nom. sg.; see 4.11);

-*ds*, -*dz*: *nudz* 'naked' (nom. sg.; see 4.7).

C) The voiced /z/ can be spelled

z except final: *zẹl* 'zeal,' *razoṇ* 'reason';

s when intervocalic in many cases; *rasoṇ*; *pausa* 'pause'; and probably also by assimilation before a voiced consonant: *almọsna* 'alms,' *isla* 'island';

ç, *cz*, *dz*, *s*, and *ss*, all sporadically;

x as /gz/: see 4.8.

Words with intervocalic /z/ often have alternate dialectal forms with Ø or -*d*-: *fi(z)ęl*, *fidel* 'faithful'; *a(z)orar*, *adorar* 'to worship.' Such forms with *d* are pronounced with the interdental voiced spirant /δ/ becoming /z/ during the twelfth century. For optional /z/ in *e*, *a*, *o* and *que*, see 2.8.

D) Intervocalic -*s*- is voiced or not, according to etymology. The manuscripts' *dousa* represents *doussa* for *dọlsa* 'sweet' (f.), but *baisar* stands for *baizar* 'to kiss' as well as for *baissar* 'to lower.' After prefixes, intervocalic -*s*- probably remains /s/ as in the component root: *resǫli* 'I resole,' *desús* 'above.' A manuscript's *pesar* might correspond to three different words: with /s/, *pessar* 'to break' or *pensar* 'to think'; and with /z/, *pesar* 'to weigh.'

E) The normalized spellings *ce* and *ci* indicate a /s/ that evolved from /ts/, as does the manuscripts' *ç* in most cases. Similarly, the /z/ represented by our normalized spelling *z* evolved from /dz/. Though these evolutions were not completed until after the twelfth century, we recommend the pronunciations /s/ and /z/, which already were usual; however, final /-ts/ where normalized as -*tz* apparently reduced more slowly to /-s/, so that it is best to pronounce these as /-ts/ unless the rhymes indicate otherwise.

The sounds spelled -*iss*- and final -*is* may have had partial palatalization in many dialects, and had full palatalization in the Southwest. This pronunciation /s̰/ is sometimes represented, after *i*, by *sh*, *x*, or *h*: *crẹisher* for *crẹisser* 'to grow,' *creix* (42:68) for *creis* 'grows,' *procezih* 'proceeds'

(180:103). Similarly, *iz* in some cases corresponds to a palatalized pronunciation with /z̯/.

4.11 /ǧ/ and /č/: Palatal Affricatives

A) The voiced palatal affricative /ǧ/--which actually includes a considerable range of sounds lying between /dž/, /d̯y/, and /dz/--is spelled

g before *e* and *i* (*y*): *gen* 'people,' *fregir* 'to fry';

j (*i* in the manuscripts) before *a*, *o*, *u*: *jọrn* 'day,' *pojar* 'to rise';

tg before *e* and *i*: *coratge* 'heart, courage';

tj (*ti* in the manuscripts) before *a*, *o*, *u*: *coratjọs* 'courageous.'

Rarer spellings are *j* (manuscript *i*) before *e* or *i* (*jen* for *gen*); *gg* (*coragge*); *ih* (*poihar*); *g* before *a*, *o*, *u* (*poga* for *pǫja* 'rises'). In many words, /ǧ/ alternates with dialectal variants:

1) /ǧ/ ~ /i̯/, both normally spelled *i* in the manuscripts. In intervocalic position, /ǧ/ predominates (3.7), thus *majọr* 'bigger' rather than *mai̯or*. Initial *i*-, where it is not the vowel /i/, is /ǧ/, not /i̯/: manuscript *ioc* is *jǫc* 'game.' But final -*i*, where not /i/, is semivocalic /i̯/: *rẹi* 'king.' Many editors leave the manuscripts' *i* in any position even where /ǧ/ is the presumed pronunciation;

2) ∅ ~ /ǧ/: *regina*, *reïna* 'queen';

3) /ǧ/ ~ /i̯d/: *cujar* (manuscript *cuiar*), *cuidar* 'to believe';

4) /g/ vs. /ǧ/ before *a*: *gal* vs. *jal* (manuscript *ial*) 'rooster,' *longa* vs. *lonja* 'long' (f.);

B) The unvoiced /č/--which has a variety of pronunciations lying between /tš/, /t̯y/ and /ts/--

is also variously spelled:

(i)ch: *chárcer* 'prison,' *dreͅ(i)cha* 'just' (f.), *fa(i)ch* 'done';

(i)g: *faig*;

(i)h: *faih*.

Ch is usual in initial and internal position; in final position -*i(g)* predominates but the others are also frequent and -*(i)th*, -*(i)gh*, -*(i)c*, etc., also occur. In all these combinations the optional *i* is probably not pronounced.

Since final -*g* can also represent /k/ (4.8), one must be careful to distinguish /č/ in, e.g., *cug* 'I believe' (also spelled *cuig*) from /k/ in, e.g., *amig* 'friend' (usually written *amic*, with devoicing of the /g/ that is seen in f. *amiga*).

Dialectally, /č/ alternates with various other sounds, all of which are common:

1) /k/ ~ /č/ (northern dialects) before *a*: *cantar*, *chantar* 'to sing'; *rica*, *richa* 'rich';

2) /č/ ~ northern /i̯t/: *fach*, *fait*; *noͅch*, *noit* 'night'; *esplechar*, *espleitar* 'to accomplish';

3) /-č/ ~ /-i̯/: *meͅch*, *mei* 'half'; *bruch*, *brui*, *bruit* 'noise'; *correͅch*, *correi*, *correit* 'strap.' The pronunciation with /-i̯/ spelled -*i* is frequent (3.7); given words have preferred forms that cannot always be explained by etymology. Furthermore, there is no reason that postvocalic -*i* cannot represent, in addition to /-i̯/, also /ǧ/ devoiced in final position to /-č/, whenever the consonantal variant occurs in other derivatives of the same root. Thus, *pueͅi*, *puej* (12:53), the 3 sg. present subjunctive of *pojar* 'to mount,' might have /-č/ just like the noun *poͅi*, *poch*, *pog* 'hill';

4) /-č/ ~ /-ts/: *brutz, corretz.*

When we find situations like *fait* in the same poem as *faich* (26:31, 54) or *fag* (84:24, 27), the best we can do is pronounce consistently within the poem, bearing in mind that outside of the rhyme an individual troubadour's own usage may be unrecoverable.

4.12 Strong /rr/ and Weak /r/: Alveolar Trills

OP has two alveolar trills. The "weak" or "simple" /r/ is formed by probably a single vibration of the tip of the tongue against the alveolar ridge; the strong /rr/ consists of several more intensive vibrations. The strong /rr/ is spelled

-*rr*-: *terra* 'earth';

rr after *l* or *n*, or in final position: *volrran* 'they will want,' *venrran* 'they will come,' *ọrr* 'he runs'; but even when these uncommon spellings do occur, they probably indicate /r/ in most cases;

r-: *rǫsa* 'rose.'

The weak /r/ is represented by *r* in other positions: *cara* 'face,' *gran* 'big,' *cǫr* 'heart.'

A palatal /r̯/, which once induced diphthongization (3.8), may still exist in some twelfth-century dialects.

4.13 /l/ and /l̆/: Non-Trilled Liquids

OP has a palatalized /l̆/ as well as a nonpalatal /l/. The latter is generally alveolar (as in modern French or Spanish), but it has a velar pronunciation /ɨ/ (as is common in English) when it occurs before a consonant, and in other positions according to the etymology. Because of this distinction, many poets strive to distinquish rhymes in /-ȩl/ and -ǫl/, and the like.

The nonpalatal /l/ is spelled

l: *lana* 'wool,' *bȩla* 'beautiful' (f.) *castȩl* 'castle';

-ll-: *bella* for *bela*.

The palatal /l̮/ (which is never initial) is spelled

(i)lh: *vȩ(i)lha* 'old' (f.);

(i)l: *me(i)lọr* 'better';

(i)li: *cava(i)liȩr* 'knight';

(i)ll: *fuȩ(i)lla* 'leaf';

(i)lli: *mo(i)lliȩr* 'woman.'

Rarer are *(i)gl*, *(i)lg*, and combinations with *y* for *i*. In all these spellings for /l̮/, the optional *i* either before or after *l*, *ll*, *lh* is probably silent, merely marking palatalization.

Since the double *ll* represents both /l/ and /l̮/, one must learn which words have which sound, either by observation or by finding the etymology or cognates in other languages. However, some words show dialectal variation, for example, *bella* 'beautiful' (f. sg.) occasionally rhymes in /-ȩ́l̮a/ rather than /-ȩ́la/, and *melor* and *fil* sometimes represent pronunciations with /l/ for the more usual /l̮/ of *melhor* 'better' and *filh* 'son.'

Particularly during the twelfth century, *l* vocalizes to *u* before a consonant, especially *d*, *t*, *n*, *s*, *z*, *ç*, *ce*, and *ci*: *mou̯t* for *mọlt* 'much,' *dou̯s* for *dọls* 'sweet,' etc. For the sake of consistency it is best to retain the *l*, pronounced as /ɫ/, even though this letter may often have been used, in the twelfth century and afterwards, to indicate the pronunciation /u̯/. In texts which portray this vocalization, we find alternations like *bel* 'beautiful' ~ *beutat* 'beauty.'

4.14 /ŋ/, /n/, /n̯/, /m/: Nasals

Velar /ŋ/ arises by assimilation of *n* to a following /k/ or /g/: *oncle* 'uncle,' *ongla* 'fingernail.' It probably also exists by syntactical phonetics between two closely linked words, as in "un gran can" 'a big dog.'

Dental /n/ is spelled *n* everywhere except before /k/, /g/, /b/, and /p/: *nǫu* 'new,' *menar* 'to lead,' *mon* 'world.' One of the most disconcerting traits of OP phonology is the optional disappearance of so-called, "unstable *n*," which we represent as *ṇ*, thus *paṇ* = *pan* or *pa* 'bread.' It occurs chiefly in final position or before flectional -*s*: *fiṇ*, *fiṇs* 'end' (obl. and nom. sg.), *boṇ*, *boṇs* 'good' (obl. and nom. sg.). A similar phenomenon occurs internally by assimilation to following *s*, *f*, and *v*: *coṇselh*, *cosselh* 'advice,' *coṇfǫrt* 'encouragement,' *coṇvenir* 'to suit.' Final -*n* is, however, stable in many words, particularly where it is followed by an unstable -*t* (4.7), as in *can(t)* 'how much,' *longamen(t)* 'for a long time.' Words with stable and unstable *n*'s, in *aman(t)* 'lover' and *maṇ* 'hand,' normally do not rhyme together.

Palatal /n̯/ is spelled

(i)nh: *se(i)nha* 'sign';
(i)gn: *ense(i)gnament* 'instruction';
(i)n: *se(i)noria* 'domain';
(i)ng: *fe(i)ngedor* 'suitor';
(i)nn: *se(i)nnor* 'lord.'

Rarer are *(i)hn*, *ne*, *ni*, *(i)ngn*, *(i)nnh*, *nyh*, and spellings with *y* for *i*; some editors even let *j* enter these groups, as in *sejnhoria* 'lordship' (42:25). In all these combinations, *i*, *y*, and *j* are probably silent, as with /l̯/. Where one is not sure if *(i)n* represents /n/ or /n̯/, one must consider rhymes, cognates, or the etymology. Final *-nh* and *-nhs* can become depalatalized: *gen(h)* 'skill,' *gen(h)s* (nom. sg.); *fen(h)* 'he pretends'; *plan(h)s* 'lament' (nom. sg.).

OP /m/ is spelled

m: *mermamen* 'diminution';

n before *b*, *p*: *senblar* 'to seem,' *enpȩri* 'empire' (both more often with *m*). By syntactical phonetics, final *-n* before a word beginning with *b*, *p*, or *m* is probably pronounced--and is sometimes written--as *m*: *em paradis* 'in paradise' (20:12), *om mais* 'when the most' (181:4).

Alternations of spelling and pronunciation involving nasals other than unstable *n* include the following:

n ~ *m*: *contar*, *comtar* 'to tell,' *son*, *som* 'sleep,' *con*, *com* 'how';

mn ~ *n(n)*: *domna*, *don(n)a* (or *dompna*, see 4.4) 'lady';

m ~ *mn*: *ome*, *omne* 'man';

n ~ *r*: *mongue*, *mọrgue* 'monk.'

Chapter 4: Exercises

A. According to the principles given in chapters 2-4, make a broad phonetic transcription of the following lines, including qualities of *e* and *o* and tonic stress

1. De sai guarda, de lai guigna (12:20)
2. E sui be fols quar m'en reguart (73:32)
3. De tal guisa que no·m puoscha aiudar (78:18)
4. Cuidon c'aia perdut son sen (145:34)

B. Under what base form would one expect to find the following words in a glossary that adopted normalized spelling as recommended in chapter 4 and in the "Normalized OP Spelling" section at the beginning of the book?

1. abbat
2. amia 'friend' (f).
3. bellazor
4. dompna
5. frẹidament
6. gęra 'war'
7. humil
8. lanquant
9. lǫcx
10. longz
11. moillięr
12. nudz
13. ǫbs
14. quatre
15. senblar
16. senyhor
17. septmana
18. sęrv
19. vẹrd
20. via 'life'

C. In each group identify the one word which is not a variant of the same word as the other two (spelling is not normalized)

1. canço, canto, chansson
2. cen, cent, cenc
3. dolç, dotz, dous
4. fach, fait, fas
5. fil, fiel, fizel
6. placa, plaça, plassa
7. placa, plaia, plaja
8. regina, reïna, renha

5
NOUNS

5.1 OP Nouns: General

The function of nouns is revealed by their inflection, the inflection of accompanying articles and adjectives, word order, or as a last resort, common sense.

The declension system depends basically on the contrast between the ending -*s* and a zero ending symbolized as ∅. However, a stem ending in a sibilant--/s/ or /č/, spelled with *s*, *ç*, *ch*, *(i)g*, *h*, *z*, *x*, etc.--generally obscures the contrast between -*s* and -∅. A noun's gender, phonetic qualities, and origin determine the structural class to which it belongs, and this in turn determines the functional significance not only of inflections but also of final consonant modifications, added final syllables, and shifting stress.

5.2 Gender in OP

OP nouns are either m. or f. A few can have both genders, such as *mar* 'sea' (usually f.), *maṇ* 'hand' (usually f.), *sanc* 'blood' (usually m.), *serpen(t)* 'snake' (about equally divided), and some of the nouns in 5.4.5. In OP, the neuter gender exists only in adjectives (7.9) and pronouns (8.5). Gender can distinguish nouns that are otherwise identical: *estat* means 'summer' when f. and 'state' when m.

Gender is often motivated by the sex of persons or animals: m. *ome* 'man,' f. *domna* 'lady,' *pọl* 'rooster,' *pọla* 'hen.' However, some nouns referring to males or to humans in general are always f.: *espia* 'spy,' *gacha* 'watchman,' *garda* 'guard,' *guida* 'guide,' *poęsta* and *poestat* 'ruler,' *trompa* and *trompẹta* 'trumpeter'; *persona* 'person,' *gen(t)* 'people.' The great majority of nouns refer to abstractions or objects, and their gender depends solely on grammatical convention, thus m. *sọl* 'sun' and f. *luna* 'moon.'

The gender of nouns can be deduced from the following evidence:

1) Suffixes, as listed in 13.7.

2) Almost all OP nouns ending in *-a* are f. (but see 5.4.5). Most f. nouns end in *-a*, but many end in a consonant (5.5.2-4) and a few end in *-e* (5.5.1).

3) M. gender is signaled by the endings *-e* (e.g., *arbre* 'tree'), with a few exceptions, and by *-i* (*somi* 'sleep').

4) Some nouns are m. because of the way they are derived, including nouns formed from infinitives (*lo parlar* 'speaking'), nouns formed from adjectives (*lo vẹr* 'truth'), and compounds of verb plus noun (*lo baticǫr* 'heartbeat').

5.3 Case and Number

OP nouns, adjectives, articles, and pronouns have two cases (subject or nominative, and object or oblique) and two numbers (singular and plural). This gives a total of four different functions, abbreviated as nom. sg., obl. sg., nom. pl., obl. pl., usually cited in that order. However, many forms are ambiguous, since no noun has more than three different forms, most have only two, and some are invariable. The only constant is that the obl. pl. almost always ends in /s/. Number is more clearly marked than case, especially in f. nouns.

Nouns out of context are best cited in the obl. sg., thus Bernart de Ventadorn (not the nom. sg. Bernartz) and *fin' amor* (the troubadours' usual term for what scholars have come to call 'courtly love'). The eventual breakdown of the case system generalized the oblique case at the expense of the subject case, except that the nom. sg. *amors* is used where one would expect the oblique, as in the title of the fourteenth-century treatise *Las Leys d'amors*.

5.4.1 M. Nouns with Nom. Sg. -s

In the nom. sg. and obl. pl., the great majority of m. nouns add *-s*, *-z* (especially after *t*), or *-x* (after *c*):

nom. sg.	*obl. sg.*	*nom. pl.*	*obl. pl.*
murs 'wall'	mur	mur	murs
sermoṇs 'speech'	sermoṇ	sermoṇ	sermoṇs
Guilhems 'William'	Guilhem		
enamoratz 'lover'	enamorat	enamorat	enamoratz
amicx 'friend'	amic	amic	amicx

Nom. sg. *-s* increasingly disappears during the thirteenth century, e.g., in No. 181; in particular, nouns whose nom. sg. traditionally ends in *-es* are often assimilated to the *fabre* type (5.4.2).

A few nouns of this class have alternate nom. pl. forms with a palatal consonant: nom. pl. *anh* ~ *an* 'years,' *auzęlh* ~ *auzel* 'birds,' *cabẹlh* ~ *cabel* 'hair(s),' *cavalh* ~ *caval* 'horses.'

5.4.2 M. Nouns without Nom. Sg. -s

Many m. nouns ending in a vowel, and especially in *-re* and *-i*, have no *-s* in the nom. sg.:

nom. sg.	*obl. sg.*	*nom. pl.*	*obl. pl.*
fabre 'smith'	fabre	fabre	fabres
bẹure 'drink'	beure	beure	beures
empęri 'empire'	emperi	emperi	emperis

Nouns ending in *-atge* sometimes join this class: *messatge* 'message,' *damnatge* 'harm,' etc.

A nom. sg. *-s*, analogical to the most frequent class of m. nouns, is early used but does not become frequent till the thirteenth century (e.g., *paires*, 137:3). However, this analogical *-s* occurs about as often as not in substantivized infinitives like *beure(s)*. Also, nouns of this group which end in *-ire* can lose the *-e* and join the m. nouns with nom. sg. *-s*, thus nom. sg. *pairs* 'father' and obl. sg. *frair* 'brother' (both 74:5).

5.4.3 M. Nouns with Three Different Forms

Some m. nouns denoting persons have three different forms; only their obl. sg. and nom. pl. are identical, and their nom. sg. lacks *-s*. These nouns fall into three classes:

A) Nouns with one syllable fewer in the nom. sg. and with stable stress; there are only two such nouns (plus their compounds):

nom. sg.	*obl. sg.*	*nom. pl.*	*obl. pl.*
coms 'count'	comte	comte	comtes
om 'man'	ome	ome	omes

B) Nouns with a constant number of syllables but with a stress shift that isolates the nom. sg. These include nouns with the obl. sg. suffix *-dọr* and a few other words:

nom. sg.	*obl. sg.*	*nom. pl.*	*obl. pl.*
trobaire 'troubadour'	trobador	trobador	trobadors
crezẹire 'believer'	crezedor	crezedor	crezedors
jauzire 'enjoyer'	jauzidor	jauzidor	jauzidors
sẹnher 'lord'	senhor	senhor	senhors
ẹnfas 'child'	ẹnfan	ẹnfan(h)	ẹnfans

And similarly: *ancẹstre*, *ancessor* 'ancestor,' *autre*, *autor* 'witness,' *pastre*, *pastor* 'shepherd,' *sartre*, *sartor* 'tailor,' *abas*, *abat* 'abbot,' *laire*, *lairoṇ* 'thief,' etc.

C) Nouns with one syllable fewer in the nom. sg. and with shifting stress. These include most nouns with the syllable *-oṇ* in the obl. sg. and a few other words:

nom. sg.	*obl. sg.*	*nom. pl.*	*obl. pl.*
bar 'nobleman'	baroṇ	baroṇ	baroṇs
companh 'companion'	companhoṇ	companhoṇ	companhoṇs
Uc 'Hugh'	Ugoṇ		
nęps 'nephew'	nebọt	nebot	nebotz
pręire, p(r)ęstre 'priest'	prevęire	preveire	preveires

All these three-form paradigms are subject to various analogies tending toward regularization. The nom. sg. often adapts to the other three forms, or to the m. nouns with nom. sg. *-s*, or to both; thus we find nom. sg. *comte*; *oms*, *omes*; nom. sg. nouns in *-aires*, more rarely in *-adors*, *-ẹires*, *-ires*; *autors*; *sẹnhers*, *senhors*; *eṇfans*; *laires*, *lairoṇs*; *bars*, *baroṇs*; *companhs*; *pręstres*, *preveires*; and the like.

On the other hand, sometimes it is the obl. sg. that adapts to the nom. sg. by taking on forms like *laire*, *bar*, *companh*, *preire*. One also occasionally finds analogical obl. pl. forms like *homs* or *companhs*.

D) Rarely, one finds dialectal nom. pl. forms in *-i* or *-ei* like *li frairei* 'the brothers.'

5.4.4 M. Nouns: Invariable

Some nouns have only one form because of the difficulty in adding *-s* to a stem ending in

1) /ts/, spelled *-ts*, *-tz*, or *-ç*: *bratz*, *braç* 'arm,' *pęitz* 'chest,' *prętz* 'worth,' *latz* 'side';

2) /s/, spelled *-s* or *-ç*: *cas* 'case,' *sirventẹs* 'sirventes,' *vis* 'face,' *tem(p)s* 'time,' *ǫps* 'need,' *vęrs* 'verse';

3) /č/, spelled *-ch*, *-(i)g*, *-h* (see 5.6,11 and 7.2).

Midons 'milady' and *sidons* 'his lady' are also indeclinable by generalization of the nom. sg. used as a vocative; and some compounds are by their nature invariable, such as *crup-en-camí* 'stick-in-the-mud' (11:48).

From the earliest documents on, indeclinable m. nouns, particularly those ending in -*rs* or simple -*s*, can add -*es* in the obl. pl.: *brasses, cases, verses,* etc. This is rare in the troubadours, but is usual after the case system breaks down.

Sometimes a properly invariable noun will become declinable through analogical removal of the final stem consonant, thus obl. sg. *Peitęus, Peiteu* 'Poitiers.'

Cǫrs 'body, person' is properly indeclinable, while *cǫr* 'heart' by its origin lacks nom. sg. -*s*. However, *cor* usually receives -*s* in the nom. sg. by analogy to the nouns with -*s*, so that its nom. sg. then becomes identical to that of *cors*. The troubadours even seem to desire ambiguity in using these two very common words; for example, *mos cors* (nom. sg.) can often be understood as both 'my heart' and 'my body, my person, I myself.'

5.4.5 M. Nouns Ending in -a

The few m. nouns ending in -*a* follow the paradigm without -*s* in the nom. sg.:

nom. sg.	*obl. sg.*	*nom. pl.*	*obl. pl.*
papa 'pope'	papa	papa	papas
profęta 'prophet'	profeta	profeta	profetas

However, some nouns of this class can also be feminine in gender and paradigm, even though they refer to male persons. Of these, *papa* and *profęta* are about equally divided in gender; *evangelista* and *patriarca* are generally m.; *dia* and *psalmista* are generally m. *Artista, ermita, ipocrita,* and *legista* are only m., while *espia* and the associated nouns given in 5.2 are only f. Of all these nouns, only *dia* appears to take, on occasion, an analogical nom. sg. -*s* (e.g., in 28:49).

5.5.1 F. Nouns without Nom. Sg. -s

F. nouns ending in -*a* and the few in -*e* have -*Ø* in the sg. and -*s* in the pl., hence with no differentiation of cases:

nom. sg.	*obl. sg.*	*nom. pl.*	*obl. pl.*
domna 'lady'	domna	domnas	domnas
maire 'mother'	maire	maires	maires

However, -*s* does rarely occur in the nom. sg. of *maire*.

5.5.2 F. Nouns with Nom. Sg. -s

F. oxytons whose stem ends in a consonant or semivowel have -*s* or -*z* in all cases except the obl. sg.:

nom. sg.	*obl. sg.*	*nom. pl.*	*obl. pl.*
flọrs 'flower'	flor	flors	flors
vertatz 'truth'	vertat	vertatz	vertatz
naus 'ship'	nau	naus	naus

By analogy with the most frequent class of f. nouns, the nom. sg. -*s* is sometimes dropped. Present participles used as f. nouns follow this paradigm, with stable -*n* and unstable -*t* (5.6,10), as does *rẹns* 'thing, person' (though it behaves somewhat differently as a pronoun, 9.8).

5.5.3 F. Nouns with Shifting Stress

Two f. nouns designating persons preserve a three-form paradigm (cf. 5.4.4):

nom. sg.	*obl. sg.*	*nom. pl.*	*obl. pl.*
mọlher 'woman'	molher	molhers	molhers
sǫr(re) 'sister'	serọr	serors	serors

One also finds analogical forms such as nom. sg. *molhęrs*, *mọlhers*, *seror*, *sǫrs*, and obl. sg. *sor*.

5.5.4 F. Nouns: Invariable

F. nouns whose stem ends in a sibilant are usually regarded as invariable, thus *lutz* 'light,' *vọtz* 'voice,' and the numerous words with the f. suffix *-ritz*, such as *emperairitz* 'empress,' *defendeiritz* 'defendress,' *perd(r)itz* 'partridge,' etc. *Laus* 'praise' is often invariable but can also be declined like *naus*. These invariable f. nouns have extended plurals in *-es* more rarely than do the corresponding m. nouns. F. compounds like *portasẹlh* 'bucket-carrier' are also invariable.

5.6 Modification of Final Consonants before -s

Certain optional alternations of final consonants occur, due to the influence of the endings *-s* and *-∅*; final *-z*: then includes the glide consonant /t/.

1) postconsonantal /-f/ ~ /-s/: obl. sg. and nom. pl. *sęrf* (or *ser*) 'servant' ~ nom. sg. and obl. pl. *sers*;

2) /-l/ ~ /-u̯s/ (3.6; 4.13): *anhęl* 'lamb' ~ *anheus* (or *anhels*, *anhelz*);

3) /-l/ ~ /-lts/: *auzęl* 'bird' ~ *auzelz* (more often *auzels, auzeus*);

4) /-l̬/ ~ /-l̬ts/, /-lts/ (4.13), or /-ls/: *filh* 'son' ~ *filhz, filz, fils* (or *filhs* /fil̬s/);

5) stable /-n̬/ ~ /-nts/: *an* 'year' ~ *ans* (more often *ans*);

6) unstable /-n/ ~ /-nts/: *fiṇ* 'end' ~ *finz* (normally *fins*);

7) /-n̬/ ~ /-nts/, /-ns/: *senh* (or *sen*) 'sign' ~ *senz, sens* (or *senhs*);

8) /-sk/ ~ /-ks/: *bǫsc* 'forest' ~ *bocs*;

9) /-st/ ~ /-ts/: *ǫst* 'army' ~ *otz, oz*;

10) dropped unstable /-t/ ~ /-ts/: *joven* (less often *jovent*) 'youth' ~ *jovenz* (more often *jovens*); and all nouns, both m. and f., derived from present participles, thus *aman* (or *amant*) 'lover' ~ *amanz* (more often *amans*);

11) /-č/ ~ /-ts/: *gauch* /gau̯č/ 'joy' ~ *gauchs, gaugs, gaugz*, etc. /gau̯č, gau̯ts/ or *gautz* /gau̯ts/. The awkward combination of /č/ plus /s/ yields either to /ts/ or to /č/, both being variously spelled (4.10-11). When we find /č/ for /-č/ + *-s*, there is no alternation and such words are invariable, with /-č/ in all forms. Invariability is indicated by spellings like nom. sg. *gaug* (hence, with /-č/ in all forms) or obl. sg. *gautz* (with /-ts/ in all forms). Solutions vary with time and place. For reading aloud, it seems best to pronounce *gauch, gauchs, gaugs, gaugz*, etc., all with /-č/, pronouncing /-ts/ only where the spelling *-tz* predominates or where required by the rhyme. Thus, if *fagz* 'fact' (nom. sg.) and *amatz* 'you love' rhyme together, both must have /-ts/.

In many of these alternations, confusion and hesitation arise from analogy and from dialectal differences. The substitute forms indicated parenthetically in the above list produce no alternation. Some purely orthographic alternations merely reflect variations in the spelling of final consonants with or without following *-s*.

5.7 Variations of Stem Consonant and Suffix Between M. and F. Nouns

If the last consonant of a noun is an occlusive or fricative, it will be voiced in the f. before *-a/s* but unvoiced in the m. when final or before *-s* (4.4). Thus we have f. *lọba* and m. *lop* 'wolf,' *druda* and *drut* 'lover,' *amiga* and *amic* 'friend,' *sęrva* and *serf* 'servant.' Another type of m./f. alternation involves dropping a consonant: *amia* and *amic* (4.8, dialectal), *sęrva* and *ser* (4.9, dialectal), *paona* and *pao*, *paon* 'peacock' (4.14). Such phenomena are more far-reaching in adjectives (7.5).

Usually the f. has *-a* while the m. does not. Another way in which m./f. pairs are distinguished is through the addition of a gender-reflecting suffix for the f. or for both f. and m., thus m. *amador* and f. *amairitz* 'lover,' *fornięr* and *forniera* 'baker,' *leoṇ* 'lion' and *leonẹssa* 'lioness,' *sartor* 'tailor' and *sartẹssa*, *sartoressa*, *sartra* 'seamstress.'

5.8 Recapitulation of M. and F. Nouns (Excluding Analogical Forms)

1) One form (invariable)

	nom. sg.	*obl. sg.*	*nom. pl.*	*obl. pl.*
m. (5.4.4)	bratz	bratz	bratz	bratz
f. (5.5.4)	lutz	lutz	lutz	lutz

2) Two forms (with stable stress)

A) with nom. sg. -*s*

		nom. sg.	*obl. sg.*	*nom. pl.*	*obl. pl.*
m.	(5.4.1)	murs	mur	mur	murs
f.	(5.5.2)	flors	flor	flors	flors

B) without nom. sg. -*s*

m.	(5.4.2)	fabre	fabre	fabre	fabres
	(5.4.5)	papa	papa	papa	papas
f.	(5.5.1)	domna	domna	domnas	domnas

3) With three different forms

A) with one syllable fewer in the nom. sg. and with stable stress

m.	(5.4.3,A)	coms	comte	comte	comtes
f.	(5.5.3)	sǫr (sǫrre)	serọr	serors	serors

B) with a constant number of syllables but with shifting stress

m.	(5.4.3,B)	trobaire	trobadọr	trobador	trobadors
f.	(5.5.3)	mọlher	molhęr	molhers	molhers

C) with one syllable fewer in the nom. sg. and with shifting stress

m.	(5.4.3,C)	bar	barọn	barọn	barọns

5.9 The Use of Cases: General

The OP declensional system is torn between conflicting tendencies toward 1) regularization of the two-case pattern, particularly by generalizing the nom. sg. ending -*s* in m. nouns, and 2) marking number at the expense of case, which is the situation in the most numerous class of f. nouns. The first of these tendencies strengthens the two-case system through analogical creation of forms like nom. sg. *fabres*, *trobaires*, and *barọns*, while the second tendency threatens the very existence of the case distinction.

From the beginning, documents sometimes blur the case distinction, particularly by using the oblique for the subject case. But in verse, where the case system enjoyed the prestige of learnèd tradition and the advantages of permitting looser and more expressive word order, confusion does not become noteworthy until the thirteenth century. It is impossible to say whether a given usage is due to the poet or scribe unless the noun in question is in the rhyme, or is elided to show -Ø rather than -*s*, or has a paradigm with a changing number of syllables. The troubadours were certainly more careful than the later copyists, who were largely non-Occitans. At any rate, the language moved irresistibly toward a sg. without -*s* and a pl. with -*s*, and by the late fourteenth century the case system had broken down even in the literary idiom.

5.10 Use of the Subject Case

The chief function of the subject case, which has a distinctive form in almost all m. nouns. and many f. nouns, is to mark the subject of a finite verb. The verb can be active: "Lo coms de Peiteus si fo uns dels majors cortes" 'The Count of Poitiers was one of the greatest nobles' (1:1); or reflexive: "Ma voluntatz s'en vai" "My will goes away' (23:41); or passive: "si fos dos ans o tres / Lo segles faihz al meu plazer" 'if for two or three years / The world were made to my liking' (36:22-23). Words in apposition to a subject are likewise in the subject case: "E·l quartz de Briva·l Lemozis, / Us joglars" 'And the fourth [is] the Limousin from Brive, / A jongleur' (54:25-26).

A noun that is introduced by a conjunction and is the subject of an understood verb, as in comparisons and similar constructions, is normally in the subject case: "nulhs autres joys tan no·m play / Cum jauzimens d'amor de lonh" 'no other joy pleases me so much / As enjoyment of far-off love' (24:45-46). Occasionally, we also find the subject case where the function seems more oblique: "atressi·m ten en balansa / Com la naus en l'onda" 'she keeps me in uncertainty / Like the ship on the sea' (29:39-40).

Linking verbs, such as those of being, seeming, or becoming, retain the subject case: "'Auzels sui'" '"I am a bird"' (17:19); "aicel jorns me sembla nadaus" 'that day seems Christmas to me' (28:46); "tals se fai cavalgaire" 'such a one acts like a knight' (15:40). Verbs taking a predicate in the subject case include *ęsser* 'to be,' *se far* 'to act like, become, pretend to be,' *se fẹnher* 'to pretend to be,' *parer*, *resemblar*, and *semblar* 'to seem, resemble,' *se sentir* 'to feel,' *se tener* 'to consider oneself,' *se tornar* and *venir* 'to become,' and passives like *ęsser elegitz* 'to be elected,' *ęsser fach* 'to be made,' *ęsser levatz* 'to be promoted,' and *ęsser apelatz* or *clamatz* 'to be called.' But some of these also on occasion admit the oblique: "Guirautz de Bornelh, / Que sembl' odre sec" 'Guiraut de Bornelh, / Who seems a dry wineskin' (54:13-14). Other expressions meaning "to be called"--*aver nom, s'apelar, nomnar, se far clamar, se far dire*, etc.--usually take the subject case, for example: "se fez dire Cercamons" 'he had himself called Cercamon' (18:2-3; but cf. "un trobador que avia nom Cercamon" 'a troubadour who had the name Cercamon,' 9:13).

The subject case is also used to address someone or something: "Auzels" 'Bird' (17:34), "Glorios Dieus" 'Glorious God' (20:19), "Amicx" 'Friend' (23:45), "miralhs" 'mirror' (37:21), "Senher marques" 'Lord Marquis' (111:1). But the oblique sometimes assumes this function: "estornel" 'starling' (16:1), "Sant Jacme" 'St. James' (20:53), "bel companho" 'fair companion' (47:6).

5.11 Use of the Oblique Case

The oblique case marks the object of a transitive verb: "Lo plaing comenz iradamen / D'un vers don hai lo cor dolen" 'I begin this lament sorrowfully / In a poem for which my heart is sad' (20:1-2). Similarly, with a term in apposition to a direct object: "ie·l doney a son senhor polin payssen" 'I gave him to his lord as a grazing colt' (2:19), and when a linking verb refers us back to a direct object: "L'appellava son ioglar" 'He called her his jongleur' (39:7). Expressions like *i a* 'there is, there are' and *vẹc vos, vẹus* 'here is, here are; behold' also normally take a direct object: "Assatz hi a pas e camis" 'There are many passes and roads' (24:26). The oblique also indicates the subject of an infinitive (12:12).

With words and names designating persons, the oblique can indicate possession, attribution, or relationship: "Per amor Dieu" 'For love of God' (24:16), "l'escola n'Eblo" 'the school of Lord Eblon' (38:23), "Lo Poch Nostra Domna" (or Santa Maria, a city). This oblique follows the other noun, except for *autrui* and often *Dęu*: "l'autrui aver" 'others' property,' "per Deu voluntat" 'by God's will.' (The preposition *de* can also be used, 13.1.)

The oblique can designate a person who receives the action indicated by a verb or noun: "Qe Cercamonz tramet n'Eblo" 'Which Cercamon sends to Lord Eblon' (20:50); "... a fenit sa demanda / So frair Richart" '... has withdrawn his claim / Against his brother Richard' (74:4-5). (The preposition *a* also indicates indirect objects, 13.1.)

The object of a preposition is in the oblique: "en eisil" 'into exile' (8:5); "per son amic" 'as her friend' (25:27).

The oblique can be used adverbially, with no preposition, with complements of measure, time, manner, circumstance, etc.: "un dorn" 'by a hand's breadth' (54:20), "trenta deniers" 'for thirty deniers,' "manhtas vetz" 'often' (29:70), "lonc tems" 'for a long time,' "totz jorns" 'every day, always' (22:15), "los sautz menutz" 'with small jumps,' "mon escien(t)" 'in my opinion' (4:22).

Chapter 5: Exercises

A. (5.2) Using as a guide the meaning, suffix, or ending, give the gender of the following nouns

1. amor 'love'	6. agradatge 'pleasure'
2. ęga 'mare'	7. empęri 'empire'
3. ardimen 'boldness'	8. pęrdre 'loss'
4. parẹlha 'union'	9. lǫc 'place'
5. agradansa 'pleasure'	10. lǫga 'place'

B. (5.4, 5.6) Give the normal complete non-analogical declension of these m. nouns

1. nom. sg. emperaire 'emperor'
2. nom. pl. fabre 'smith'
3. obl. pl. jauzidors 'enjoyers'
4. nom. sg. gatz 'cat'
5. nom. pl. bratz 'arms'
6. obl. sg. evangelista 'evangelist'
7. nom. pl. pǫch 'hill'
8. obl. pl. omes 'men'

C. (5.5-6) Give the normal complete non-analogical declension of these f. nouns

1. obl. sg. sazọn 'season'
2. obl. sg. esperansa 'hope'
3. obl. pl. partz 'parts'
4. nom. pl. vẹrges 'virgins'
5. obl. sg. molhęr 'woman'
6. obl. pl. trichairitz 'trickstress'

D. (5.10-11, 5.4-5) Indicate the correct cases by adding needed endings

1. Cercamon___ si fo uns joglar___ ...

2. Chantar___ no pot gaire valer, / Si d'ins dal cor___ no mou lo chan___

3. Sor___, del banh___ nos apareillem (8 syllables)

4. Del com___ de Peitieu me plaing / Q'era de Proeza___ compaing___

5. Gasco___ cortes, nominatiu, / Perdut avez lo segnoriu___

6. Pro ai del chan___ essenhador___ / Entorn mi et ensenhairit___

7. ... flor___ d'albespi___ [pl.] / No·m platz plus que l'yvern___ ...

8. Ueit jorn___ ez encar mais estei / En aquel forn___

9. Ami___ Peirol___, malamen / vos anatz ...

10. ... membre·us del bar___ / Que denant vos jai pelegri___

6
ARTICLES

6.1 The Article: General

The article specifies the sense of the following noun as being general, particular, etc.; it agrees with the noun in number, case, and gender. The noun is usually expressed but may be understood ("una cruzela" 'a cruel one,' "la plus cara" 'the dearest one') or represented by a pronoun ("lo meu" 'mine,' "lo cal" 'which'). The definite article is more common than the indefinite article, while the partitive is comparatively rare, but all three expand their roles, particularly during the thirteenth century. During the same century, as with nouns, the oblique case begins to push out the subject case.

6.2 The Indefinite Article

The indefinite article follows the pattern of *murs* and *domna*:

	masculine	*feminine*
nom. sg.	uṇs	una (often un' before a vowel)
obl. sg.	uṇ	
nom. pl.	uṇ	unas
obl. pl.	uṇs	

The singular generally presents a newly characterized or previously unmentioned noun: "Farai un vers de dreyt nien" 'I will make a poem about nothing at all' (3:1). The various forms of *uṇ* also appear as an indefinite pronoun (9.8) and a numeral (9.9).

Forms with initial *h-* are not rare: *hun*, etc. The form *us* is more common than *uns*; and the rare form *u* is found chiefly before nasal consonants. The manuscripts and some editions often represent the indefinite article and the numeral "one" by the signs ·*i*·, ·*j*·, ·*I*·.

The plural is uncommon; it is translated as 'some' or left untranslated in English. It designates pairs of objects, collective nouns, nouns whose singular is not normally used, and occasionally other objects: "us gans, unas sabatas" '(a pair of) gloves, shoes'; "us sautiers, us candeliers, us sonetz" '(some) psalters, candlesticks, tunes' (54:10, 11, 76).

6.3 The Definite Article: Forms

<table>
<tr><th></th><th>full forms</th><th colspan="2">contracted forms</th></tr>
<tr><td>masculine</td><td></td><td>proclitic</td><td>enclitic</td></tr>
<tr><td>nom. sg.</td><td>lọ; lẹ; li</td><td rowspan="2">l'</td><td rowspan="2">·l</td></tr>
<tr><td>obl. sg.</td><td>lo; le</td></tr>
<tr><td>nom. pl.</td><td>li; lhi, los</td><td>(l')</td><td>usually ·il(l), ·l, ·lh</td></tr>
<tr><td>obl. pl.</td><td>lọs; lẹs</td><td>---</td><td>·ls; ·lz</td></tr>
<tr><td>feminine</td><td></td><td></td><td></td></tr>
<tr><td>nom. sg.</td><td>la; li, lhi</td><td rowspan="2">l'</td><td>(·l, ·lh)</td></tr>
<tr><td>obl. sg.</td><td>la</td><td>(·l)</td></tr>
<tr><td>pl.</td><td>las</td><td>---</td><td></td></tr>
</table>

Some texts show a totally different "sigmatic" series: *sọ, sos, sa, sas, zọ,* etc.

Elision of the sg. article to *l'* is almost universal in the m. and is usual in the f. However, *la* is often retained before the numeral *un/a*: *la una* 'one' (4:37). Postvocalic *lo* and *los* almost always contract, particularly in verse: *e·l, e·ls* 'and the.' The rare enclisis of *la* is chiefly a metrical convenience: "e·l flors reviu" 'and the flower revives' (100:15). The m. nom. pl. *li* is treated enclitically ("e·lh vielh" 'and the old,' 79:2) more often than proclitically ("l'auzelh" 'the birds,' 14:10; but "li aucel," 7:2, with *li* retaining syllabic value).

When the m. article occurs between certain common prepositions and a noun beginning in a consonant, the preposition and article can combine as one word:

	m. obl. sg.	*m. obl. pl.*
a 'to'	al	als
com, con 'with'	cọl	---
dẹ 'of'	dẹl	dels
en 'in'	ẹl	els
pẹr 'for'	pẹl	pels
sus 'on'	sul	suls

However, the full forms remain possible; and reduction is not usual for *com* and *per* and is rare for *sus*. The contracted pl. forms occasionally end in *-lz*. One also finds the conjunction *com, con* 'as' combining with the article to form *cọl* or, less often, *cols* (better written *co·l, co·ls*, just as *e·l* is preferable for *e lo*).

When an *l* resulting from a reduction of the article occurs between two vowels, medieval scribes and modern editors have generally preferred proclitic treatment, thus "e l'argen" 'and the money' or "de l'argen." Some use the raised dot with an enclitic article: "a·ls joves" 'to the young' (79:2).

6.4 The Definite Article: Use

The definite article usually individualizes a precise object, person, or concept; these can be unique ("lo solelh" 'the sun') or expressly particularized ("lo vescoms de Ventadorn" 'the Viscount of Ventadorn'), or they can have been previously referred to. Another use of the definite article has a strong, almost demonstrative force: "Lo plaing comenz iradamen" 'I begin this lament with sorrow' (20:1). At the opposite extreme is a weak, generic usage, usually with plural nouns: "De las domnas me dezesper" 'I despair of ladies' (37:25).

The definite article is used with parts of the body when their possessor is clear: "fetz li taillar la testa" 'he had his head cut off' (118:13). It also has a distributive meaning with temporal expressions: "una vegada l'an" 'once a year.' See 9.2 for the definite article used as a pronoun.

6.5 The Partitive Article

The partitive article has two series of forms, one identical to the preposition *dẹ*, *d'*, and the other identical to *de* plus the definite article (thus: *del*, *de la*, *dels*, *de las*). Its use is optional, and it is translated into English as 'some' or is often left untranslated.

The original and most common function of the partitive article is to indicate an unspecified portion of an uncountable substance. That is, it has the function of the indefinite article before non-count nouns. Thus, alongside "beure vi" 'to drink wine' (with no article) we find "beure de vi" with the same meaning, while "beure del vi," which at first meant 'to drink some of the [previously specified] wine,' soon became synonymous to the other two expressions.

The partitive began also to be used with other sorts of nouns. Thus with abstract nouns: "Et elh eis sent del espaven" 'And he himself feels terror' (54:75). With count nouns, the partitive took on a plural form which functions essentially as an alternative plural of the indefinite article (the plural *uns*, etc., being restricted to use with pairs, etc.): "de sos sirventes" (71.II:17) or "dels sieus sirventes" (81:13-14) 'some of his sirventes.' Occasionally, one even finds the partitive used with the subject of a verb or with the object of a preposition.

With a negative, the simple form *d(e)* is preferred to the compound forms *del*, etc.: "Non ai de sen per un efan" 'I don't have (enough) sense for a child' (27:45). So too when an adjective precedes the noun: "d'aquel vi" '(some of) that wine,' "de bo vi" '(some) good wine,' "de caitivetz vers" 'wretched verses' (9:9), "de grans bes" 'great rewards' (71.I:12). *D(e)* by itself is also used when an adjective stands alone, the noun being understood: "n'i a de grans" 'there are big ones,' "n'i a d'altres" 'there are others.' *De* can also be used with adverbs of quantity (9.8) and numerals (9.9).

6.6 Non-Use of Articles

No article is generally needed when it would have little or no semantic value, principally in the following cases:

A) A noun is already sufficiently particularized by its own meaning or its qualifiers, thus

1) almost always with proper names, usually with months, and often with days: "Guilhem" 'William,' "febrer" 'February,' "dimartz" 'Tuesday'; however, names accompanied by an adjective take the article: "lo bels Narcisus" 'the handsome Narcissus' (37:24);

2) with geographical terms: "a Tolosa" 'to Toulouse,' "en Provensa" 'in Provence,' "de Fransa" 'from France,' "Si com clau mars e Durensa" 'As the sea and the Durance enclose' (87:10). But when an adjective is added, the article is used: "Tolosa la gran" 'great Toulouse'; and rivers take the article about as often as not: "(lo) Roẓer" 'the Rhone';

3) often with ethnic names: "Felon Gascon et Angevi" 'The villainous Gascons and Angevins' (8:16);

4) before certain adjectives that sufficiently limit or determine the following noun, namely unstressed possessive adjectives (8:13), fractions and cardinal numerals (9.12), negative adjectives (13.3), and generally interrogative and indefinite adjectives (9.9, 9.11);

5) with linking verbs that introduce or stand in apposition to a predicate noun: "fo moiller del rei Enric d'Engleterra, maire del rei jove" 'was the

wife of King Henry of England, (and the) mother of the young king' (1:6).

B) The noun is nonparticularized, especially

1) when its sense is general and unrestricted (even when there is a qualifying adjective): "Domna fai gran pechat mortal / Que no ama cavalier leal" 'A lady commits a great mortal sin / If she doesn't love a loyal knight' (4:7-8); "Reiesme son, mas reis no ges" 'There are kingdoms, but no king at all' (76:17);

2) with unqualified abstractions, qualities, and elements: *bontat* 'goodness,' *aigua* 'water,' *fręg e calọr* 'cold and heat,' *aur e argen* 'gold and silver.' Such terms are often regarded as personifications (whether printed with an initial capital letter or not): *natura* 'nature,' *fortuna* 'fortune,' *amor* 'love,' *mesura* 'moderation,' *prętz* 'merit,' thus in context: "no·i gardet sen, ni gentilessa, ni honor" 'she did not heed wisdom or nobility or honor' (26:21);

3) with negations (13.3), as in the last example under B1), above, or in "Non volc mais muiller" 'He never wanted a wife' (44:11); also in *ni* ... *ni* ... 'neither ... nor ...' and *sens* ... *ni* ... 'without ... or ...';

4) in conditions implying hypothetical or denied existence: "s'agues bon destrier" 'if I had a good steed' (86:1).

C) The noun is combined with other words to form a closely-linked unit, thus

1) with a preposition plus an unmodified noun: "En chaval, armatz, ses temor" 'On horseback, armed, without fear' (80:23);

2) with two coordinated nouns of general meaning: "noih e jorn" 'night and day';

3) in locutions where a verb and direct object form one sense unit: "aver razon" 'to be right,' "aver moiller" 'to have a wife,' "aver nom" 'to be named,' "tenir viatge" 'to make a trip';

4) in generic comparisons: "plus ez blanca qu'evori" 'she is whiter than ivory' (5:13).

Chapter 6: Exercises

A. (6.3) Supply the correct form of the definite article; determine genders from 5.2, 13.7, or a dictionary

1. E sa maire calfava ___ forn / Et amassava ___ issermen
2. Si tuit ___ dol e ___ plor e ___ marrimen / E ___ dolors ...
3. ___ nuech vai e ___ jorns ve / ... / E ___ alba no·s rete

B. Insert the proper forms, if needed, of the appropriate articles, or of the preposition *de*

1. ... fo ... ___ fils d ___ sirven e d ___ fornegeira
2. Non a ni ___ sima ni ___ raïtz
3. "Mas trop vezem anar per ___ mon / ___ folla gent"
4. Qu'en ___ joi d ___ amor ai et enten / ___ boch' e ___ olhs e ___ cor e ___ sen

5. E cantava mielhs d ___ home d ___ mon, e fo ___ bos trobaire
6. ... ac per ___ moiller ___ duquessa d ___ Normandia
7. ... si fo ___ chastelas d ___ eveschat d ___ Peiregorc, ___ senher d ___ chastel que avia ___ nom ___ Autafort
8. ... se deletava molt en dire ... ___ similitudines d ___ bestias e d ___ ausels e d ___ omes, e d ___ sol e d ___ estellas
9. ___ Emperador avem d ___ tal maneira / Que non a ___ sen ni ___ saber
10. Senes ___ breu de ___ parguamina
11. Ni tan d ___ ira non ac de se
12. Lanquan ___ jorn son lonc en ___ may / M'es belh ___ dous chans d ___ auzelhs de lonh
13. ... no·m laisset re / Mas ___ dezirer e ___ cor volon
14. ___ proesa grans qu'el vostre cors s'aizina / E ___ rics pretz qu'avetz

7
ADJECTIVES

7.1 OP Adjectives: General

OP adjectives (including present and past participles when these are used adjectivally) reflect gender, number, and case. While each noun inherently possesses m. or f. gender, each adjective is m., f., or neuter according to the noun, pronoun, or unexpressed referent which it qualifies. As with articles and pronouns, an adjective's number and case depend on its function in the sentence.

Morphologically, adjectives comprise two main groups: 1) those that distinguish gender in all four forms; and 2) those whose m. and f. differ only in the nom. pl.

Adjectives follow the same pattern as corresponding nouns; thus *feloṇ* 'evil,' *glotoṇ* 'greedy,' etc., follow the model of *baroṇ* (5.4.3,C). Synthetic comparatives (7.11) are also three-form adjectives; for other types of special adjectives, see 8.12, 9.2, 9.4-5, and 9.8.

7.2 M. Adjectives

Almost all m. adjectives follow the same pattern as the *murs* class of m. nouns (5.4.1):

nom. sg.	*obl. sg.*	*nom. pl.*	*obl. pl.*
bęls 'beautiful	bel	bel	bels
fizẹls 'faithful'	fizel	fizel	fizels
amans 'loving'	aman	aman	amans
amatz 'loved'	amat	amat	amatz

Rarely, one finds dialectal forms of the nom. pl. in a palatalized consonant (*amach*; cf. 5.4.1) or in *-i* (*beli*; cf. 5.4.3,D).

Like the *fabre* type of m. nouns (5.4.2), m. adjectives in *-e* usually do not take nom. sg. *-s*:

nom. sg.	*obl. sg.*	*nom. pl.*	*obl. pl.*
paubre 'poor'	paubre	paubre	paubres
fẹble 'weak'	feble	feble	febles

Similarly, *agre* 'bitter,' *alęgre* 'happy,' *altre* 'other,' *nẹgre* 'black,' *tendre* 'tender,' *salvatge* 'wild,' and sometimes adjectives in *i*: *savi* 'wise,' etc. An analogical nom. sg. *-s* is not rare: "autres" (24:45), "salvatges" (2:15). The final nom. sg. *-e* almost always elides before a vowel: "autr' escondich" 'another excuse' (78:13).

M. adjectives are invariable when their stem ends in a sibilant: *divęrs* 'diverse,' *fals* 'false,' *francẹs* 'French,' *gloriọs* 'glorious,' *joiọs* 'joyous,' and all others in the common suffixes *-ẹs* and *-ọs*. But as with invariable nouns (5.4.4), an analogical *-es* sometimes appears, particularly in later texts, in the obl. pl. and even the nom. pl., thus giving *diverses*, *glorioses*, etc. Adjectives ending in /-č/, like the corresponding nouns, become invariable when inflectional *-s* is absorbed into the final /-č/: nom. sg. *perfęg(z)* and obl. pl. *perfegz*, pronounced with

/-č/ or /-ts/, become identical in pronunciation to obl. sg. and nom. pl. *perfech, perfeg,* etc.

Also invariable are the few adjectives in -*ọr* derived from Latin genitive plurals: *paganor* 'pagan,' *sarrazinor* 'Saracen,' etc. *Prọs* 'excellent' is often invariable, having nom. sg. and obl. pl. *pros* and obl. sg. and nom. pl. *pros* or *proṇ*. On the other hand, sometimes a properly invariable adjective becomes declined through analogical removal of the final stem consonant, thus in the m. nom. sg. *malva(i)tz, malvat* 'bad' and *verais, verai* 'true.'

7.3 F. Adjectives

Most f. adjectives, including all past participles, have identical nom. and obl. forms in each number and correspond to the f. nouns in -*a* (5.5.1):

nom. and obl. sg.	*nom. and obl. pl.*
bę̧la 'beautiful'	belas
paubra 'poor'	paubras
falsa 'false'	falsas
amada 'loved'	amadas

Adjectives whose m. forms end in an unstressed vowel follow this same pattern: *savi, sávia* 'wise' (see 3.10), *ambigu, ambîgua* 'ambiguous.' The f. ending -*a* is generally elided before a vowel, as in "la bon' esperansa" 'good hope' (29:37).

Many f. adjectives, including those ending in -*al*, -*ẹl*, -*il* or derived from present participles, are declined like *flọrs* (5.5.2) and hence are identical to m. adjectives like *bę̧l* except for the nom. pl.:

nom. sg.	*obl. sg.*	*nom. pl.*	*obl. pl.*
fizẹls 'faithful'	fizel	fizels	fizels
fǫrtz 'strong'	fort	fortz	fortz
amans 'loving'	aman	amans	amans

Similarly *brẹu* 'short,' *gentil* 'noble,' *jọvẹn* 'young,' *lẹu* 'easy,' *mortal* 'mortal,' *vẹrt* 'green,' etc.

However, some f. adjectives which properly are without -*a* receive an analogical -*a* during the literary period, and hence show dual declensions:

nom. sg.	*obl. sg.*	*nom. and obl. pl.*
grans 'big'; granda	gran; granda	grans; grandas
valens 'worthy'; valenta	valen; valenta	valens; valentas

And similarly *cruzẹl(a)* 'cruel,' *jauzen(ta)* 'joyous,' *plazen(ta)* 'pleasing,' etc. Though the tendency to add -*a* appears in the twelfth century, only in *gran* does it become common before the fifteenth century.

Invariable f. nouns (5.5.4) remain invariable when used adjectivally, thus *trichairitz* 'deceitful,' etc. Also invariable in the f. are the few adjectives in -*ọr* (7.2), as in "la gen paganor" 'the pagan people,' and also the adjective *prọs* 'excellent,' except that alongside *pros femna* 'good woman' one finds the compound *profemna*, *pro femna*.

7.4 Modifications of Final Consonants before -s

The same sorts of alternation of final consonants occur in adjectives where -*s* and -∅ contrast as in the corresponding nouns (5.6):

1) postconsonantal /-f/ ~ /-s/: obl. sg. and nom. pl. *salf* (or *sal*) 'safe' ~ nom. sg. and obl. pl. *sals*

2) /-l/ ~ /-u̯s/: *natural* 'natural' ~ *naturaus* (or *naturals*, probably also pronounced with /-au̯s/)

3) /-l/ ~ /-lts/: *sọl* 'alone' ~ *solz* (more often *sols*)

4) /-l̮/ ~ /-l̮ts/, /-lts/: *vȩlh* 'old' ~ *velhz*, *velz* (or *velhs*)

5) unstable /-n/ ~ /-nts/: *fiṇ* 'fine' ~ *finz* (or *fins*, *fis*)

6) /-sk/ ~ /-s/: *frẹsc* 'fresh' ~ *fres* (or *frescs*)

7) /-st/ ~ /-ts/, /-s/: *trist* 'sad' ~ *tritz*, *tris* (or *tristz*)

8) dropped unstable /-t/ ~ /-ts/: *corren* (or *corrent*) 'rapid' ~ *correnz* (or *correns*); *gran* (or *grant*) 'big' ~ *granz* (or *grans*)

9) /-č/ ~ /-ts/: *fach* 'done' ~ *fatz* or ~ *fachs*, *fagz*, etc. when these are pronounced /fatz/ (4.10,B; such words can also be invariable, 7.2; see also 5.6,11)

On the whole, these alternations arise from regular phonetic evolution; however, they are often obscured by analogy or by phonetic reductions such as /ts/ > /s/ (4.10). There are also purely orthographic alternations such as *-t* ~ *-z*; *-nt* ~ *-nz*; *-chs*, *-gz*, etc. representing /č/ ~ *-ch*; *-c* ~ *-cx*, *-x*, *-cz*; etc.

7.5 Variations of Stem Consonant between M. and F.

Alternations of stem occur (as in nouns, 5.7) whenever a stem-final consonant behaves differently in the f. before *-a(s)* and in the m. when word-final or before *-s*.

A consonant which is voiced and/or palatalized before *-a(s)* will always be unvoiced and will often be nonpalatalized when it is final or precedes *-s* (or *-z*, *-x*):

		fem. sg.	*m. obl. sg.*
1)	/b/ ~ /p/	ǫrba 'blind'	orp
2)	/d/ ~ /t/	muda 'mute'	mut
3)	/d/, /z/ ~ /t/	nuda, nuza 'naked'	nut
4)	/d/, /z/ ~ /Ø/, /t/	cruda, cruza 'raw'	cru, crut
5)	/č/ ~ /k/	francha (franca) 'noble'	franc
6)	/g/ ~ /k/	larga 'large'	larc
7)	/g/, /ǧ/ ~ /k/	longa, lonja 'long'	lonc
8)	/ǧ/ ~ /č/	mięja (mieia) 'half'	miech (miei)
9)	/i̯d/, /ǧ/ ~ /i̯t/, /č/	fręida, freja 'cold'	frech, freit
10)	/s/ ~ /ts/	faitissa 'pretty'	faititz
11)	/v/ ~ /f/, Ø	salva 'safe'	salf, sal
12)	/z/ ~ /s/	cortẹsa 'courtly'	cortẹs
13)	/(i̯)z/ ~ /(i)ts/	malva(i)za (malvada) 'bad'	malva(i)tz (malvais, malvat)

However, many adjectives have /s/, /t/, or /č/ in both the m. and the f. Thus with /s/: *dọus/sa* 'gentle,' *gras/sa* 'fat,' *grǫs/sa* 'big.' With /t/: *azaut/a* 'skillful,' *devǫt/a* 'devoted,' *petit/a* 'small'; in the diminutive suffix *-ẹt/a*, such as *alegrẹt/a* 'joyous'; and usually in a consonant plus *-t*, such as *cobęrt/a* 'covered,' *cọrt/a* 'short,' *mǫrt/a* 'dead' (but *sọrda* ~ *sort* 'deaf'). And with /č/ or /t/: *dich/a*, *dit/a* 'said,' *drẹ(i)ch/a*, *dre(i)t/a* 'straight,' *fach/a*, *fait/a* 'done.'

All past participles in *-ada/-at*, *-ida/-it*, and *-uda/-ut* follow the alternation of 2), above; however, many irregular past participles follow 12) (e.g., *prisa/pris* 'taken,' or else have no alternation.

A consonant in the f. can correspond to Ø in the m., as in 4) and 11) above, particularly in adjectives with unstable *-n* and *-t*:

	fem. sg.	*m. obl. sg.*
14) /n/ ~ Ø	bona 'good'	boṇ
15) /nda/ ~ /n/	blonda 'blond'	blon
16) /nta/ ~ /n/	genta 'nice'	gen(t)

Finally, a consonant in the f. can correspond to a semivowel in the m.:

17) /v/ ~ /u̯/	nǫva 'new'	nou
	viva 'alive'	viu

7.6 Other Variations between M. and F. Adjectives

Some adjectives have an additional syllable in the f.: f. sg. *cọbeza*, *ǫrreza*, *sábeza*, *tębeza* 'desirous, horrible, agreeable, tepid' correspond to the m. forms *cobe*, *orre*, *sabe*, *tebe*. Such adjectives have alternate forms such as f. sg. *orrẹza*, *orra* and m. nom. sg. *cobẹs*, *tebẹs*. The difference between m. and f. is also noteworthy in adjectives derived from three-form nouns (5.4.3,C): f. sg. *glọta*, *fẹla* 'greedy, bad,' m. nom. sg. *glot*, *fel*, m. obl. sg. *glotoṇ*, *feloṇ*, etc. As in the nouns, we find analogical forms like f. sg. *felona* (also *felonẹssa*), m. nom. sg. *fels*, and m. obl. sg. *fel*.

Some adjectives have suffixes that differ in the m. and f.: f. *francẹsca* (or *francesa*), m. *francẹs* 'French.' Adjectives in *-ięr/a* have a multiplicity of forms: f. sg. *primiera*, *-ieira*, *-eira*, m. obl. sg. *primier*, *-ieir*, *-er*, *-eir*, etc. *Piu* 'pious' has *pia* as its f.

Other adjectives show optional alternations: f. sg. *viva* 'alive' ~ m. obl. sg. *vięu* (or *viu*; see 3.11); *nǫva*, *nuęva* (or *nuova*) 'new' ~ *nuou* (or *nou*; see 3.8).

7.7 Recapitulation of Major M. and F. Types

M. with nom. sg. *-s*, f. in *-a*:

	nom. sg.	*obl. sg.*	*nom. pl.*	*obl. pl.*
m.	bęls	bel	bel	bels
f.	bela	bela	belas	belas

M. with nom. sg. *-s*, f. without *-a*:

m.	fizẹls	fizel	fizel	fizels
f.			fizels	

M. without nom. sg. *-s*, f. in *-a*:

m.	paubre	paubre	paubre	paubres
f.	paubra	paubra	paubras	paubras

Invariable m., f. in *-a*:

m.	fals	fals	fals	fals
f.	falsa	falsa	falsas	falsas

7.8 Use of M. and F. Adjectives

Adjectives agree in gender, case, and number with the noun or pronoun which they modify: "lo veiran jov' e mesqui" 'they will see him (to be) young and weak' (8:20). Case usage with linking verbs is determined as for nouns (5.10): "Que·s fai de son trobar trop bauz" 'Who acts too proud about his song-writing' (54:56). *Se tener per* 'to consider oneself' takes the subject case, e.g., with *pagatz* '(well) paid,' *rics* 'rich'; but *se tener a* takes the oblique. When an adjective modifies two or more nouns simultaneously, it normally agrees with the nearest noun: "Verais lums e clartatz" 'True light and brightness' (47:1).

Adjectives used adverbially (13.2) normally remain invariable, as do participles with a verbal function (12.3).

7.9 Neuter Adjectives

Unlike nouns, adjectives have a neuter. Existing only in the nom. sg., it is the same as the m. nom. sg. minus *-s*. It is common in words indicating a personal reaction ("m'es bel, bon, gen" 'it is pleasing to me'; "m'es fer, greu, estranh," 'it is unpleasing to me') or an opinion ("m'es parven, semblan" 'it seems to me'). The neuter is used only when the subject is impersonal or is a neuter pronoun: "De lai don plus m'es e bel" 'From there [her] of which (whom) it is most pleasing to me' (7:7); "E·lh lauza so que no·lh es gen" 'And urges her (to do) what is not pleasing to her' (28:35). Constructions where a postponed clause is the subject of a passive verb also fall in this category, thus "non fo crezut que ... " 'it was not believed that ... ' (66:6).

Except in the set expressions consisting of personal pronoun plus *ęsser* plus adjective, the m. form with -*s* often replaces the neuter. Thus we generally find "es vers" 'it is true' and "es dreitz" 'it is just' (the /-s/ ending is perhaps due to these words being interpreted as m. nouns). Similar expressions with nouns are "m'es mestiers" 'it is necessary for me' (with the -*s* often being dropped by analogy to the neuter adjectives) and "vejaire m'es" 'it seems to me' (without -*s* because of being treated as a noun of the *fabre* class, or else by analogy to the neuter adjectives).

7.10 Position of Adjectives

Adjectival position is quite free. Short adjectives generally precede the noun: "bel amic" 'fine friend,' "bona domna" 'good lady.' Their postposition, being unusual, adds force: "almorna gran" 'great pity' (27:48). Demonstrative, possessive, and indefinite adjectives and those expressing quantity ("mantas vetz" 'many times,' "tantas dolors" 'so many woes') also generally precede the noun. Most adjectives, however, are quite mobile: "l'erba fresca" 'the fresh grass' and "drut leyal" 'faithful lover' differ only stylistically from "la fresc' erba" and "leyal drut."

The adjective can be separated from its noun by an adverb like *mọlt* 'very' or, exceptionally, by a verb and any related elements: "Canson non fetz neguna" 'He made no song at all' (51:7).

When two or more adjectives modify one noun, they normally remain in their usual position, with a coordinating conjunction preceding the last in a series: "Ai, bon' amors encobida, / Cors be faihz, delgatz e plas" 'Ah, good desired love, / Well-formed, slender and smooth body' (38:50-51).

7.11 Comparatives of Superiority: Forms

The comparative of superiority is normally formed by adding *plus*, *mais*, or rarely *męlhs* (literally 'better') before the adjective, thus "plus dur" 'harder.' As opposed to such analytic (two-word) comparatives, a number of common monosyllabic adjectives have synthetic (one-word) comparatives:

positive: *m. obl. sg.*	*comparative:* *m. nom. sg.*	*comparative:* *m. obl. sg.*
bęl 'beautiful'	bel(l)aire, bel(l)ázer	bel(l)azọr
bọn 'good'	męlher, mięlher	melhọr
gen 'nice'	gẹnser, jẹnser, gẹncer	genzọr, gensọr
gran 'big'	májer, máger, máier, maire	majọr, maior
mal 'bad'	p(i)ęger, p(i)ęjer, p(i)ęier, peire	pejọr, peior
pauc 'small'	men(d)re, meindre	menọr

These have the shifting stress and the three different forms characteristic of nouns like *trobador* (5.4.3,B) and *molhęr* (5.5.3). The m. and f. are hence identical except that the f. nom. pl. has *-s*, as in, for example, mf. nom. sg. *męlher*, mf. obl. sg. and m. nom. pl. *melhọr*, f. pl. and m. obl. pl. *melhors*.

Several additional synthetic comparatives are rare and do not seem to use the nom. sg.: *alzọr*, *aussor*, *auzor* from *alt* 'high'; *forzọr*, *forsor* from *fọrt* 'strong'; *lonhọr* from *lonc* 'long'; and, lacking a positive degree, *sordejọr*, *sordeior* 'worse'; a few others are attested only once or are of dubious existence.

One often finds an analogical nom. sg. *-s*: *gẹnsers*, *májers*, *mẹlhers*, *menres*, etc. Less often, one finds nom. sg. forms like *gensọrs*, *maiọrs*, *melhọrs*, *menọrs*. Analogical obl. forms like *gẹnser*, *máier*, *mẹlher*, *menre* are rare.

7.12 *Comparatives of Superiority: Use*

Most of the synthetic forms are optional; they are used regularly only for *bọn*, *gen*, *gran*, *mal*, and *pauc*. The synthetic comparative tends to lose its force, as shown by constructions like *plus alzor*, *plus major*, *plus melhor*, *plus sordejor*. *Alzor* occurs most often with an absolute superlative meaning: 'very high.' Comparatives can be reinforced through the adverbs of quantity *assatz*, *mọlt*, and *trọp* (9.8) or expressions like "per un cen" 'in a proportion of a hundred to one.'

When the second term of the comparison is expressed, it is introduced by *que* (normally with the subject case) or *de* (normally with the oblique, but sometimes with the subject case, by analogy to *que*): "plus ez blanca qu'evori" 'she is whiter than ivory' (5:13); "es meindre d'En Borneil un dorn" 'he is lesser than Lord Borneil by a hand's breadth' (26:6).

7.13 Comparatives of Inferiority and Equality

The comparative of inferiority is formed with *men(h)s*: *menhs dur* 'less hard.' The second term, if any, is introduced by *de* or *que*.

The comparative of equality 'as ... (as)' is formed with the adverbs *aissí*, *enaissí*, *tan*, *si*, *atretan*, *atressí*, etc. The second term, if any, is introduced by *com*, *quan*, or *que*: "Ni anc de nul companho / Companha tan greus no·m fo" 'Nor ever of any companion / Was the company so disagreeable to me' (34:7-8).

7.14 Superlatives

The relative superlative is formed by adding the definite article before the comparative adjective: "Am la plus bel' e la melhor" 'I love the most beautiful and the best one' (27:18). But the article is usually not repeated when the adjective follows the noun: "la domna plus franca" 'the most noble lady.' The term of comparison, if any, is introduced by *de*: "la melhor de totas" 'the best one of all.' There are also a few learnèd superlatives in *-isme*: *autisme* 'highest,' *carisme* 'dearest,' *santisme* 'holiest.'

The absolute superlative is formed with *mọlt*, *beṇ*, *assatz*, *trǫp*, *trę̧s*, *fǫrt*, etc.: "el era mot avinens hom e cortes" 'he was a very attractive and courtly man' (66:11-12). The same function is served by the prefix *sobre-*: *sobrebę̧l* 'very beautiful,' *sobreboṇ* 'very good,' *sobrevalẹn* 'of very great worth.'

Chapter 7: Exercises

A (7.2-4, 7.7). Give the non-analogical m. and f. paradigms

1. paubre   2. cortẹs   3. gentil

B (7.4-5). Supply the f. if the m. is given, and vice versa:

1. lonc: duret _______ sason lor jois
2. frech: Car fin' amors m'asegura / De la _______ bisa
3. salva, sana: Tan com sia _______ ni _______
4. boṇ, jauzion: _______ domna _______

C (7.2-9). Add proper endings or apostrophes as needed

1. Lo vers es fi___ e naturau___
2. Et el o saup e fo tris___ e dolen___
3. [La duquessa] era jove___ e gai___ e de gran ___ valor
4. Bel___ domna e pro___
5. Fer___ vos deu esser et esqui___
6. Quar vei mort___ joven e valor

D (7.11-14). Give the correct comparative or superlative for the adjectives indicated, using analytic forms where they exist

1. gran: Lo coms de Peiteus si fo uns dels _______ cortes del mon
2. gen, avinen: Que tramet a la _______ / E a la _______
3. pauc: S'eu no pren / D'aquestz dos mals lo _______
4. bela: Con plus vos gart, m'etz _______

5. bọn: E _______ es, qui·l joi aten
6. lonh, mal: E sai, si la fezes _______, / Ades la trobara ________

E (7.12-14; ch. 5-6). Give the other three non-analogical forms

1. los majors homes
2. los melhors senhors
3. las gensors serors

8
PERSONAL AND POSSESSIVE PRONOUNS AND ADJECTIVES

8.1 M. and F. Personal Pronouns: Uncontracted Forms

Like nouns, adjectives, and articles, OP personal nouns possess the properties of gender, case, and number; and like verbs, they possess three persons.

For personal pronouns, we will not use the traditional terms "strong" (or "stressed") and "weak" (or "unstressed"), which correspond more to historical criteria than to what is known about the rhythm of the OP phrase. Rather, we will use the four terms heading the chart below. The disjunctive pronoun is usually tonic and is frequent in the rhyme, whereas both these circumstances are infrequent for the other three types of pronoun, which are usually unstressed adjuncts to an adjoining verb.

		subject	*disjunctive*	*indirect object*	*direct object*
1 sg.		(i)ȩu	mẹ, mi ⟶	⟶	⟶
2 sg.		tu	tẹ, ti ⟶	⟶	⟶
3 sg.	*m.*	ẹl(h), il(h)	lui, el(h)	l(h)i	lọ
	f.	ẹl(h)a, il(h)	l(i)ȩi(s), el(h)a	l(h)i	la
1 pl.		nọs ⟶	⟶	⟶	⟶

	subject	*disjunctive*	*indirect object*	*direct object*
2 pl.	vọs →	→	→	→
3 pl. m.	il(h), el(h)	el(h)s ←	lọr, lur (m. and f.)	los
f.	el(h)as →	→		las
			ẹn, n(ẹ)	lo
neuter	lo (rare)		(h)i, y	(h)ǫ

Only the third person formally differentiates the genders or more than two of the four functions. The various forms for any one function appear to be used interchangeably and often exploited for metrical convenience. Purely orthographic variants include *ill* for *ilh*, *ẹlla/s* for *el(h)a/s*, *yęu* for *ieu*, and *ylh* for *ilh*. Infrequent variants that affect pronunciation are *mẹi* and *tẹi* for disjunctive *me* and *te* (see 3.7), *ẹu/s* for *el/s*, *lu* for *lui* (see 3.7), and *lọrs* for *lor*.

8.2 Personal Pronouns: Contracted Forms

Like articles, the indirect and direct object pronouns usually contract before or after a vowel:

	proclitic		*enclitic*	
	indirect	*direct*	*indirect*	*direct*
1 sg.	m' →	→	·m →	→
2 sg.	t' →	→	·t →	→
3 sg. m.	(l'; lh') (m. and f.)	l' (m. and f.)	(·lh, ·l) (m. and f.)	·l
f.				---
1 pl.	---	---	·ns →	→

	proclitic		*enclitic*	
	indirect	*direct*	*indirect*	*direct*
2 pl.	---	---	·us →	
3 pl. m.	---	---	---	·ls
f.	---	---	---	---
neuter	n'	l'	·n, ·i	·l

Purely orthographic variants of *·lh* are *·ll*, *·ill*, and *·il*. Occasional variants that affect pronunciation include *·u* for *·l* (thus *no·u* for *noṇ* + *lo*), *·s* for *·us* after an *o* (thus *no·s* for *noṇ* + *vos*), *vọ·* for *vos* (thus *vo·n* for *vos* + *ne*), and *·nz* and *·lz* for *·ns* and *·ls*. Finally, *si·us* sometimes becomes *si·eus* (see 3.11).

Li contracts less frequently than the others. Otherwise, proclitic elision is almost universal; rarely does one find examples like "me a mes" 'has put me' (59:32).

Indirect and direct object pronouns almost always contract after certain common monosyllables (*e* 'and,' *ǫ* 'or,' *ọ* 'where,' *ni* 'nor, or,' *que* 'that, which; what,' *qui* 'who,' *si* 'if; indeed,' etc.), after the pronouns *lọ*, *la*, *li*, and *sǫ*, and after some common polysyllables like *aissî* 'as' and *ara* 'now.' For example, we find *e·m*, *que·t*, *qui·l*, *si·ns*, *so·us*, *ara·ls*, etc. Even after words other than such common ones as these, enclitic contraction occurs in verse more than four times out of five, thus "sembla·us" 'it seems to you' (46:49). But full forms may be retained for the sake of clarity, emphasis, or metrics, as in "e peza me" 'and it grieves me' (28:28) or "membre vos" 'may you recall' (93:59). No enclitic contraction is possible after semivowels, hence "calfei me" 'warmed myself' (4:41).

Disjunctive pronouns do not contract. The only subject pronouns that contract are *(i)ę̀u*, which generally becomes *(i)e* before an enclitic (*e·us* for *eu vos*, *e·n* for *eu en*, etc.), and *nọs* and *vọs*, which can lose their *-s* before an enclitic (e.g., *no·n* and *vo·n* for *nos en* and *vos en*).

8.3 Use of Personal Pronouns: General

For addressing a single person, the 2 pl. expresses the respect due to superiors like a king or lady. Both the *tu* and *vọs* forms are used for God, Christ, and the Virgin Mary, as well as for abstractions and personifications like *Amor* 'Love' and *Mercẹ* 'Mercy.'

The adjective *altre* reinforces *nos* and *vos* to indicate a nation ("nos altre Provensal" 'we Provençals') or any group contrasted with another ("nos altre ... vos altre"). However, the sense often weakens to merely 'we' and 'you.'

A frequent circumlocution for the personal pronoun is the possessive adjective plus *cǫrs*, literally 'body': *mọs cors* 'I,' *vǫstre cors* 'you,' *son cors* 'he, she.' The lady is so fundamental in the troubadours' poetry that her presence is often indicated by a f. pronoun which either has no antecedent or technically refers back to *Amor*. When it is not clear whether the f. pronoun designates the lady or Love, the ambiguity is probably intentional.

Where one pronoun represents antecedents of mixed gender, the m. pl. pronoun is used. OP does not usually represent inanimate things by m. and f. pronouns, but rather by neuter personal or demonstrative pronouns (8.6, 9.3); however, m. and f. pronouns are used for animals.

8.4 Use of Subject Pronouns

The distinctiveness of most OP verbal inflections usually suffices to indicate the person and number of the subject. Hence, the subject pronoun is used mainly for the sake of clarity, contrast, emphasis, or possibly metrics. For example, here one might look for a third-person subject unless the first-person *eu* were specified: "Messongers en fos eu e faus!" 'Would that I were a liar and deceiver about this!' (28:26). The next example shows a contrast between the subjects of two clauses: "digas li·l meu afaire / Et ilh diga·t del seu ver" 'tell her about me / And may she tell you the truth about herself' (52:3-4). The next case emphasizes the poet's own importance while also bringing the verse up to the right number of syllables: "Ieu sui Arnautz qu'amas l'aura" 'I who gather the wind am Arnaut' (68:43).

The subject pronoun generally precedes the verb (but see 13.6); they may be separated by object pronouns, adverbs, adverbial phrases, etc.

With imperatives, the subject pronoun is not usual: "Escoutatz!" 'Listen!' (12:4); but exceptionally: "als avols tu·l sela e·l rescon" 'hide and conceal it from the base ones' (142:55 bis).

8.5 Use of M. and F. Indirect and Direct Object Pronouns

The direct object pronoun is the direct object of a verb. The indirect object pronoun has a variety of meanings generally translated into English using *to*, *towards*, *for*, *from*, *concerning*, etc.: "El li descobri l'amor qu'el li avia" 'He revealed to her the love which he had for her' (58:15); "Be·m parra joys quan li querray / ... l'alberc de lonh" 'Joy will appear to me when I ask of her / ... shelter from afar' (24:15-16). The indirect object pronoun in the so-called "ethical dative" indicates than an action occurs to the benefit or detriment of the speaker or grammatical subject: "E di·m a la gensor" 'And tell the nicest one for me' (29:74). For a possessive meaning, see 8.12.

Object pronouns are generally repeated with each of two or more verbs: "Totas las dopt' e las mescre" 'I fear and mistrust them all' (37:31); but they can be omitted when the sense is perfectly clear: "la amet senes veser" 'he loved her without seeing [her]' (39:22).

8.6 Use of Neuter Personal Pronouns

ǫ and *lọ*, translated as 'it, this' or sometimes untranslatable, generally refer to a previously mentioned concept or thing: "E fai o mal qui lo; [i.e., lo·i] cossen" 'And whoever lets him do this, does badly' (54:39). Normally no neuter pronoun is used in expressions like "eu soi" 'it is I' or with impersonal verbs like *cal* 'it is necessary.'

The form *en* is used before a verb and *ne* after; *n'* is proclitic before a verb, while *·n* can be attached to almost any word ending in a vowel. These forms, which generally replace *de* plus a noun or pronoun, are translated as 'of it, from it, of them, from them' and the like: "Aquil n'an joja" 'Those derive joy from this' (20:43).

En replaces the partitive article plus a noun or pronoun: "en volh" 'I want some (of it).' It often stands for the referent of a number or an adverb of quantity: "C'una·n volh e·n ai volguda" 'For I want and have wanted one (of them)' (38:6). As here, it can replace a third-person (or rarely first- or second-person) personal pronoun referring to people; in comparisons it replaces *de* plus a third-person pronoun: "Qu'ie·n sai gensor et bellazor" 'For I know a nicer and more beautiful one than she' (3:35) ("que el" is also possible, e.g., 81:4). Frequently, though, the sense of *en* is too weak to be translatable, especially in fixed expressions like "tornar s'en" (or "tornar se") 'to return.'

I, which usually replaces the prepositions *a* 'to' or *en* 'in' plus a noun or pronoun, is translated as 'to it, in it, there' or the like: "Ni no·i vei melhuramen" 'Nor do I see any improvement in this' (38:28). The expression *i a* (or merely *a* by itself, or *a·i* in cases of inversion) means 'there is, there are': "E no·i ac cog" 'And there was no cook' (4:45).

8.7 Position of Indirect and Direct Object and Neuter Pronouns

Usually the indirect and direct object and neuter pronouns immediately precede the verb, as in all the examples given so far. However, the pronoun generally follows the verb when the verb is introduced by *pǫis*, *aprę̧s* , or *adonc* (e.g., 71.II:16). Postposition of the pronoun predominates after a subordinate clause introduced by a subordinating conjunction (e.g., 60:11-12) and after the coordinating conjunction *e*: "e platz me" 'and it pleases me' (100:7), less often "e·m platz" (100:10). Finally, postposition of the pronoun is virtually obligatory when the pronoun would otherwise begin the sentence (ignoring any preceding vocatives): "Cavallier, datz mi cosselh" 'Knights, give me advice' (2:22).

In compound tenses, the pronoun normally precedes the auxiliary verb, the usual order being pronoun + auxiliary + participle (e.g., 37:22), or, in completely initial position or after a vocative, participle + pronoun + auxiliary (e.g., 37:54), but after the conjunction *e*, generally auxiliary + pronoun + participle.

With an infinitive, the word order pronoun + conjugated verb + infinitive predominates: "ela non l'auza regardar" 'she does not dare look at him' (181:16).

8.8 Order of Two Pronouns Together

When two object pronouns come together, the direct object normally precedes the indirect object, thus *·l mi* (41:5), *·l lor* (78:9), *la m'* (73:24), *·ls vos* (107:53), etc. However, one finds exceptions to this rule; in particular, a third-person indirect object often precedes a first- or second-person direct object, e.g., *lor me* (86:3), or *li·m* rather than *me li*; and this is always the case when the direct object is reflexive. With an infinitive, two pronouns normally go together before the conjugated verb, no matter which verb they logically refer to: "Quan a vos plac que·us mi laissetz vezer" 'When it pleased you to let me see you' (119:2).

Neuter pronouns follow m. and f. pronouns, and *en* precedes *i*, thus *la·n* (84:26), *·lh o* (37:52), *·us o* (30:34), *n'i* (145:29), etc.

After *lọ* and *la*, the indirect object *li* almost always becomes *i* in order to avoid an accumulation of *l*'s, thus *lo·i* and *la·i*, both usually monosyllabic. However, combinations like *lo·lh* (34:34) and *la·il* (72:11) remain possible. Where two third-person pronouns would come together, sometimes only *li* is kept (often, however, best interpreted as *l'i* for *lo·i* or *la·i*): "... se ella per temps passat no li avia fach plazer, qu'ella li volia far ara" '... if she had not given him pleasure in the past, that she wished to give it to him now' (61:27-28).

8.9 Use of Disjunctive Pronouns

The disjunctive pronoun normally does not depend on a conjugated verb, but rather is used

1) after a preposition: "de mi" 'about me' (25:7), "en lor" 'in them' (37:26), including before an infinitive: "per voluntat de liei vezer" 'from a desire to see her' (21:5);

2) after an infinitive: "d'amar leis" 'of loving her' (but "de l'amar" is also possible; see 8.7);

3) introducing a relative clause: "am leis qui ..." 'I love her who ...';

4) rarely, in place of a demonstrative pronoun (see 9.2);

5) in apposition to a direct object: "los vezem, lui e sos amics" 'we see them, him and his friends';

6) as object of a gerund: "leis aman ..." 'while loving her ...';

7) in absolute constructions: "me presen" 'I being present,' "lui renhan" 'during his reign.'

For the sake of special emphasis, contrast, or clarity, a disjunctive pronoun sometimes is used in place of a direct or indirect object pronoun: "E lui apel' om Cossezen" 'And him they call "Charming"' (54:78); "Car ieu l'am tant e liei non cau" 'For I love her so much and to her it doesn't matter' (23:38). When the disjunctive pronoun functions as an indirect object, the preposition *a* is obligatory with *ẹl*, *ela*, *els*, or *elas*, thus "non las ausava dire ad ella" 'he did not dare tell them to her' (58:9-10; but *a* is optional before *lę̣is* and *lui*: "(a) leis platz" 'it pleases her,' "(a) lui es semblans" 'it seems to him.'

In addition, the disjunctives *leis* and *ẹlhs* are sometimes used as subjects. Conversely, *tu* rarely replaces the disjunctive: "per tu" 'for you.' And occasionally, the f. indirect object *li* or the m. disjunctive *lui* replaces the disjunctive f. *leis*.

8.10 Pronominal Verbs

The first- and second-person reflexive pronouns are identical with the non-reflexive forms, while the third person has a special form, *se* or *si*, contracted to *s'*, *·is*, *·s*. Word order is as for other unstressed pronouns (8.7-8).

The reflexive pronoun refers to the subject of the clause, and can be an indirect object or, as in this example, a direct object: "el se crozet a mes·se en mar" 'he took the cross and took to the sea' (21:5). The reflexive pronoun can be the object of a preposition: "de me" 'over myself' (37:17), "en se" 'in himself' (154:36); but in this function the third person plural generally uses the disjunctive *lọr* (or, less often, *ẹls*, *elas*): "las dompnas valenz lo partran entre lor" 'the noble ladies will share it among themselves' (156:9).

In a certain number of specific circumstances, pleonastic verbal pronominalization can be considered obligatory, namely after negative *saber*, after indefinites meaning 'whatever' and the like ("qui que·m sia" 'whoever I may be,' 15:22), and in "si·s vol" 'if he wishes.' Pronominalization is also frequent, with some slight stylistic value, for the first verb in a narrative, particularly in *vidas* and *pastorelas* ("L'autre jorn, m'anava" 'The other day I was going,' 172:1) and in various types of parallelism, comparison, and contrast ("atrestan se·n faria us pins" 'a finch would do as well,' 54:35), including interpolated expressions in direct discourse ("'Toza,' fi·m ieu" '"Girl," said I,' 15:15). In addition, a pleonastic pronoun, adding nothing save perhaps a slight subjectivity or emphasis, is frequent with verbs expressing change, rest, perception, and mental effort, thus: "Ni mal no·m sent" 'Nor do I feel pain' (19:32); "Suau s'estes lo reis ... / E dormis se planamen" 'The king would be tranquil ... / And sleep peacefully' (86:26-27).

Pronominal verbs also have a reciprocal meaning: "tuich trei se clamavon 'Bertran' l'uns l'autre" 'all three called each other "Bertran"' (55:10-11). This reciprocal pronoun can be replaced by the terms which often reinforce it, namely *entre lor*, *mest lor* 'among them(selves),' *ambedui* 'both,' and *l'uns (a) l'autre* '(to) one another': "l'us l'autre non cossen" 'they do not tolerate each other' (2:9); "Totas cridan ... / L'un' a l'autre" 'They all shout to each other' (109:118-19).

Finally, the reflexive construction can have a passive value: *se dire* 'to be said,' *se vendre* 'to be sold,' *se mirar* 'to be seen,' etc.

8.11 Possessive Pronouns and Adjectives: Forms

Possessive pronouns and adjectives have two series of forms, known as strong and weak, in the singular, but only one series in the plural. Both series identify the person and number of the possessor as well as the gender, case and number of the possessed. The usual forms are:

	1 sg. strong	*1 sg. weak*
m. nom. sg.	m(i)ęus	mọs
obl. sg.	m(i)eu	mọn
nom. pl.	m(i)ei	m(i)ei
obl. pl.	m(i)eus	mos
f. sg.	mia, mieua	ma, mi
pl.	mias, mieuas	mas
neuter sg.	mieu	---

	2 sg. strong	*2 sg. weak*
m. nom. sg.	t(i)eus	tọs
obl. sg.	t(i)eu	tọn
nom. pl.	t(i)ei	t(i)ei
obl. pl.	t(i)eus	tos

	2 sg. strong		*2 sg. weak*
f. sg.	tua, tọa, tieua		ta, ti
pl.	tuas, toas, tieuas		tas
neuter sg.	tieu		---
	3 sg. strong		*3 sg. weak*
m. nom. sg.	s(i)ęus		sọs
obl. sg.	s(i)eu		sọn
nom. pl.	s(i)ei		s(i)ei
obl. pl.	s(i)eus		sos
f. sg.	sua, soa, sieua		sa, si
pl.	suas, soas, sieuas		sas
neuter sg.	sieu		---
	1 pl.	*2 pl.*	*3 pl.*
m. nom. sg.	nǫstre	vǫstre	
obl. sg.	nostre	vostre	lọr, lur
nom. pl.	nostre	vostre	lọr, lur
obl. pl.	nostres	vostres	lọr, lur
f. sg.	nostra	vostra	lọr, lur
pl.	nostras	vostras	lọr, lur
neuter sg.	nostre	vostre	

Less-used strong or weak forms are m. nom. pl. *tọi, sọi, tui, sui*. Less-used strong forms are m. nom. pl. *meu, teu, seu*; f. sg. *tia, sia*, f. pl. *tias, sias*. We also find an analogical m. obl. pl. (and rarely nom. sg.) adjective *lọrs* or *lurs* and analogical m. nom. sg. *nostres* and *vostres* (see 7.2: *paubre*).

The possessive pronoun, as well as the possessive adjective when separated from its noun, belongs to the strong series and is capable of carrying tonic stress.

Mia, etc., are occasionally treated as monosyllabic (see 3.10). A final vowel normally elides before a vowel: "m'arma" 'my soul' (70:12), "s'uxor" 'his wife' (10:18), "la nostr' amor" 'our love' (7:13); but exceptionally we find "sa ira" 'her anger' (6:26), "sa onor" 'her honor' (30:22).

8.12 Use of Possessive Adjectives and Pronouns

	attributive adjective	*predicate adjective*	*pronoun*
weak series	without article	--	--
strong series	with or without art.	without art.	with art.

The weak possessive series is only attributive and lacks the article: "mos pretz" 'my merit' (29:7), "son dous chantar" 'his sweet singing' (22:6), "sos sirventes" 'his sirventes' (71:II,17), "sas alas" 'its wings' (37:2).

The strong series gives slightly more emphasis: "al mieu pro" 'to my advantage' (40:3), "lo sieus sers" 'her servant' (70:16), "las soas chanssos" 'his songs' (66:4). The article is optional: "la soa dompna" (61:12-13) or "soa domna" (33:11), both 'his lady.' The strong series also serves, without the article, in predicative position: "Ni no fui meus de l'or' en sai" 'Nor was I mine from that hour forth' (37:18).

Preceded by an indefinite article or a numeral, the strong possessive adjective means 'of mine,' etc.: "una soa domna" 'a lady of his' (56:18-19), "doas soas fillas" 'two daughters of his' (39:26-27).

A loosely construed possessive appears in constructions like "son plach" 'agreement with her,' "la soa batalha" 'battle with it,' "son damnatge" 'harm to him,' or "vostre jois" 'joy caused by you' (57:4).

The pronominal function is performed by the strong form preceded by the definite article: "Dreitz es qu'ieu lo mieu refranha" 'It is right that I should modulate mine' (22:7). The neuter possessive functions as a predicate adjective ("aisso es nostre" 'this is ours') or as a pronoun ("lo mieu" 'mine, my property').

Possession can also be expressed 1) through a juxtaposed oblique noun (5.11); 2) through *de* or *a* plus a personal pronoun, producing a stronger impact and in the 3 sg. clarifying the sex of the possessor: "·l maritz de leis, ·l maritz de ela" 'her husband' (85:31, 32); 3) through an indirect object pronoun, particularly with parts of the body: "la doussor c'al cor li vai" 'the sweetness that goes to his heart' (37:4).

Chapter 8: Exercises

A. For the subject pronouns and noun phrases which are supplied, give the proper disjunctive, indirect object, direct object, or reflexive forms

1. eu: Sapchatz qu'a _____ fo bon e bel
2. eu: Et eu calfei _____ volentiers
3. ela: Amigu' ai ieu, no sai qui _____ es

4. a mon fil: Faran _____ mal tut li plusor
5. a Deu; eu; el: E prec _____ que _____ reteng' am _____
6. vos; vos: Mas _____ non cal, si d'amor no _____ sove
7. eu; el: Tant _____ rancur de _____ cui sui amia
8. ela: Mon chantar, que de _____ mou
9. nos: Q'eras _____ a mostrat Mortz que pot faire
10. elas: ... car tan _____ es sobreira

B. Insert the appropriate neuter pronouns

1. S'anc li fi tort qu'il m'_____ perdon
2. Cel que·us a tan gen formada, / Me _____ do cel joi qu'eu _____ aten
3. E·m combatey sotz la tor ... / E _____ fuy nafratz
4. Que yeu _____ dic per Dieu, qu' _____ sia plus amatz

C. Complete with possessive adjectives and pronouns

1. Totz lo joys del mon es n_____
2. Qu'aja m_____ manz soz s_____ mantel!
3. Aissi torn eu, domna, en v_____ merce
4. Ieu l'autrei m_____ cor e m_____ amor, / M_____ sen, m_____ huoills e m_____ vida
5. Qu'el s_____ cors sobretracima / Lo m_____ tot
6. Me fan l_____ amor estranha

9
OTHER PRONOUNS AND SPECIAL ADJECTIVES

9.1 Demonstrative Adjectives and Pronouns: General

Demonstratives point to the real or imagined location of objects, persons, or concepts. Most OP demonstratives serve as both adjectives and pronouns, but a few others are pronominal only. The demonstratives of proximity and remoteness both include short forms as well as long ones with an extra initial syllable. The short forms have a weaker impact, are often qualified by following expressions, and are the more common in the troubadours.

9.2 Demonstratives of Proximity and Remoteness

The adjective 'this' and pronoun 'this (one)' are expressed, in order of frequency, by the short forms *cẹst*, *ẹst*, and the long forms *aquẹst*, *aicẹst*, all declined on the following model:

nom. sg. m.	cẹst	*f.*	cesta, cist
obl. sg.	cest		cesta
nom. pl.	cist		cestas
obl. pl.	cestz, cests, cetz		cestas

Initial *c-* can become *s-*; the m. nom. sg. can take *-s*. Rare or dialectal forms include m. nom. sg.

ist, *aquist*, m. nom. pl. and obl. pl. *aquest*, and m. nom. pl. *aquisti*.

The adjective 'that' and pronoun 'that (one)' are expressed, in order of frequency, by *cẹl*, *aquẹl*, and *aicẹl*, *aissel*, all declined on this model:

nom. sg. m.	cẹl(h)	*f.*	cel(h)a, cil(h)
obl. sg.	cel(h)		cel(h)a
nom. pl.	cil(h)		cel(h)as
obl. pl.	cel(h)s		cel(h)as

Initial *c*- can become *s*- (or rarely *sc*-). The f. -*l*- and m. -*lh(s)* can both be spelled *ll* without changing the pronunciation. M. -*l* can vocalize preconsonantally to -*u*. The m. nom. sg. (and rarely nom. pl.) can take -*s*. Rarely the m. nom. sg. is *cil(h)* and the f. nom. sg. *cilh* or *cilha*. Occasional expanded forms of the obl. sg. (and rarely the nom. sg.) pronoun are m. *cel(l)ui* and f. *cel(i)ęi(s)*; for examples, see 9.7.

The long forms are used for emphasis or metrical convenience, thus "d'aquest segle flac" 'from this weak world' (75:25) alongside "en est segle dolen" 'in this grieving world' (75:3).

Rarely, a personal pronoun or definite article is used as a demonstrative: "lor de Tolosa" 'those from Toulouse,' "e·lh de Monclar" 'and those from Monclar.'

9.3 Neuter Demonstrative Pronouns

The neuter demonstrative pronoun has a short form and two long ones, namely *sǫ* (*zo*, *ço*), *aissǫ* (*aisǫ*, *aiçǫ*, *aizǫ*, etc.), and *aquǫ* (*acǫ*, *achǫ*). All are invariable and are translated as 'it, this, that.' The short forms, weaker in force, are more frequent in the troubadours. Uninflected forms of other demonstrative pronouns, such as *aquẹst*, may also be used as neuter pronouns. For *h(ǫ)* and *lǫ*, see 8.6.

The neuter demonstrative can refer back to something previously mentioned (including a m. or f. impersonal noun): "Can lo maritz a la moiller fai dol / So es guerra" 'When the husband displeases his wife, / It's war' (139:11-12). Or, it announces something to come: "So diz n'Agnes a n'Ermessen: / "Trobat avem ... " 'Lady Agnes said this to Lady Ermessen: / "We have found ... "' (4:31-32). As in these examples, the neuter demonstrative can be the subject or direct object of a verb, and it can also have a disjunctive function: "per so" 'because of that,' etc.

Generally, the short forms precede the verb while the long ones follow.

9.4 Other Demonstrative Terms

The intensifying demonstratives, generally translated with the aid of 'self,' are *ẹis/sa* (rarely *eus*, *es*, *eps*), *mezẹis/sa* (or *meteis*, rarely *medeis*; or *-eus*, *-es*, *-eps*); and *medẹsme* (*mezesme*, *mesesme*, *meesme*). The long forms are more frequent in the troubadours. These are all declined like *bęl*, except that the m. of *eis* and its compounds is normally invariable but can have nom. pl. *eisi* and, more often, obl. pl. *eisses*. These terms reinforce a noun or more often a personal pronoun: "ieu mezeys" 'I myself' (6:45), "si maseissa" 'herself' (56:23), "lor mezeis" 'themselves' (179:36).

9.5 Relative Pronouns and Adjectives

The relative pronoun exists in two series:

	pronoun; people	*pronoun; things*	*pron. or adj.; people, things*
subject	qui, quẹ	que	lo cals
'of ...'	(de) cui; don(t)	de que; don(t)	del cal
indirect object	(a) cui	a que	al cal
direct object	cui, que	que	lo cal
disjunctive	cui	que	lo cal

Only the series based on *cal* is declinable to reflect gender and number, following the model of *fizẹl*. Variant forms have *qu* for *c*- and -*lz* for -*ls*. *Qui* has the variants *qi* and rarely *ki*. *Que* before a vowel becomes *qu' c'*, or less often *quez* or *ques*. *Don(t)* has a variant *dun(t)*.

The usage of these forms fluctuates somewhat. As a subject, *qui* occasionally replaces *que* for things: "Ab mon cor, qui s'es enpres" / ..." 'With my heart, which has undertaken / ...' (165:10). On the other hand, if the context is clear, a relative subject pronoun can be omitted, notably in negative and/or comparative constructions: "anc no vitz nulh aman, / Melhs ames" 'you never saw a lover / Who loved better' (31:21-22). *Cui* in its various uses can be replaced by *qui* or *que*: "domna ... / A qui nom plagues ma dolors" 'a lady ... / To whom my pain might not be pleasing' (106:18-20); "lo Senher ... / Per qu'ieu veirai l'amor de lonh" 'the Lord ... / By whom I'll see far-off love' (24:8-9).

With *cui*, in the indirect object function, *a* is optional: "Dieus, a cui la grazis" 'God, to whom I give thanks for her' (42:12); but "Mas eu, que planh e plor, / Cui jois non a sabor" 'Except me, who lament and weep, / For whom joy has no savor' (31:7-8); and similarly for *de*. Without any preposition, *que* can be used in expressions of time: "Selh dia / ... qu'ie·us perdria" 'The day / ... that I lost you' (107:26-28); for temporal *que* considered as a conjunction, see 13.4). Also, with a whole clause as antecedent, *que* can refer to a previously mentioned concept: "lo vol perdre, en que faill malamenz" 'he wants to lose it, in which he badly errs' (156:6). Similarly, we find *per que* and *don* with the meaning 'because of which' (e.g., 53:20, 23:7); with the meaning 'from where,' the spelling *d'on* is preferable to *don*. The relative pronoun or adverb *on*, literally, 'where,' can mean 'in whom, in which, with whom,' etc.: "na Salvaga, on prez es" 'Lady Salvatja, in whom is merit' (150:2).

The relatives usually follow immediately their antecedent, but not always: "A vos o dic c'auzitz" 'I say it to you who have heard' (50:12). There is some tendency to replace a prepositional relative by *que* followed later by a personal pronoun, thus *que* ... *lor* for *a cui*, *que* ... *ab el* for *ab cui*, and *que* ... *en* for *de que*, *don*: "Per mal que la·n vueilh encolpar" 'For pain of which I wish to accuse it' (13:34).

The forms with *cal* add specificity or slight emphasis: "Rambauz lo cals det la meitat d'Aurenga al Hospital" 'Raimbaut, who gave half of Orange to the Hospitalers (39:29). As a relative adjective, *cal* adds precision: "fetz mantas bonas chansos de la comtessa, las quals cansos mostren ..." 'he made many good songs about the countess, which songs show ...' (58:18-19).

9.6 Interrogative Pronouns and Adjectives

The interrogative forms are like those of the relatives, except that *que* normally remains impersonal:

	pronoun; people	*pronoun; things*	*pron. or adj.; people, things*
subject	qui	quẹ	cals; quin(h)s
'of...'	(de) cui	de que	de cal; de quin(h)
indirect object	(a) cui	a que	a cal; a quin(h)
direct object / *disjunctive*	cui	que	cal; quin(h)

There is the inevitable confusion of forms: *que* for *cui* or *qui*, *qui* for *cui*, etc. Prevocalic *que* usually gives *qu'*, *c'*, *quez*, or *ques*. *Cal*, especially when meaning 'which,' can be preceded by the definite article. Other interrogatives are *quin(h)* and *can(t)* (9.8), both declined like *bęl*: "cantas penas?" 'how many sufferings?'

For the use of interrogative terms in direct and indirect questions and in exclamations, see 13.5.

9.7 Combinations of Relatives and Other Pronouns

The demonstrative and relative pronouns can combine to designate specific persons or things. They often evoke the lady: "Celeis cui am de cor e de saber, / ... volrai dir" 'To her whom I love with heart and wisdom, / ... I'll say' (132:1-2); or the deity: "eu irai m'en a scellui / On tut peccador troban fi" 'I'll go to him / In whom all sinners find peace' (8:27-28). This is the most frequent use of the demonstrative forms *celui* and *cel̨ęis*.

Such combinations can also have an indefinite value translated as 'he who, whoever,' etc.' "sel que de mi l'apenra" 'anyone who learns it from me' (25:33); "aissilh que so camiador" 'those who are inconstant' (106:42-43). The combination of a neuter demonstrative and a relative also carries an indefinite meaning: *aquǫ* (or *sǫ*, *zo*) *que* 'what' (54:48), *so* (or *zo*) *que* 'what' (118:16) or 'the fact that' (167:35), *acho don* 'that of which' (7:6), etc. This neuter construction can also poetically designate a female person: "S'ieu am so que ja no·m veira" 'If I love one who will never see me' (25:8).

The personal pronoun, particularly *lęis*, can also be combined with a relative pronoun to designate a specific person: "Vas leis que·m destrui" 'Towards her who destroys me' (37:30).

The combination of a relative pronoun with *que* produces the so-called indefinites of generalization, namely *qui que* 'whoever'; *cui que* 'whomever'; *que que* 'whatever'; *cal que*, *calque* 'whatever, whichever, some; however'; *on que* 'wherever.' For example (with *qui que* used for *cui que*): "de qui qu'el fos fils" 'of whomever he was the son' (26:11). Of these indefinites of generalization, only *cal que* can be adjectival: "cal que dousa sabor" 'some sweet taste' (27:10).

9.8 Indefinite Pronouns, Adjectives, and Adverbs

Indefinites designate persons, objects, qualities, and quantities which are not closely specified. In addition to the combinations discussed in 9.7, the relatives *qui* and *que* by themselves can have an indefinite meaning. In particular, *qui* (and less often the indirect object *cui*) with no expressed antecedent can mean 'whoever, one who, he who,' etc., thus: "No sap chantar qui so non di" 'Someone who doesn't say the melody doesn't know how to sing' (25:1). *Qui ... qui* indicates two indefinite subjects: "Qui·l fer en gauta, qui en col" 'One strikes him on the cheek, the other on the neck' (145:39). For *qui* meaning 'if someone,' see 12.9.

Similarly, *que* sometimes stands alone to mean 'what': "nos a mostrat Mortz que pot faire" 'Death has shown us what it can do' (93:23). And with a m. nom. sg. adjective, *que* means 'something': "Que fals faras e que leugiers" 'You will do something faithless and irresponsible' (57:27); the construction seems to be elliptical: "... something (that a) faithless (person would do)."

Besides negating words (13.3), indefinites include many other types, declined like *bęl* or *uṇ* unless otherwise specified.

Words meaning 'each (one), every (one)':

cada: indeclinable adjective (with numbers and measurements of time)

c(h)asque: indeclinable adjective

c(h)ascuṇ: pronoun and adjective

cada uṇ: pronoun, rarely adjective

quec̣, quega: pronoun and adjective

un quec̣, unquec: pronoun

Expressions of quantity, all capable of being adjectives, pronouns, and adverbs unless otherwise indicated:

assatz and *pron̩* 'enough; much, many': adverbs

main(t), man(h)t 'many (a), many a one': adjective, pronoun

men(h)s 'less': adverb

menut (f. *-da*) 'little; in rapid succession'

mọlt 'much, many; very'

(un) pauc '(a) little; few'

(un) petit (f. *-ta*) '(a) little'

plus, pus 'more': adverb

tamanh 'so great': adjective

tan(t), ta(m), aitan(t), aita(m) 'so much, so many; so'

trǫp 'much, many; very; too (much)'

As adverbs of quantity, all these usually take partitive *de* before a qualified noun: "assatz de cansos" 'quite a few songs' (129:2-3); the opposite order is rarer: "de joy assatz" 'much joy' (14:35). But adverbs of quantity can also function without *de*: "assatz hi a pas" 'there are many steps' (24:26); "pro vetz" 'enough times.' Without *de*, they are usually treated as adjectives when an adjectival form exists, thus "tropas domnas" 'too many ladies' compared with the more frequent "trop de domnas." However, even with *de*, the expression of quantity can also be variable by attraction: "en petita d'ora" 'soon'; "tanta d'honor" 'so much honor.' For comparisons introduced by *(ai)tan*, see 13.2.

Indeclinable pronouns and/or adverbs designating quantity:

al(s), au 'something else, anything else'

alque(s) 'something; somewhat' (occasionally adjectival)

altretan(t), atre(s)tan(t) 'as much, so much; similarly'

calacom 'something, a little'

que(s)acom, que(s)acomet 'a little'

The pronoun *reṇ* 'someone, something; anyone, anything' varies from the declension of the noun *reṇ* (5.5.2) in that the properly nom. sg. *reṇs* is used as the obl. sg. sometimes for things and generally for persons; this pattern also holds for compounds like *al(d)rẹ* 'something else' and *calque reṇ* 'something,' except that the pronoun or adverb *gran reṇ, ganreṇ* 'much, many; very; a long time' is indeclinable. The last of these can function as an adverb of quantity: "gran ren d'autrez castels" 'many other castles' (39:2).

Tọt 'all'--pronoun, adjective, adverb--has many forms:

m. nom. sg.	totz, tutz	*f. sg.*	tota
m. obl. sg.	tot, tut		
m. nom. pl.	tuit, tu(i)ch, tug, tot, tut, tutz	*f. pl.*	totas
m. obl. pl.	totz, tutz, tugz		

Tot means 'every' with a singular noun, but 'all' when preceded by a definite article, thus "tot jorn" 'every day; always' but "tot lo jorn" 'all day.' *Tot* by itself is a neuter pronoun meaning 'everything'; and *tot* enters readily into compounds, notably with neuter demonstrative pronouns, e.g., "tot aisso" 'all that.'

Other indefinites include the following:

alcant 'some(what)': pronoun, adjective, adverb (diminutive: *alcantẹt*)

alcuṇ 'some (one), any (one)': pronoun, adjective

altre '(an)other (one)': pronoun, adjective; declined like *paubre*, usually with no preceding article

a(l)tretal, atrestal 'some; like, such (a)': pronoun, adjective, adverb; declined like *fizẹl*

altrui '(of, to) someone else': oblique pronoun corresponding to *altre*

can(t) 'how much, how many; as much (as), as many (as)': pronoun, adjective, adverb; *tot cant* means 'all that ...'

(h)om, (h)on 'one': subject pronoun; occasionally with the definite article or with an analogical *-s*

plusọrs 'several': pronoun, adjective; the nom. pl. has no *-s*

quiacom 'so': adverb

tal, aital 'such (a) (one), someone': pronoun, adjective; declined like *fiẓel*, with no preceding article; the corresponding adverb is *talmẹn*

uṇ '(any)one': pronoun, adjective; identical to the article

9.9 Numerals

The first three cardinal numerals are declinable:

m. nom.	uṇs	*m. obl.*	uṇ	*f.*	una
	dui, doị		dos		doas
	trẹi		tres, treis		tres

Some substitution of forms occurs, as in m. obl. *dui*, f. *dos*, m. nom. *tres*. *Uṇ* also can have the special meaning 'a single' or 'the same': "Bon' amors a un uzatge / Co·l bos aurs" 'Good love has the same custom / As good gold' (53:II, 41-42). As '(the) one' opposed to 'the other,' we find *la un* (6.3), *laün*, *l'un*: *la un pę* 'one foot.' A compound of *dos* meaning 'both' is m. *amdọs*, nom. *-dui*, *-doi*; f. *amdoas* (both also *an-*, *ab-*, *ambe-*).

The numbers 4 through 16 are *catre*, *cin(c)*, *s(i)ęis*, *sęt*, *ǫit* (*uęit*, *uęch*, *ǫig*), *nǫu* (*nuęu*), *dętz* (*dęi*), and then, ending in *-ze*, *onze*, *dọ(t)ze*, *trẹ(t)ze*, *catǫrze*, *quinze*, *sętze* (*sedze*), probably all pronounced with /dz/, simplifying to /z/ in many cases. The other "teens" are formed by addition: *detz e set*, *detz e oit*, *detz e nou*.

The multiples of 10 are *vin(t)*, *trenta*, *caranta*, *cinquanta*, *se(i)ssanta*, *setanta*, *catre vin(t)*, and *nonanta* (*noranta*, *novanta*). Digits are normally added after *e*: *vint e uṇ*, *trent' e dos*, etc.

Multiples of *cen(t)* '100' take an *-s* in the oblique: nom. *dui cen*, obl. *dos cens*. There are also special forms for 200 (m. *docẹn*, *dozen*, *dosen*; f. *docentas*, *dozentas*) and 300 (m. *trecẹn*, *tresen*). The plural of *mil* '1000' is *milia*, *millia*, *mila*, *melia*, *miria*, thus *dos* (or *doa*) *milia*, *tres* (or *tria*) *milia*, *catre milia*, etc. The noun *millięr* (*melier*) and also *cen* when it functions as a noun take *de*: "cinc milliers de cavals" '5000 horses,' "cen (de) baizars" '100 kisses,' etc.

An example of a complex number is "cen e quatre vint e ueit" '188' (4:80). Roman numerals were generally used in writing; e.g., for 188, ·C·XX·IIII·VIII· or ·C· e quatre ·XX·VIII.

The only multiplicative term is *dọble* 'double'; after that, one uses *tres vẹtz*, literally 'three times,' etc. The distributive function is expressed by *dos a dos* 'two by two,' *tres a tres*, etc.

The first six ordinals have special forms which are declined like the sg. of *bęl* except that *tęrtz* is indeclinable: 1. *premięr*, *prim(i)er*, *primeir*, *prum(i)er*, also *primairaṇ*, *primeiraṇ*, and also *prim* (which more often means 'fine,' etc.); 2. *segon(t)*; 3. *tęr(t)z*, *ters*; 4. *cart*; 5. *quin(t)*; 6. *sęst* (more frequently *seizeṇ*, *seizena*). All other ordinals are formed by adding m. *-eṇ/s*, f. *-ena/s* to the cardinal: m. obl. sg. *seteṇ*, *ocheṇ*, *noveṇ*, *detzeṇ*; *detz e seteṇ*; *vinteṇ*; *quatre vinteṇ*; etc. In 30-70 and 90 the *-a* drops before *-eṇ* is added: *trenteṇ*, etc. The corresponding adverbs are *premieramen* 'firstly,' etc. Ordinals also serve as fractions: *lo centeṇ* 'the hundredth part.'

Chapter 9: Exercises

A. (9.1) Supply demonstratives of proximity

1. Qu'ieu veya s_____ amor de lonh
2. C'ai_____ dui träidor
3. Chantarai d'aq_____ trobadors

B. (9.1) Supply demonstratives of remoteness

1. Trobey sola ... / S_____ que no vol mon solatz

2. C'ai_____ jorns me sembla nadaus
3. E tenia lo·i a solatz, e tug aq_____ que o sabion

C. (9.3, 9.5, 9.7) Supply relative and neuter demonstrative pronouns
1. Car no vol s_____ _____ om deu voler
2. Ac_____ es carnz _____ non pot esser neta
3. El fetz una canson, _____ comensa
4. Ilh es c_____ per _____ eu chan e plor
5. A l'ora _____ ce fo deliz

D. (9.6) Supply the proper interrogatives
1. _____·m conselhatz?
2. _____ flors?
3. Domnas i a de mal conselh / E sai dir _____

E. (9.8) Supply indefinites for the indicated meaning
1. each: Com _______ ab sa par s'aizi (7 syllables)
2. many: _______ li vengront de grans aventuras
3. anything, as much as: E _______ no·n sai mas ______ n'aug dir
4. so much; such a: Pastorgar _______ bestia / En ______ terra

F. (9.9) Translate in the m. obl. form
1. eleventh   2. eighty-nine   3. 517

10
VERBS: FORMS

10.1 Categories of the OP Verb

OP verbs possess the following formal properties:

2 voices: active, passive
6 moods: personal: indicative, subjunctive, conditional, imperative
impersonal: infinitive, participle (and gerundive, 12.3)
8 tenses: simple: future, present, imperfect, preterit
compound: future perfect (or future anterior), compound past, pluperfect, past anterior
3 persons: first, second, third
2 numbers: singular, plural

10.2 Conjugations

OP verbs fall into three conjugations, for which our nomenclature and model verbs will be:

A-verbs: infinitives in -*ar*: *amar* 'to love'

E-verbs: infinitives in -*re*, -*er*, -*ẹr*: *vendre* 'to sell'

I-verbs: infinitives in -*ir*, including *isc*-verbs:

florir 'to flower'; and non-*isc*-verbs: *partir* 'to depart.' Only the A- and I-*isc*-verbs are "living" conjugations, that is, are capable of forming new verbs in OP.

Another division is that between weak verbs, in which the preterit is stressed on the ending, and strong verbs, in which stress normally falls on the base in the 1 sg., 3 sg., and 3 pl. of the preterit, the 1-3 sg. and 3 pl. of the conditional B, and often in the past participle. All verbs with infinitives in -*ẹr* are strong; the exclusively or predominantly weak E-verbs have infinitives in -*re* and rarely -́*er*. In addition, many properly strong verbs sometimes take weak endings by analogy. All A- and I-verbs are weak; on the other hand, despite their infinitives, *far* * (*faire*) 'to do,' *merir* * 'to deserve,' and *venir* * 'to come' are basically strong E-verbs. Verbs followed in this chapter by a *, including all strong verbs, have special forms which are given in chapter 11. Many other verbs show consonantal or vocalic alternation without being considered special verbs as long as these alternations follow certain regular patterns.

10.3 Infinitives and Series of Endings

Many verbs have two or more infinitives. This causes no problem as long as all variants correspond to the same conjugation. However, some verbs have infinitives that correspond to different series of endings; for these, we indicate which series of endings are to be used. However, a few verbs like *benezir** 'to bless' and *legir** 'to read' combine weak I and strong E forms corresponding to their I- and E-infinitives.

10.4 Bases and Stems

Each verb form is built around a base which carries the fundamental semantic weight; for example, *am-* conveys the idea of loving. To this base are added a tense/aspect (T/A) marker and, in conjugated categories, a person/number (P/N) marker. For example, the 1 pl. imperfect indicative *amavam* has the base *am-*, the T/A marker *-ava*, and the P/N marker *-m*. In many verbs, the base takes on different allomorphs, or configurations determined by the associated category and markers. For example, the verb *dever** 'to owe' has the base allomorphs /dev-/, /deu̯-/, /dei̯-/, /deg-/, and /dek-/ (ignoring variants). The stem is the appropriate base allomorph plus the T/A marker; for example, the stem of *amavam* is /amava-/. The ending is the T/A and P/N markers taken together; thus in *amavam* and *am* 'I love,' the endings are /-avam/ and Ø (zero-grade).

The most important base, which we will call the "P-base," is most conveniently derived by removing the ending from the 1 pl. present indicative. Thus, our four model verbs have the P-bases *am-*, *vend-*, *part-*, and *flor-*, while *dever** has the P-base *dev-*. Certain verbs also have special bases for one or more of the following: the singular present indicative, the present subjunctive, base-stressed forms of the present system, the preterit, and rarely the past participle. These other bases almost always stand in a relation of consonantal or vocalic variation to the P-base.

10.5 Stress

Stress can be final or penultimate in OP verbs, but never antepenultimate. Thus the 3 sg. present indicative of *cambiar* 'to change' and *tremolar* 'to tremble' is *cambía* and *tremǫla*. Throughout a given category of one verb, stress remains on the same syllable counting from the end of the word, except that it is always on the final syllable in the 1 and 2 pl. The base is normally stressed (in all except I-*isc*-verbs) in the 2 sg. imperative and the 1-3 sg. and 3 pl. present indicative and subjunctive, as well as in some other categories of strong E-verbs.

10.6 Tense/Aspect and Person/Number Markers

Every verb category has a T/A marker, which can be Ø. The first vowel in the T/A marker of the majority of forms in a given category is called the "thematic vowel" (ignoring the infix -*isc*-). The A-, E-, and I-verbs are named after their respective thematic vowels.

There are two basic series of P/N markers, one for the preterit and the other, rather different, for all other conjugated categories.

The 1 and 3 sg. usually have the P/N marker Ø and therefore often coincide formally. Ambiguity is somewhat reduced by the development of the optional 1 sg. indicative markers -*i* after consonants (10.9) and -*c* in a few verbs (10.10); and in the 3 sg. preterit of I-verbs, of optional -*it* and -*ic* (10.17).

The 2 sg. has -*s* or, with a supporting vowel, -*es* (10.11), except for -*st* (occasionally -*s*) in the preterit and -Ø in the imperative.

The 1 pl. marker -*m* takes, in some dialects, the form -*n*. The 2 pl. marker -*tz* can also be spelled -*z*; but some dialects have -*t* and, by the thirteenth century, we often find the reduction -*s*; thus *vendętz*, *vendez*, *vendet*, *vendęs* all signify 'you sell.' The 3 pl. marker -*n* often drops from -*ọn* and preterit -*rọn*. When -*an* and -*en* appear as the rare -*ant* and -*ent*, it is in northern border dialects or (probably then with silent -*t*) through learnèd influence.

10.7 Isc-*Verbs*

Most I-verbs have a special "*isc*-stem" formed by adding an extra syllable -*isc*-, -*iss*- or -*is* before the P/N marker in the 1-3 sg. and 3 pl. of the present indicative, in all forms of the present subjunctive, in the 2 sg. imperative, and often in the present participle. The traditional name for these verbs is "inchoative." In Latin, verbs designated by this term, which means 'inceptive,' indicate the beginning of an action or state; a few OP *isc*-verbs retain this nuance.

The three persons of the singular present indicative and 2 sg. imperative generally end in -*is*. This confusion is partly alleviated by the alternate endings -*isc* in the 1 sg. and -*isses* in the 2 sg. indicative, producing the distinctive paradigm *jo florisc*, *tu florisses*, *el florîs*.

The form -*issọn* (-*issen*) dominates in the 3 pl. present indicative, but -*iscọn* is not rare. Forms with -*isc*- dominate in the present subjunctive, but those with -*iss*- also exist, and in fact prevail in the 3 pl. The infix has a palatal variant which can be written with *sh* or, rarely, with -*h*: *jo florish*, *il florishoṇ*, etc. (see 4.10, E). When we refer in general to *isc*-verbs or to the infix -*isc*-, it is understood that all the above variants are included.

Verbs ending in the suffix -*ezir* or -*zir* normally take -*isc*-, -*iss*-, -*is*, such as *enfolezir* 'to become crazy,' *envelhezir* 'to age,' *envelzir* 'to make base,' *esclarzir* 'to make clear,' *obezir* 'to obey,' etc. Such verbs generally reflect the idea of beginning or becoming.

Most other I-verbs also take -*isc*-, but the following and their compounds do so only sporadically or to the extent here indicated:

auzir* 'to hear'
bandir 'to banish'
bastir 'to build'
blandir 'to court'
bolhir 'to boil'
bondir 'to resound'
cobrir* 'to cover'
colhir* 'to gather' (but -*isc*- is not rare in the 3 sg. pres. ind. of *acolhir* 'to welcome')
cosir* 'to sew' (predominantly an E-verb)
croissir 'to crack'
cropir, crupir 'to crouch'
discernir, decernir 'to discern'
dormir 'to sleep' (but -*isc*- is not rare)
eissir* 'to go out'

escantir 'to extinguish' (about half and half)

escarnir, esquernir 'to mock' (-*isc*- in indicative, generally not in the subj.)

escremir 'to defend'

esparnir se 'to burst'

espelir 'to tell' (but with -*isc*- as 'to hatch'

estormir 'to attack'

falhir 'to fail' (-*isc*- is not uncommon in the pres. ind.)

ferir* 'to strike' (also E-verb)

fugir* 'to flee'

gandir 'to escape' (about half and half)

garentir, guirentir 'to guarantee' (-*isc*- in pres. ind. but not subj.)

garnir 'to supply' (-*isc*- in pres. ind. but not subj. or part.)

gauzir* 'to enjoy' (-*isc*- is not uncommon except in the pres. part.)

gequir, giquir 'to leave' (also -*isc*- especially in the sg. pres. ind.)

glatir 'to bark'

grondir 'to grunt, scold'

gron(h)ir 'to scold, growl' (also -*isc*- in pres. ind.)

guerpir, gurpir, grepir, grupir 'to leave' (about half and half in pres. ind.; *isc* in subj.)

legir* 'to read' (including *elegir* 'to elect'; also E-verb)

luzir* 'to shine'

mentir 'to tell a lie'

so-mergir* 'to submerge' (also E-verb)

merir* 'to deserve' (also E-verb)

so-monir* 'to summon' (also E-verb)

morir* 'to die'

obrir* ' to open'

ofrir* 'to offer' (but -*isc*- can occur in 1 and 3 sg. pres. ind.; also E-verb)

omplir, emplir 'to fill' (about half and half in pres. ind., more -*isc*- in subj.; including *complir* 'to achieve')

partir 'to depart' (-*isc*- is not rare)

pen(e)dir*, (re)pentir 'to repent' (also E-verb)

perir 'to perish' (-*is(c)*- usual in 3 sg. but not 1 sg.)

plevir* 'to pledge' (but -*is(c)* is common in 1 and 3 sg. pres. ind.)

pruzir 'to itch'

pudir 'to stink'

querir* 'to seek' (also E-verb)

regir* 'to rule' (also -*is* in 3 sg. pres. ind.)

resplandir* 'to shine' (but -*isc*- in the 1 sg. and rarely 3 sg. pres. ind.; also E-verb)

sal(h)ir 'to jump; to go out' (rarely -*isc*-)

seguir* 'to follow' (also E-verb)

sentir 'to feel'

servir 'to serve' (about half and half)

sofrir* 'to suffer' (like *ofrir*)

tossir, tussir 'to cough'

venir* 'to come' (predominantly E-verb)

vertir 'to turn' (about half and half)

vestir 'to clothe' (sometimes -*is* in 3 sg. pres. ind.)

Some verbs properly with -*isc*- occasionally lack the infix, particularly in the present participle, e.g., *floren* for *florissen*. On the other hand, the properly non-*isc*-verbs are occasionally contaminated by the more numerous *isc*-class, except in the present participle; and the postclassical period further extends -*isc*-.

10.8 Paradigms for Simple Verb Categories

The following table of our five model verbs italicizes -*isc*- and endings and capitalizes the stressed (or only) vowel or diphthong. Chapter 11 describes all strong verbs and others whose bases vary from the paradigms given here other than by consonantal or vocalic alternation.

A-verbs	*weak E-verbs*	*strong E-verbs*	*I-verbs (non-*isc*)*	isc-*verbs*
infinitive				
am*Ar*	vEnd*re*	pEn*re**, prEnd*re*	part*Ir*	flor*Ir*
pres. ind.				
Am(*i*)	vEn	prEn(*c*)	pArt	flor*Ís*(*c*)
Am*as*	vEn*s*	prEn*s*	pArt*z*	flor*Ís*(*ses*)
Am*a*	vEn	prEn	pArt	flor*Ís*
am*Am*	vend*Em*	prend*Em*	part*Em*	flor*Em*
am*Atz*	vend*Ętz*	prend*Ętz*	part*Ętz*	flor*Ętz*
Am*oṇ*, Am*an*	vEnd*oṇ*	prEnd*oṇ*	pArt*oṇ*	flor*Issoṇ*
imperative				
Am*a*	vEn	prEn	pArt	flor*Ís*
am*Atz*	vend*Ętz*	prend*ętz*	part*Ętz*	flor*ętz*

A-verbs	*weak E-verbs*	*strong E-verbs*	*I-verbs (non-*isc*)*	isc-*verbs*
pres. subj.				
Am	vEnd*a*	prEng*a*	pArt*a*	florI*sca*
Am*s*	vEnd*as*	prEng*as*	pArt*as*	florI*scas*
Am	vEnd*a*	prEng*a*	pArt*a*	florI*sca*
am*Em*	vend*Am*	preng*Am*	part*Am*	flor*iscAm*
am*Ẹtz*	vend*Atz*	preng*Atz*	part*Atz*	flor*iscAtz*
Am*ọn*	vEnd*an*	prEng*an*	pArt*an*	florI*scan*
pres. part.				
am*An(t)*	vend*En(t)*	prend*En(t)*	part*En(t)*	floriss*En(t)*
impf. ind.				
am*Ava*	vend*Ia*	prend*Ia*	part*Ia*	flor*Ia*
am*Avas*	vend*Ias*	prend*Ias*	part*Ias*	flor*Ias*
am*Ava*	vend*Ia*	prend*Ia*	part*Ia*	flor*Ia*
am*avAm*	vend*iAm*	prend*iAm*	part*iAm*	flor*iAm*
am*avAtz*	vend*iAtz*	prend*iAtz*	part*iAtz*	flor*iAtz*
am*Avọn, -Avan*	vend*Iọn, -Ian*	prend*Iọn, -Ian*	part*Iọn, -Ian*	flor*Iọn, -Ian*
future				
am*arAI*	vend*rAI*	prend*rAI*	part*irAI*	flor*irAI*
am*arÁs*	vend*rÁs*	prend*rÁs*	part*irÁs*	flor*irÁs*
am*arÁ*	vend*rÁ*	prend*rÁ*	part*irÁ*	flor*irÁ*
am*arEm*	vend*rEm*	prend*rEm*	part*irEm*	flor*irEm*
am*arẸtz*	vend*rẸtz*	prend*rẸtz*	part*irẸtz*	flor*irẸtz*
am*arÁn*	vend*rÁn*	prend*rÁn*	part*irÁn*	flor*irÁn*
cond. A				
am*arIa*	vend*rIa*	prend*rIa*	part*irIa*	flor*irIa*
am*arIas*	vend*rIas*	prend*rIas*	part*irIas*	flor*irIas*
am*arIa*	vend*rIa*	prend*rIa*	part*irIa*	flor*irIa*
am*ariAm*	vend*riAm*	prend*riAm*	part*iriAm*	flor*iriAm*
am*ariAtz*	vend*riAtz*	prend*riAtz*	part*iriAtz*	flor*iriAtz*
am*arIan*	vend*rIan*	prend*rIan*	part*irIan*	flor*irIan*

A-verbs	weak E-verbs	strong E-verbs	I-verbs (non-isc)	isc-verbs
preterit				
am(I)Ȩi	vend(I)Ȩi	prIs	partÍ	florÍ
am(I)Ȩst	vend(I)Ȩst	prezIst	partIst	florIst
amȨt	vendȨt	prẸs	partÍ	florÍ
amEm	vendEm	prezEm	partIm	florIm
amȨtz	vendȨtz	prezẸtz	partItz	florItz
amȨroṇ	vendȨroṇ	prẸIroṇ	partIroṇ	florIroṇ
impf. subj.				
amȨs	vendȨs	prezẸs	partÍs	florÍs
amȨsses	vendȨsses	prezẸsses	partIsses	florIsses
amȨs	vendȨs	prezẸs	partÍs	florÍs
amessEm	vendessEm	prezessEm	partissEm	florissEm
amessȨtz	vendessȨtz	prezessẸtz	partissẸtz	florissẸtz
amȨssen	vendȨssen	prezẸssen	partIssen	florIssen
cond. B				
amȨra	vendȨra	prẸIra	partIra	florIra
amȨras	vendȩras	prẸIras	partIras	florIras
amȨra	vendȨra	prẸIra	partIra	florIra
amerAm	venderAm	preirAm	partirAm	florirAm
amerAtz	venderAtz	preirAtz	partirAtz	florirAtz
amȨran	vendȨran	prẸIran	partIran	florIran
past part.				
amAt	vendUt	prẸs	partIt	florIt

10.9 The Present System and -Ø, -e, -i

The "present system" comprises the present indicative, subjunctive, imperative, and participle.

When the usual ending is -Ø, certain verbs take a final supporting *e* or *i*. Some of the consonant combinations that for ease of pronunciation in the preliterary period required this supporting vowel changed phonetically by the twelfth century, but the supporting vowel normally remains wherever it was once present. The supporting vowel is needed when the base ends in the following sounds:

1) any consonant plus a liquid, thus *siscle* 'I pipe' (43:45), and similarly for *alegrar* 'to delight,' *comprar* 'to buy,' *emblar* 'to steal,' *enclostrar* 'to cloister,' *entrar* 'to enter, *mostrar* 'to show,' *obrar* 'to fashion,' *omplir* 'to fill,' *on(d)rar* 'to honor,' *parlar* 'to speak,' *semblar* 'to seem,' *tremblar* 'to tremble,' etc.

2) a semivowel plus a liquid, when the semivowel is derived from a consonant, thus *·m liure* 'I give myself up' (5:7), and similarly for *aproimar se* 'to approach,' *repairar* 'to go,' etc.

3) vocalic *i* plus a liquid, where the *i* has absorbed a consonant (though in such cases, the supporting vowel is sometimes dropped), thus in *albirar* 'to consider,' *cossirar* 'to consider,' *dezirar* 'to desire,' etc.

4) a labial (including *u* from a vocalized consonant) plus a dental where a posttonic Latin vowel between them has fallen, thus *dọpti* 'I fear' (19:50), and similarly for *endeutar* (*endeptar*) *se* 'to become indebted,' *reptar* 'to blame,' etc.

5) a consonant plus /ǧ/, or intervocalic /ǧ/ when its usual spelling is *tj* or *tg* (see 4.11,A), thus *alongi* 'I prolong' (179:5), and similarly for *camjar* 'to change,' *domesjar* 'to tame,' *escomenjar* 'to excommunicate,' *manjar* 'to eat,' *venjar* 'to avenge,' etc.

6) usually, a consonant plus *m* or *n*, when a post-tonic Latin vowel between them has fallen, thus *mẹrmi* 'I lack' (128:31), and similarly for *blasmar* 'to blame,' *esmar* 'to esteem,' etc.

A supporting vowel is often extended to forms that do not require it, particularly in A-verbs and even more so with bases ending in a vowel plus *r*. Thus, *azirar* 'to hate,' *esclairar* 'to brighten,' *mirar* 'to look at,' *restaurar* 'to restore,' *sospirar* 'to sigh,' *virar* 'to turn,' and the like take the optional final vowel about as often as not. When the base contains tonic *i*, the troubadours prefer the final vowel *-e* even in the 1 sg., no doubt in order to avoid two *i*'s in successive syllables; only rarely does one find forms like *albiri* 'I consider.'

The 1 sg. has *-e* in other scattered instances such as *torne* (54:57) for *tọrn* 'I turn,' but in general it prefers the more distinctive *-i*, as in *nadi* 'I swim' (66:10), *resoli* 'I resole' (73:29), *tremi** 'I fear' (3:19), *josti* (128:47) for *jọst* 'that I joust,' and the whole series of verbs rhyming with *dǫli* 'I plane' and *esmęri* 'I grow purer' in No. 68.

Nevertheless, in the 1 sg. the troubadours use *-i* less and *-e* much less than the -Ø ending. Some common forms, such as *ai**, *fau(c)**, *sọi**, and *vau(c)** 'I have, make, am, go' have no corresponding dissyllabic variant; and the troubadours hardly ever use *-i* in I-verbs, where *-is(c)* is felt as a sufficiently distinctive marker (although by the fourteenth century we do find forms like *noirishi* for *noirisc* 'I nourish').

The 3 sg. indicative has *-e* as its normal supporting vowel, though one does find occasional forms like *cobri* (181:29, from *cobrir** 'to cover'). The 3 sg. subjunctive shows an even clearer preference for *-e* as supporting vowel, e.g., *iutge* (126:51, from *jutjar* 'to judge'), *membre* (90:37, from *membrar* 'to be reminded'). The unnecessary *-e* on 3 sg. subjunctives such as *tire* (69:42, from *tirar* 'to irritate') becomes more common by the fourteenth century (e.g., 180:24, 97, 112, etc.).

10.10 Present Indicative 1 sg. -c

A number of verbs have in their 1 sg. present indicative a *-c* that is a base-consonant either throughout (*pęc*, from *pecar* 'to sin') or in alternation with other consonants (*pręc*, from *pregar* 'to pray,' *cenc*, from *cẹnher** 'to gird,' and similarly in *nh*-verbs; see 10.12). Reinforced by the example of the *-is(c)* that appears in the majority of I-verbs, *-c* became particularly associated with the 1 sg. present indicative and in a few cases, can be seen as a genuine ending. Thus we find *dauc* from *dar** 'to give,' *estauc* from *estar** 'to stay,' *fa(u)c* from *far** 'to do,' and *vauc* from *anar** 'to go.'

10.11 The Present System: Other

In the 2 sg. of verbs whose base ends in *nh*, *lh*, and sometimes *l*, an optional spelling with *-z* reflects the insertion of a glide /t/; thus, from *lonhar* 'to remove,' *trebalhar* 'to work,' and *apelar* 'to call,' we find on occasion the 2 sg. present subjunctives *lonhz*, *trebalhz*, and *apęlz*. Depalatalization of

-*nhz* and -*lhz* to -*nz* and *lz* (or of -*nhs* and -*lhs* to -*ns* and -*ls*) is also possible.

The 2 sg. takes a supporting vowel (before the -*s*) wherever the 1 sg. does, and often, in addition, where a group of two sibilants would otherwise occur. In these cases, the -*s* ending becomes -*es*, as in *comples* (*complir** 'to achieve'), *parles* (subjunctive, *parlar* 'to speak'), and *cręzes* (*cręire** 'to believe'). Especially in later texts, this -*es* ending can be extended to other verbs, thus *esgardes* for *esgartz* 'you look at' and *partes* for *partz* 'you depart.'

The 2 pl. -*tz*, in the imperative, can elide before ·*us*, e.g., *mete·us* from *mętre** 'to put.' The 3 pl. ending -*an* is reserved for the indicative of A-verbs and the subjunctive of other verbs, while the more frequent forms in -*on* are applied to the indicative and subjunctive of all conjugations; -*on* does not elide but can support enclitics, as in *canto·l* for *canton lo* 'they sing it.' A second nondiscriminating ending, -*en*, as in *canten*, *venden*, *parten*, *florissen*, is less common and dialectal.

The subjunctive is used as the imperative of *aver**, *ęsser**, *saber**, *voler**, and also, in the plural, *auzir**, *cręire**, *dire**, *vezer**, and some other verbs with less regularity.

10.12 Base-Consonant Alternation in the Present System

As in nouns (5.6-7) and adjectives (7.4-5), the final consonant of verb bases often changes because of the following inflection. These changes, which are the most far-reaching in the strong verbs, usually represent a normal adaptation to phonological conditions. Only *isc*-verbs are, because of their infix, exempt from these alternations.

The first and most frequent type is exemplified by the following patterns:

	A-verbs	*E-verbs*	*non*-isc *I-verbs*
infinitive	trobar 'to find'	pęrdre 'to lose'	seguir* 'to follow'
pres. ind.			
sg. 1	trǫp	pęrt	sęc
sg. 2		pertz	secs
sg. 3		pert	sec
pres. subj.			
sg. 1	trop		
sg. 2	trops		
sg. 3	trop		
impv.			
sg.2		pert	sec

Similarly we find the following alternations, here represented by the infinitive and 1 sg. present indicative:

1) other voiced/unvoiced pairs: *salvar* 'to save' ~ *salf*, *auzar* 'to dare' ~ *aus*, *cujar* 'to believe' *cuch*;

2) /v/ ~ /u/: *abrivar* 'to hasten' ~ *abriu*;

3) /z/ or /s/ ~ /ts/: *prezar* 'to esteem' ~ *pretz*, *cassar* 'to hunt' ~ *catz*;

4) /nd/ or /nt/ ~ /n/: *blandir* 'to court' ~ *blan*, *chantar* 'to sing' ~ *chan* (in the occasional spellings like *bland* and *chant*, the final consonant is probably silent);

5) /n/ ~ -ṇ: *donar* 'to give' ~ *doṇ*

6) /z/ ~ Ø (or sometimes /s/): *lauzar* 'to praise' ~ *lau(s)*.

The second type of consonant alternation affects E- and I-verbs in which a consonant not present elsewhere appears in the present subjunctive (and often also the 1 sg. present indicative), for example:

		non-nh *verbs*	nh-*verbs*
infinitive		çreire* 'to believe'	venir* 'to come'
pres. subj.	*sg. 1*	creia	venga
	sg. 2	creias	vengas
	sg. 3	creia	venga
	pl. 1	creiam	vengam
	pl. 2	creiatz	vengatz
	pl. 3	creian	vengan
pres. ind.	*sg. 1*	crei (cre)	venc

We find the following subtypes, here represented by the infinitive and the 3 sg. present subjunctive:

1) *l* ~ *lh*: *caler** 'to be important' ~ *calha*;

2) /z/ or /v/ ~ /i̯/ or /ǧ/: *tazer** 'to be silent' ~ *taia*, *aver** ~ *aia* (see 3.7);

3) /is/ ~ /sk/: *conọisser** 'to know' ~ *conosca*;

4) *n* ~ *ng* or *nh*: the forms given in the above chart for *venir** have a parallel series all with *nh*: present subjunctive *venh*- and 1 sg. present indicative *venh*. This group of "*nh*-verbs" includes the following and their compounds: *cẹnher** 'to gird,' *contránher** 'to force,' *fẹnher** 'to feign,' *fránher** 'to break,' *jọnher** 'to join,' *ọnher** 'to anoint,' *pẹnher** 'to paint' (and compounds meaning 'to push'), *plánher** 'to lament,' *pọnher** 'to prick,' *penre**

'to take,' *(re)maner** 'to remain,' *so-monre** 'to summon,' *e-strẹnher** 'to squeeze,' *e-stẹnher** 'to extinguish,' *tánher** 'to be fitting,' *tẹnher** 'to color,' *tener** 'to hold,' and *venir** 'to come.'

10.13 Base-Vowel Alternation in the Present System

Where the base vowel develops differently when stressed and unstressed, we find alternations such as the following:

1) Stressed /ę/ and /ǫ/ ~ unstressed /ẹ/ and /ọ/ > /u/ and occasionally > /ü/: *pęrt* 'he loses' ~ *perdem* 'we lose,' *dǫrm* 'he sleeps' ~ *dormem, durmem* 'we sleep' (see 3.4).

2) Diphthongized *ię* and *uǫ* > *ue* (3.8) ~ unstressed *e* and *o*: 1 sg. present indicative *quięr* and 3 sg. present subjunctive *quię(i)ra* ~ *querer** 'to seek,' 3 sg. present indicative *fuǫlha, fuęlha* ~ *folhar* 'to leaf.' Where stressed /ę/ and /ǫ/ can diphthongize before *r*, we often find an intercalated *i*, as in 1 sg. present subjunctive *fię(i)ra* ~ *ferir** 'to strike.'

3) Pretonic *i* sometimes optionally dissimilates to *e* before tonic *i*, and similarly pretonic *e* to *i* before tonic *e*, as in *fenit* (past participle) ~ *finir* 'to finish,' and *sirven* (present participle) ~ *servir* 'to serve.' Similarly, an alternation of pretonic *ei* to *i* can occur as in *eissir** 'to go out' (cf. 3.7).

4) When stressed, the base of a few verbs has an additional syllable, thus 3 sg. present indicative *ajuda* and subjunctive *ajut* ~ *aidar* 'to help'; 1 sg. present indicative *man(d)uc* and 3 sg. *manduja,*

manjuia, and 3 sg. present subjunctive *manjuc* ~ *manjar* 'to eat'; and 3 sg. present indicative *paraula* ~ *parlar* 'to speak.' However, one base tends to supplant the other: *ajud-* dominates even in base-unstressed forms like the infinitive *ajudar* (though sometimes we find *aid-* in a base-stressed form like 3 sg. present indicative *aida*), while *manj-* and *parl-* dominate in the other two verbs, in the usual 3 sg. present indicatives *manja* and *parla* (though forms like the infinitive *paraular* do exist).

10.14 The Present Participle

The present participle is formed very regularly from the P-base (except for *ęsser**) plus *-an(t)* in A-verbs and *-en(t)* in others; *-iss-* is usually, but not always, inserted in *isc*-verbs. The *t* may or may not be actually pronounced when it remains reflected in spellings like *-ant*, *-anz*, *-antz*. When it functions as an adjective or noun, the present participle is declined like *fizẹl*; but when used as a verb (12.3), it remains invariable, identical to the m. and f. obl. sg.

10.15 The Imperfect Indicative

The imperfect endings shown in 10.8 are added to the P-base except for *ęsser**). In the 3 pl., *-avoṇ* and *-ioṇ* are more common than *-avan* and *-iaṇ*, while *-aven* and *-ien* are less usual. The endings *-ia*, etc., are normally dissyllabic, but sometimes count as one syllable (3.10). The 3 pl. rarely has a final *-t*, and *iauṇ* occurs in some documents.

10.16 *The Future, Conditional A, and Infinitive*

The conditional A is also known as the "new conditional" and, confusingly, as both "first" and "second conditional"; it also serves as "future imperfect" or "future in the past." Its T/A marker, like those of the future and the infinitive, always includes an *r*, and it always has the same stem as the future, for example, in 3 sg. *naisserá* and *naisseria* from *náisser** 'to be born.' As in this example, all three categories almost always have the same base, which is the P-base except in some E-verbs such as *mover**, which has the future and conditional A stem *mour*-.

The P/N markers of the future and conditional are as in most other categories (10.6) except for *i̯* in the 1. sg. future. The resulting endings are the same as the imperfect of E- and I-verbs (10.8). Rarer endings are, in the future, 1 sg. -*ẹi*, -*ey* (*metrey** 'I will put,' 122:62), 1 pl. -*am*, 2 pl. -*atz*, 3 pl. -*ant*, *aun*, *au*; and, in the conditional A, 3 pl. -*ioṇ*, -*ien*, -*iau*.

A-verbs sometimes show a weakening of *ar* to *er*, thus *cuieriant* 'they would believe' (179:34). In E-verbs, after an *l* or *n*, we often find the glide consonant *d* intercalated before *r*, as in *(re)man(d)ra** 'he will remain,' and similarly for *caler**, *tener**, *toler**, *valer**, *venir**, *voler**.

For phonetic reasons, some I-verbs often drop the *i* in combinations like -*rtir* (*partrai* 'I will leave') and -*stir*- (*bastra* 'he will build'), and similarly *mentir* 'to lie' and *vestir* 'to clothe,' and even more regularly so in -*rir*-, thus *garrá* 'he will be cured,' from *garir*, and similarly for *ferir**, *merir**, *morir**, *perir* 'to perish,' etc.

When the first component of the future corresponds in form to an infinitive, then one or more pronouns can intervene between it and the ending, thus *comtar l'as* 'you will tell it' (16:8), *aucir m'ant* 'they will kill me' (96:13), *partir m'ai* 'I will leave' (96:24), *laissar m'o ai estar* 'I will let it be' (82:27). This separable construction is much rarer in the conditional.

10.17 Weak Preterits

The "preterit system" comprises the preterit, imperfect subjunctive, conditional B, and past participle. The preterit itself determines that all A- and I-verbs and a minority of E-verbs are weak (10.2), having stressed preterit endings in all six persons like *amar*, *partir*, *florir* and *vendre* (10.8). The following E-verbs and their compounds have weak preterits, with strong variants only as here indicated:

batre 'to beat'
(es)coissendre 'to scratch'
ọser* 'to sew' (also an I-verb)
crẹire* 'to believe'
descendre 'to descend'
espandre* 'to spread' (also an I-verb)
fendre 'to split' (but *de-fendre** is strong)
fondre* 'to melt'
fọtre 'to have sexual intercourse with'
iráisser* se 'to become angry' (preterit-base; also strong
mẹisser* 'to pour a drink' (preterit-base)
náisser* 'to be born' (preterit-base; also strong)
páisser* 'to feed' (preterit-base; also strong)

pendre 'to hang' (compounds include *despendre* 'to spend')

pẹrdre 'to lose'

rendre, rẹdre, 'to yield'

rompre 'to break'

sẹgre* 'to follow' (also an I-verb)

tẹisser* 'to weave' (can be preterit-base; also strong)

tendre* 'to stretch' (rarely strong)

tondre 'to shear'

vẹncer* 'to conquer' (preterit-base)

viure* 'to live' (preterit-base; also strong)

Almost all weak preterits are formed with the P-base. However, the verbs indicated above as "preterit-base"--namely *viure** plus a few entirely or predominantly weak verbs with infinitives in *-ér*--have a special preterit-base (as well as a subjunctive-base) in /k/: *irasquẹt**, *mesquẹt**, *nasquẹt**, *pasquẹt**, *tesquẹt** (and *teissẹt*), *venquẹt**, and *visquẹt** (see also *e-legir**). In addition, most strong verbs have occasional weak preterit forms constructed on their preterit-base. Conversely, several of the preterit-base weak verbs just listed, as well as a few other predominantly weak verbs, have alternate strong forms, particularly with 3 sg. *-c* (10.18A).

The 1 and 2 sg. undiphthongized endings *-ẹi* (or *-ey*) and *-ẹst* are more common than diphthongized *-iẹi* (*-iey*) and *-iẹst*. The 2 sg. *-st* sometimes reduces to *-s*: *am(i)ẹs*, *partis*, etc. The 3 sg. normally has a *-t* in A- and E-verbs but only rarely in I-verbs (*sentit* 'he felt,' 137:6). The 2 pl. of

A- and weak E-verbs has -*ẹtz* with open /ẹ/; and the 3 pl. -*ẹron*, -*iron* can become -*ẹren*, -*iren*.

The 3 sg. of I-verbs not infrequently has a -*c* which distinguishes it from the 1 sg. pret., thus *acuillic* 'she welcomed' (26:43), *fenic* 'he came to his end' (26:51), *el se partic* 'he left' (153:15), also many of the rhyme words in No. 140, and with particular frequency *moric** 'he died.' This 3 sg. -*c*, of analogical origin like the 1 sg. present indicative -*c* (10.10), is occasionally extended to A- and weak E-preterits, thus *chantẹc* 'he sang,' *dẹc** 'he gave,' *entendẹc* 'he heard,' *estẹc** 'he stayed,' etc.

There is some evidence of a southwestern dialectal 3 sg. preterit in -*á*; in troubadour poems and biographies, however, such forms are better interpreted as being morphologically present. See 12.5, as for the rare preterit periphrasis formed with *anar**.

10.18 Strong Preterits

A) Strong preterits are distinguished from weak ones by three factors: a) they are base-stressed in the 1 sg., 3 sg., and 3 pl.; b) their endings -Ø, -*ist*, -Ø, -*em*, -*ẹtz*, -*ẹtz*, -*ron* (less often -*ren*) differ from the corresponding weak preterit endings except in the 1 pl.; and c) they are built on a preterit-base which is almost always different from the P-base and restricted to part or all of their preterit system.

Strong verbs are traditionally divided into three classes according to whether in Vulgar Latin their perfect T/A marker had /s/, /u̯/, or neither. Our own purely synchronic classification will discern six classes: *c/g*, *ec/eg/*, *s/s*, *s/z*, *up/ub*, and strong throughout. In the first five of these classes, the first indicated sound of each pair occurs in the 1 and 3 sg. and the other sound elsewhere (except in some 3 pls.).

For each class, we give only the 3 sg. of representative verbs; chapter 11 shows significant variations from the pattern, weak forms when they are at all frequent, and many other verbs of the various classes, including some with multiple allegiance. Compounds normally follow the same patterns as the simple roots, although not all forms are always attested for either.

1) *C/g* preterits, about thirty in all, can be formed by removing the last consonant of the P-base (except *l*, *n*, and *r*) and any preceding semivowel, and then by adding *-c* or *-g(u)-*. Model: *dever** 'to owe': *dẹc, deguist, dẹc, deguem, deguẹtz, dẹgroṇ*.

In addition, a few of the predominantly weak preterit-base E-verbs (10.17) have alternate strong forms with *-c* in the 3 sg. only, thus *nasc* from *náisser** 'to be born' and similarly for *tẹisser** 'to weave' and *viure** 'to leave.' Also, a few otherwise weak preterits have alternate 3 sg. strong forms in *-ęrc*, thus *sofęrc* from *sofrir** 'to suffer' and similarly for *obrir** 'to open' and its compound *cobrir** 'to cover.'

The 3 sg. *-c* evidently marks a point of contact between strong and weak verbs. Like certain weak verbs (10.17), some predominantly strong verbs took on a 3 sg. preterit *-ic*, as in *as-sic* from *as-sezer** 'to place.'

2) *Ec/eg* preterits add *-ec* and *-eg(u)* to their P-base, as in *parer** 'to appear': *parẹc, pareguist, parẹc, pareguem, paregụetz, parẹgrọn.* The final *-ec* usually has /ẹ/ but sometimes /ę/ as in weak forms.

3) *S/s* preterits have /s/, normally spelled *ss* or postconsonantal or final *s*, except for scattered forms with *z* representing /z/. In general, one can derive these preterit-bases by taking the P-base, removing only the second of two consonants, and adding /s/. The major exception is the verbs with infinitives in *-ńher* listed in 10.12, which have preterit-bases in *-i̭s* and only scattered examples in *-i̭ns* or *ns*. About forty verbs follow the model of *dire** 'to say': *dis, dissist, dis, dissem, dissẹtz, dirọn.*

4) *S/z* preterits can in general be formed by taking the P-base, removing the final consonant or consonant group, and adding /s/ in the 1 and 3 sg. and /z/ elsewhere. Some twenty verbs follow the model of *rire** 'to laugh': *ris, rizist, ris, rizem, rizẹtz, rirọn.*

5) *Up/ub* preterits follow the model of *saber** 'to know': *saup, saubist, saup, saubem, saubẹtz, saubrọn* or *sauprọn.*

6) "Strong throughout" preterits have 2 sg., 1 pl., and 2 pl. endings are reduced to *-st*, *-m*, and *tz*, respectively, thus from *ęsser** 'to be' *fui, fust, fọ, fom, fọtz, fọrọn*, and similarly *fi* and *vi*, etc., from *far** 'to do' and *vezer** 'to see.'

B) The strong 1 and 3 sg. are almost always identical. However, several 1 sgs. have the base vowel *i* corresponding to 3 sg. *ẹ*, thus 1. sg. *cric* ~ 3 sg. *crẹc* from *crẹisser** 'to grow.' In addition, the 1 sg. can be optionally distinguished by diphthongization (3.8), as in *puǫc, puęc* from *poder** 'to be able.' Another less common means of distinguishing the 1 sg. is to use the weak P/N marker *-î*, thus *beguî* from *bẹure** 'to drink,' and *dissî* from *dire**. There is also evidence of an unstressed 1 sg. P/N marker *-i*, thus *bẹgui*, and *dissi*. In the 3 sg. of normally strong preterits, weak forms, rarer than in the 1 sg., are taken from the weak E-conjugation, thus *agųet* from *aver**.

In strong as in weak preterits, the 2 sg. *-st* occasionally reduces to *-s* and the 2 pl. *-tz* more often so. It should be noted that the 2 pl. has *-ẹtz* rather than the *-ętz* of weak E-preterits.

In the 3 pl., the contact of a base-final consonant with the ending-initial *r* often produces phonetic alterations. One solution, in *s/z* and *s/s* verbs, is to insert a glide *d* or *t* (4.4), thus *aucisdroṇ* and *duistroṇ* from *aucire** 'to kill' and *duire** 'to lead.' A second solution in *s/z* and *s/s* verbs is to drop the final base consonant, thus *auciron* from *aucire**. When the tonic vowel is not *i*, a /i̯/ is often inserted, thus *mẹ(i)roṇ* from *mẹtre** 'to put.' A third solution is to drop the *r* itself, thus *vǫlgoṇ* from *voler** 'to want.' Given the multiplicity of solutions, it is not surprising that many strong verbs develop weak 3 pl. preterits, either in exclusivity or in competition with strong forms, thus *prezęrọn* from *penre** 'to take.'

10.19 The Imperfect Subjunctive

The imperfect subjunctive has only weak forms except for the three verbs with "strong throughout" preterits. In other verbs, the imperfect subjunctive is quite regularly constructed on the preterit-base, with the endings shown in 10.8; the 1 sg. and 3 sg. are hence identical, for example, in *deguẹs* from *dever**. Forms built on strong preterit stems have tonic /ẹ/, while those built on weak stems have /ę/ or /i/.

Alternate forms used on occasion by the troubadours include 1) the 2 sg. in *-ęs* instead of *-ęsses*; 2) all six persons with *a* as the final vowel, thus the 1 sg. in *-ęssa*, *-issa*, or *-ẹssa*, the 1 pl. in *-ęssam* or *-issam*, etc.; and 3) the plural of A-verbs in *-assem*, *-assẹtz*, *-assen*.

A few verbs with *c/g* or *up/ub* preterits have optional syncopated 1 and 2 pl. imperfect subjunctives with partial assimilation of the voiced consonant to the following *s*, thus, from *aver**, 1 pl. *aguessem* or *acsem* and 2 pl. *aguessẹtz* or *acsẹtz*, and similarly for *dever**, *jazer**, *poder**, *saber**, *tener**, and *voler**. Rarely, the P-base can intrude into the imperfect subjunctive, as in *pla(i)nguẹs*, *plaissẹs* from *plánher** 'to lament.'

10.20 The Conditional B

The conditional B, also called "old conditional" and, confusingly, both "first" and "second conditional," is formed from the preterit-base plus the endings shown in 10.8.

A-verbs also have a rarer form *cantara*, *cantaras*, etc. The conditional B of strong verbs can usually be formed by removing the -*oṇ* of the 3 pl. preterit form with *r* and adding -*a*, -*as*, -*a*, -*am*, -*atz*, -*an*: thus, from *dever**, *dẹgroṇ* gives 1 and 3 sg. *dẹgra*. The 1-3 sg. and the 3 pl. are strong in most strong verbs.

Where a weak preterit is in competition with the strong one, the conditional B can also have dual forms, as in *dira* and *dissęra* from *dire**; but many uncommon verbs do not have the conditional B attested at all.

10.21 The Past Participle

In A-verbs and almost all I- and weak E-verbs, the past participle is formed by adding -*at*, -*it*, and -*ut*, respectively, to the P-base, thus *amat*, *partit*, *florit*, *vendut*. These have their feminine in -*da* and the plural in -*tz* and -*das*, like the adjective *mut* (7.5,2). Occasionally, -*ida* reduces to -*ia* (4.7).

A few weak verbs have dual participles corresponding to parallel paradigms, as in *seguit* ~ *segut* from *seguir**, *sęgre* 'to follow.' The few weak or predominantly weak E-verbs whose preterit uses a base in *k* (10.17) add -*ut*/-*uda* to that base, thus *irascut* from *iráisser** 'to become angry.' A few weak verbs have strong past participles, thus *mǫrt* and *rọt* (or *romput*) from *morir** 'to die' and *rompre* 'to break.'

The situation is far more complex for verbs with strong preterits, about half of which have strong past participles, while quite a few have both strong and weak participles. One finds the following types, with examples:

A) strong participles:

1) ending in base-final *-s* and identical to the 3 sg. preterit: *aucis, auciza* from *aucire** 'to kill,' *cọrs/a* from *cọrre** 'to run';

2) in postconsonantal *-t/a*: *tǫlt* from *tǫlre** 'to take away,' *cobęrt* from *cobrir** 'to cover,' *quist* from *quęrre** 'to seek';

3) in *-(i)ch/a* ~ *-(i)t/a*: *dich, dit* from *dire** 'to say,' *frach* ~ *frait* from *fránher** 'to break,' *planch* ~ *plaint* from *plánher* 'to lament';

B) weak participles:

1) in *-ut, -uda*: *begut* from *beure** 'to drink,' *saubut* and *sauput* from *saber** 'to know';

2) in *-at, -ada*: *estat* from *ęsser** (borrowed from *estar** 'to stay');

3) in *-it, -ida* (corresponding to alternate I-infinitives): *cabit* from *caber** 'to fit.'

10.22 Compound Verb Categories

Compound verbs consist of a form of the auxiliary *aver** or *ęsser** plus a past participle. Examples for *amar*, in the 1 sg. when feasible, follow:

names	*examples*	*auxiliary*
comp. past	ai amat	pres. ind.
perf. subj.	aia amat	pres. subj.
past imper.	aias amat	pres. imper.

names	*examples*	*auxiliary*
past gerundive	aven amat	pres. part.
plupf. ind.	avia amat	impf.
fut. perf.	aurai amat	future
comp. cond. A	auria amat	cond. A
past inf.	aver amat	inf.
past anterior	ac amat	pret.
plupf. subj.	agueṣ amat	impf. subj.
comp. cond. B	agra amat	cond. B

It should be noted that what we call "compound past" is also known as "present perfect" and simply "perfect" (a term that is also sometimes applied to the preterit).

The following types of verbs are conjugated with *ęsser**:

1) passives (10.23, 12.10)

2) pronominal verbs (8.10), for example: "Peire Vidals saup qu'En Barrals se era levatz" 'Peire Vidal knew that Lord Barral had arisen' (84:14-15).

3) intransitive verbs denoting motion, the cessation of motion, birth, death, etc., including in general the following (and their compounds when of related meaning, unless otherwise indicated): *anar** 'to go,' *a-parer** 'to appear,' (not *parer*) *arribar* 'to arrive,' *cambaterrar* 'to dismount,' *cambiar* 'to change (oneself),' *cazer** 'to fall,' *comensar* 'to begin' (not + *a* + infinitive), *cọrre** 'to run' (not compounds), *crebar* 'to break,' *crẹisser** 'to grow; happen,' *descavalcar* 'to dismount,' *descendre* 'to descend,' *desplazer** 'to displease,' *devalar* 'to descend,' *doblar* 'to double,' *eissir** 'to go out,' *entrar* 'to enter,' *escapar* 'to escape,' *estǫrser**

'to escape,' *falhir* 'to forsake; vanish' (but not as 'to go astray'; also *de-* 'to fail, lack'), *fendre* 'to split,' *finir* 'to die' (only this sense), *fránher** 'to break,' *fugir** 'to flee' (usually), *gandir* 'to vanish; escape,' *levar* 'to rise,' *membrar* 'to call to mind' (impersonal), *mermar* 'to diminish,' *montar* 'to mount,' *morir** 'to die,' *mover** 'to move,' *mudar* 'to change,' *náisser** 'to be born,' *negar* 'to drown,' *partir* 'to leave,' *passar* 'to pass (away),' *penre** 'to result' (impersonal), *perir* 'to perish,' *pojar* 'to climb,' *remaner** 'to remain; cease,' *repairar* 'to return,' *repauzar* 'to rest,' *restar* 'to remain,' *resuscitar* 'to come back to life,' *revertir* 'to return,' *reviure** 'to come back to life,' *salhir* 'to go out' (but not compounds), *saltar* 'to jump' (usually), *secar* 'to dry,' *sọrger** 'to rise,' *tardar* 'to be late' (impersonal), *tornar* 'to return,' *trabucar* 'to stumble,' *venir** 'to come' (and compounds except *con-*), *virar* 'to turn,' *volar* 'to fly.'

However, certain verbs of motion, especially *anar** and *cọrre**, tend to take *aver** when the manner (usually time or distance) is expressed without a destination: "Anat *ai* cum cauz' enversa" 'I have gone like a crazy person' (43:33).

*Aver** is conjugated with itself: *ai agut* 'I have had.' *Ȩsser** can be conjugated with either auxiliary: *ai estat* or *sọn estatz* 'I have been.' In addition, the construction *sọn agutz*, denoting existence, is quite common. The verb *estar** 'to remain' has the same past participle as *ȩsser* but is conjugated only with *aver**: *ai estat*, etc.

A supercompound series with two past participles, of the type *an agut cantat* 'they sang,' with equivalent forms in other categories, is rather rare (see 12.10).

10.23 The Passive Voice

Simple passive forms consist of the auxiliary *ęsser** plus a past participle, thus "aissilh ... son mielhs amat" 'those ... are better loved' (106:42-43) and "Per nos er Domas envasitz" 'by us Damascus will be invaded' (112:85). Compound categories are formed with a compound form of *ęsser* (usually conjugated with itself) plus a second past participle, for example, the passive compound past "es estatz acuzatz o lauzeniatz" 'he has been accused or slandered' (180:175). In theory every active category of transitive verbs has a corresponding passive.

Chapter 10: Exercises

A. (10.1-16) Identify the following forms

1. amas (amar)
2. florissoṇ (florir)
3. falh (falhir)
4. vens (vendre)
5. parles (parlar)
6. vengan (venir)
7. vuǫlhas (voler)
8. cantavam (cantar)
9. prendiatz (prendre)
10. esclarzissen(t) (esclarzir)
11. sabratz (saber)
12. valdrias (valer)

B. (10.18) Give the 3 sg. and 1 pl. preterit

1. bẹure (like dever)
2. cazer (like parer)
3. cẹnher (like dire)
4. aucire (like rire)

5. recẹbre (like saber) 6. vezer (like ęsser)

C. (19.19-23) Identify the following forms

1. vendęs (vendre) 4. agram saubut (saber)
2. paregratz (parer) 5. sọn estada (ęsser)
3. aguẹsses frach (fránher) 6. an estat cobęrt (cobrir)

D. Fill in the correct forms of the indicated verbs

1. forsar, destrẹnher (both 1 sg. pres. ind.):
   Per que mon cor ________ e ________
2. pregar (1 sg. pres. ind.), guidar (3 sg. pres. subj.): E ________ Dieu Jhesu que·m ________
3. menassar, maldire, jurar, rire, parlar, saber, far (all 3 sg. pret.): L'uns _______, l'autre _______, / L'autre _______ e l'autre _______, / L'autre _______ e non _______ que, / L'autre _______ metolas dese

E. Identify and give alternate forms

1. contendi (contendre) 3. tęsc (teisser)
2. moric (morir) 4. decsẹtz (dever)

11
SPECIAL VERBS

Most weak verbs follow faithfully the model paradigms of *amar*, *vendre*, *partir*, and *florir* (10.8), while many others differ from these only by regular phonological developments such as alternation of base consonants or vowels (10.12-13). Some weak verbs take an obligatory or optional supporting vowel in certain forms (10.9); and many variant endings coexist, particularly in the present system (10.11). Other verbs have alternate forms due to varying solutions in the development of vowels and consonants (chapters 3-4). None of these features renders a verb "special."

This chapter gives paradigms only for verbs having one or more "special" forms that could not be predicted or often even identified only from the material included in chapter 10. These include all strong verbs plus a few weak ones. Of these verbs, we give only the unpredictable forms. Forms not included here are sometimes unattested but more often are regularly derived, as explained in chapter 10. Unless otherwise specified, therefore, most categories use the P-base (as shown by the first form given for the 1 pl. or other plural person of the present indicative, or the 3 sg. if no plural form is given); but the preterit-base (as shown by the 2 sg., 1 pl. or 2 pl. preterit) is used in the imperfect subjunctive and conditional B (or, in the latter, the base of the 3 pl. preterit, if distinct); the stem of the future and conditional A is identical to the first indicated infinitive as far as the *r*; and the 2 sg. and 2 pl. imperative have the same form as the 3 sg. and 2 pl. present indicative, respectively. Our goal is to allow recognition of forms encountered in reading, not to list all attested forms. Therefore, we give the minimal number of forms needed to identify bases and stems, for example, only the m. obl. sg. of participles and often only the 3 sg. for each conjugated category. When we give other forms, it is in the usual order, separated by semicolons: 1 sg.; 2 sg.; 3 sg.; 1 pl.; 2 pl.; 3 pl. (though not necessarily including all of these). The reader should be able to derive readily the forms we omit. For example, the information that *bẹure* has a *c/g* preterit with 3 sg. *bẹc* suffices to produce the preterit paradigm *bẹc*, *beguist*, *bẹc*, *beguem*, *beguẹtz*, *bẹgroṇ*, the imperfect subjunctive *beguẹs*, etc., and the conditional B *bẹgra*, etc. For strong verbs we will, however, give alternate weak forms whenever they seem frequent, even if regularly derived from the P-base. Multiple solutions are listed in their approximate order of frequency, separated by commas, but with the rarer forms given in parentheses.

We give simple verbs alphabetically under their most frequent infinitive, and compound verbs under their basic root, even when the latter is uncommon, as in *(re)manẹr*, or has no independent existence, as in *de-strẹnher*. However, if there is only one prefixal form and no simple form, we alphabetize under the prefix. We identify compounds only where they might cause difficulty, and give their forms only where the corresponding simple forms seem unattested.

In most cases we use normalized spellings as long as they are actually attested, e.g., -*tz* where it may reduce to -*s*, *l* where it may vocalize to *u*, and -*ch* where it may also be spelled -*g* or -*h*. Similarly, we normally give only the P/N and T/A markers for which chapter 10 has indicated priority, e.g., 3 pl. -*on̥* except for -*en* in the imperfect subjunctive; and we prefer the supporting vowels 1 sg. ind. -*i* and 3 sg. -*e*. However, we retain the non-normalized spellings for forms that are so rare that their normalized spellings seem unattested. We also indicate, at the beginning of each entry, base-vowel alternations and other base variants (except normal devoicing of consonants in final position); by applying these alternations, the reader can derive other forms than those listed. We also show the conjugation if not clear from the first infinitive given, and the preterit class for strong verbs. For the sake of completeness we give some forms attested only in non-troubadour texts (except for the Franco-Provençal epic *Girart de Rossillo* and the 14th-century *Leys d'amors*), if these forms are lacking in the troubadours; but we have not knowingly included forms based solely on conjecture, textual emendation, or extrapolation from other forms and categories, unless we so indicate. Finally, we omit some rare forms where alternate forms are common.

abauzir 'to be fitting.' Pres. ind. *abau* (only attested form).

anar (ir) 'to go.' Pres. ind. *vau(c) (vac); vas; va; anam; anatz; van.* Fut. *anará, irá.*

ardre 'to burn': *s/s*. Pres. subj. *arda, arga.* Pret. *ars.* Past part. *ars* (*ardit*).

assire: see *sezer.*

aucire: see *au-cire.*

auzir 'to hear': I non-*isc*; dialectally *auv-*. Pres. ind. *auch, au; aus, auzes; au, autz, aus; auzem.* Pres. subj. *auja* (*auga*). Impv. *au; aujatz.*

aver 'to have': *c/g*; initial *h-* is frequent, as is final *-y* for *-i*. Pres. ind. *ai* (*ęi, iei*); *as; a; avem; avetz; an* (*ant, auṇ*). Pres. subj. *aia.* Imper. uses subj. Impf. *avia.* Fut. *aurá.* Pret. *aic, aguî, ac, aiguî; aguist; ac, aguęt; agroṇ, aguęroṇ, agoṇ.* Impf. subj. *aguẹs* (*aguessa*); *aguessem, acsem.* Past part. *agut, avut* (*aüt*).

benezir, benedir, bendir, bezenir, beneïr 'to bless': I-*isc* and E *s/s*. Pres. ind. *benezisc; benezem.* Pres. subj. *benezia* (*benezischa*). Pret. *benezî; benezist; benezî, benezic, benezîs.* Impf. subj. *benezîs.* Past part. *benezit, beneït, benezeit, benedit.*

bẹure 'to drink': *c/g*. Pres. ind. *beu* (*bevi*); *beves; beu; bevem.* Pres. subj. *beva* (*bega*). Pret. *bẹc* (*beguî*); *beguist.* Part part. *begut.*

braire 'to cry.' Pres. ind. *brai*. Pres. subj. *braia*. No pret. system.

bruire, bruir, brugir, brugire, bruzir 'to make noise': E-verb (present system only) and I-*isc* (rarely in present system). Pres. ind. 1 sg. *embrugis, esbruis*; 3 sg. *brui, bruig*. Pres. subj. *bruia*. Pres. part. *brugen, bru(z)en*. Pret. *bruî, brugî, bruzî*. Past part. *brugit*.

caber, cabir 'to fit': *up/ub*. Pres. ind. *cap; cabem*. Pres. subj. *cápia*. Pret. *caup*. Impf. subj. *caupẹs*. Past part. *cabit*.

caler 'to be necessary' (impersonal): *c/g*. Pres. subj. *calha*. Fut. *cal(d)rá*. Pret. *calc*. Past part. *calgut*.

cazer, caer 'to fall': *ec/eg* and weak; often *ch*-. Pres. ind. *caz, cai; cas, cai; cai, ca, cas; cazem*. Pres. subj. *caia*. Fut. *cairá*. Pret. *cazę̣t, cazẹc, cazę̣c; cazeguem; cazẹgron, cazę̣groṇ, cazeroṇ*. Impf. subj. *cazẹs*. Cond. B *cazẹgra*. Past part. *cazut, cazegut*.

de-cẹbre 'to deceive,' *aper*- 'to perceive,' *re*- 'to receive,' etc.: *up/ub*. Pres. ind. *decep; recebem*. Pres. subj. *recẹpia, recepcha* (extrapolating from 2 sg. and 1 pl.). Pret. *decẹup* (*decep*); *deceubem; deceubroṇ, deceuboṇ, deceuproṇ*. Impf. subj. *deceubẹs, apercebẹs, receupẹs* (judging by 1 sg.). Past part. *receubut, receuput* (*receut*).

en-cendre 'to kindle,' *a*- 'to light,' etc.: *s/z*. Pres. ind. *encent; encendon*. Pres. subj. *encenda*. Pret. 1 sg. *azẹis*; 3 sg. *encendę̣t, acẹs*. Past part. *encẹs, acendut*.

cẹnher 'to gird': *s/s*. Pres. ind. 1 sg. *cenc, cenh*; 3 sg. *cenh*. Pres. subj. *cenga, cenha*. Pret. *cẹis*. Past part. *ce(i)nt, cenh, cench*.

au-cire, aucir 'to kill,' *recire* 'to cut off,' etc.: *s/z*; also *aus(s)-, auz-*. Pres. ind. *aucî; aucîs, aucîs; aucî, aucîs; aucizętz, auciętz*. Pres. subj. *aucia, auciza*. Impf. *aucizia*. Pret. *aucîs; aucizem; auciroṇ, aucizęroṇ, aucisdroṇ, aucizoṇ*. Impf. subj. *aucizẹs, auciẹs*. Past part. *aucîs*.

claure 'to close': *s/z*. Pres. ind. *clau; clauzem*. Pres. part. *clauzen, clauen*. Pret. *claus*. Impf. subj. *clauzẹs*. Past part. *claus, clus* (adj.) (*clauzit*).

con-cluire, -cluzir 'to conclude,' *a-* 'to enclose,' *re-* 'to close up,' etc.: *s/z*. Pres. ind. *conclui; aclutz*. Pres. part. *concluen*. Pret. *reclus*. Past part. *aclus*.

cobrir: see *obrir*.

es-cọdre 'to thresh,' *res-* 'to save,' *se-, so-* 'to shake': *s/z*. Pres. ind. *escot* (*escotz*). Pres. subj. *escoda, escota*. Fut. *secodrá*; (*escodirán*). Pret. *socọs, secodęt; rescozon*. Past part. *escọs*, f. *escossa*.

colhir 'to gather,' *acolhir* 'to welcome,' etc.: non-*isc* (with some exceptions); often forms in *cu-*, usually unstressed; often with stressed *cuę-, cuo-*; sometimes *l* for *lh*. Pres. ind. *culh; cǫlhs, cols; colh, col, aculhîs; colhem*.

cǫlre 'to venerate': *c/g*. Pres. ind. *col, coli; cols; col*. Pret. *cǫlc*. Past part. *colt*.

complir: see *omplir*.

conọisser (*conọsser*) 'to know': *c/g*. Pres. ind. *conosc*, *conois*, *conosci*; *conoisses*; *conois*; *conoissem*. Pres. subj. *conosca*; *conoscatz* (*conoguatz*). Impv. *conoscatz*. Fut. *conoisserá* (*conoirá*); (also 2 sg. *conoisirás*). Cond. A *conoseria*. Pret. *conuc*, *conoc*, *conoguî*; *conoguist*; *conoc*; *conogroṇ*, *conogoṇ*. Past part. *conogut*, *conegut*.

contránher 'to cripple': *s/s*. Pret. *contrais*. Past part. *contrach*.

cọrre, *cọrrer* 'to run,' *socorre*, *socorrir*, *se-* 'to help,' etc.: *ec/eg* and *s/s*; sometimes *-r-* for *-rr-*. Pres. ind. *cor*; *correm*. Fut. *corrá*, *correrá*. Pret. *corrẹc*, *corrȩc*, *cọrs*; *corrẹgroṇ*, *corregoṇ*. Past part. *corregut*, (*so*)*cors*, *secorrit*.

cọser, *cosir* 'to sew': weak E. Pres. ind. *cos*; *cosem*. Past part. *cosit*, *cosut*.

cǫzer, *cǫire* 'to cook': *c/g*. Pres. ind. *cotz*; *cozetz*. Pres. subj. *coja*. Fut. *cozerai*. Pret. *cǫc*. Past part. *coit*, *coch* (*cozit*).

crẹire (*creẹr*, *crẹr*, *-crezẹr*) 'to believe': weak E; sometimes *-d-* for *-z-*. Pres. ind. *cre*, *crei*, *crezi*; *cres*, *crezes*; *cre*, *crei*; *crezem*. Pres. subj. *creia*, *creza*, *crea* (1 sg. also *crega*). Impv. *crei*, *cre*; *crezatz*. Pres. part. *crezen* (also *recreen*). Impf. *crezia*; (3 pl. also *creyan*). Fut. *creirá* (*credrá*). Pret. *crezȩt*, *credet* (3 pl. also *creeren*). Impf. subj. *crezȩs* (3 pl. also *creessen*). Past part. *crezut*, *cregut*, *crezegut* (*creüt*).

crẹisser 'to grow': *c/g*. Pres. ind. *creis*. Pres. subj. *cresca*. Pret. 1 sg. *cric*; 3 sg. *crẹc*. Impf. subj. *creguẹs*. Past part. *cregut*.

crẹmer 'to fear': no pret.; cf. *trẹmer*. Pres. ind. 1 sg. *cremi*. Pres. subj. *crẹmia*. Past part. *crems*, *cremut*.

dar 'to give'; base for all categories is *d-*. Pres. ind. *dau*; *das*; *da*. Pret. *dęt*, *dęc*; *dęroṇ*, *deiroṇ*.

dever 'to owe': *c/g*. Pres. ind. *dẹi*, *dech*; *deus*, *deves*; *deu*; *devem*. Pres. subj. *deia*, *deja*. Fut. *deurá*. Pret. *dẹc*, *deguî*; *deguist*; *dec*. Cond. B *degra* (*deura*). Past part. *degut*.

devire, *devir* 'to divide, decide': E-verb (the the only forms seem to be those given; *devezir* 'to explain' and *dividir* 'to divide' are I-*isc* verbs). Pres. ind. 1 sg. *devís*. Past part. *devís*.

dire, *dir* (*dîzer*) 'to say,' *escondir(e)* 'to refuse,' *maldir(e)* 'to curse,' etc. (cf. *benezir*): *s/s*; with scattered I-*isc* forms in compounds; sometimes *-ch-* for *-ss-*. Pres. ind. *dic*, *dig*, *diu*, *escondic*, *escondisc*, *esconditz*; *ditz*, *dizes*, *dis*; *di*, *ditz*, *dis*; *dizem*; *dizętz*, *dissętz*; *dizoṇ*. Pres. subj. *diga*, *dia* (also *malezischa*). Impv. *di* (*dic*); *digatz*. Fut. *dirá* (*dizerá*). Pret. *dis*, *dissî*, *dissist* (*dizist*); *dis*; *dissem*; *dissẹtz*; *diroṇ*, *dissęron* (*dissoṇ*). Impf. subj. *dissẹs*. Cond. B *dira*, *dissęra*. Past part. *dit*, *dich*.

dolẹr 'to suffer': *c/g*; often *-uę-*, *-uǫ-* for stressed *o* before *lh*. Pres. ind. *dǫl*. Pres. subj. *dolha*. Impv. *dol*; *dolhatz*. Pret. *dǫlc*, *dolguî*; *dolguist*, *dolc*. Past part. *dolgut*.

dozer (infinitive unattested) 'to teach': *s/s*; partially absorbed by *duire*; only the following categories seem attested. Pres. part. *dozen*. Fut. *dozerá*. Pret. *duǫis*. Past part. *dǫch*, *duę(i)ch*, *duęit*.

duire, durre 'to lead, teach,' *aduire* 'to bring to,' *esduire* 'to remove,' etc.: *s/s*. Pres. ind. *dui, duc;* 3 sg. *dui, dutz, dus* (*duich*); *duzem*. Pres. subj. *duga, esduia*. Fut. *duirá, dur(r)á*. Pret. *duis; duissẹtz; duissęron* (*duistrent, duystrunt*). Impf. subj. *duissẹs* (*adusẹs*). Past part. *duch, duit, dut, duich*.

eissir, issir (*geissir*) 'to go out': I non-*isc; ei-* often becomes *i-* and, when stressed, *ięi-*. Pres. ind. *ięsc, isc;* 3 sg. *ẹis, eissem, issem; issętz, eissetz; eissoṇ*. Pres. subj. *iesca, isca; iscam; iscatz; escoṇ*. Pres. part. *issen, eissen*. Impf. *issia, eissia*. Fut. *issirá, istrá*. Cond. A *eisseria*. Pret. *issî, eissî*. Impf. subj. *issîs, eissîs*. Past part. *issit, eissit, issut, eissut*.

erẹbre (*erebir*) 'to save': *up/ub*. Pres. ind. *ereb*. Pres. subj. 2 sg. *erepchas*. Pret. *erẹup*. Past part. *ereubut* (*erebit*).

ẹrger, ẹrzer, erdre 'to be attached, raise,' *adẹrzer, a(d)erdre* 'to raise; attach, be attached' (also 'to make provision for,' of different origin but with the same forms insofar as attested), *condẹrger, dẹrzer, derdre, endẹrzer, esdẹrzer*, all 'to raise'; *s/s*. Pres. ind. *ẹrc;* 3 sg. *ertz, ders* (also *derc*?). Pres. subj. *erga*. Pret. *ẹrs*. Past part. *ers*.

escondre, escondir 'to hide': weak and *s/z*. Pres. ind. *escon; escondem*. Fut. *escondirán*. Pret. *escondęt, escọs*. Past part. *escondut, escọs, escǫst* (*escondit*).

escriure, escrire (*escrir*) 'to write': *s/s*. Pres. ind. *escriu; escrius, escrives; escriu; escrivem*.

Pres. subj. *escriva* (*escria*). Pret. *escris*, *escrius*; *escrissist*; *escris*, *escrius*. Impf. subj. *escriussẹs*. Past part. *escrich*, *escrit*, *escriut*.

espandre, *espandir* 'to spread': weak E and I-*isc*. Pres. ind. *espan*, *espandis*; *espandoṇ*. Pres. subj. *espanda* (*espandischa*). Pret. *espandęt*. Past part. *espandut*, *espandit*.

espárzer, *espárser*, *espárger*, *espardre* 'to spread': *s/s*. Pres. ind. *esparc*; *esparges*; *espartz*, *espars*. Pres. subj. *esparga*. Fut. *esparserá*. Pret. *espars*. Past part. *espars*.

esp(e)rẹisser, *desp(e)rẹisser* 'to wake': *ec/eg*. Pres. ind. 1 sg. *esp(e)resc*; 3 sg. *espreis*. Pres. subj. *espresca*. Impf. *despereissia*. Pret. *esp(e)rẹc*, *esp(e)ric*. Impf. subj. *espreguẹssan*. Past part. *espęrt*.

ęsser, *estre* 'to be': strong throughout. Pres. ind. *soṇ*, *sọi*, *sui*; *(i)ęst*, *(i)es* (*siest*); *ẹs* (*ęs*, *est*, *'s*); *em* (*sem*, *ęsmes*); *ętz* (*ęst*, *sęs*); *soṇ*, *son* (*sont*, *sun*, *sunt*). Pres. subj. *sia*, *sẹia*. Impv. uses subj. Impf. *ęra* (*sia*); *eram* (*eravam*); *eratz* (*eravatz*). Fut. (rarely *sir-* or *sar-*) *serai*, *ęr*; *serás*; *será*, *er*, *ert*; *serem*; *serẹtz*; *serán*. Cond. A *seria* (rarely *sir-*, *sar-*). Pret. *fui* (*fọ*); *fust*, *fost*; *foṇ*, *fonc* (*fu*, *fọc*, *font*, *fun*, *fom*); *fom*; *fotz*; *foroṇ*. Impf. subj. *fọs*, *fossa*. Cond. B *fọra*. Past part. *estat*.

estar 'to stay': occasionally *ist-* or *st-* for *est-*. Pres. ind. *estau*, *estauc*, *estei*; *estás*; *estai*, *está*; *estam*; *estatz*, *estaitz*; *están*. Pres. subj. *estia*, *estẹia* (*estei*); *estias*; *estia*, *estei*; *esteia*; *estem*;

estẹz; estian. Impv. *estai; estatz, estętz, estaitz.* Pret. *estęt, estęc.*

estẹnher: see *tẹnher*.

far, faire, -fire, -fir, etc. 'to make, do': E-verb, *s/z* and strong throughout. Pres. ind. *fatz, fas, fauc, fau* (*fac*); *fas*; *fai, fa*; *fam, faim*; *faitz, fazętz, fatz*; *fan* (*fauṇ*). Pres. subj. *fassa, faza* (*facha*). Pres. part. *fazen*. Impf. *fazia*. Pret. *fi, fis* (*fezí*); *fezist, fezís*; *fẹtz, fes, fe*; *fezem, fem* (*fim*); *fezẹtz, fetz*; *feiroṇ, feroṇ* Impf. subj. *fezẹs*; *fezessem*; *fezessẹtz, fessetz*; *fezessen, fessoṇ*. Cond. B *fẹira, fera*. Past part. *fach, fait, faich, -fit*

de-fendre 'to defend,' *offendre* 'to offend': *s/z* (but *fendre* 'to split' is purely weak E). Pres. ind. *defẹn*; *defens, offendes*; *defẹn, defent*; *defendoṇ*. Pret. 1 sg. *defẹs*. Impf. subj. *defendęs*. Past part. *defẹs, defendut*.

fẹnher 'to feign': *s/s*. Pres. ind. *fenh, fenc*; *fenhs* (*fenhes*); *fenh, fen*; *fenhoṇ*. Pres. subj. *fenha, fenga*; 3 sg. *fenha*; *fenhatz*; *fenhoṇ, fengoṇ*. Pret. *feis* (*feissí*); *feissist*. Past part. *feint, fench*.

ferir 'to strike,' *preferir* 'to prefer,' *proferir, profęrre* 'to offer,' *referir, referre* 'to refer': I non-*isc*, with isolated strong E forms in compounds; often stressed *ię* or *ięi* for *e*. Pres. ind. *feri, fer*; *f(i)ers*; *fer*; *ferem*. Pres. subj. *fera*. Fut. *ferrá*. Pret. *feri(c)* (*profęrc*?); (*profergo*?). Past part. *ferit, ferut, -fęrt*.

fǫire, fudir 'to dig': *s/s*. Pres. ind. *fǫ, fǫs; fozem*. Pret. *fǫs*. Impf. subj. *fossẹs*. Past part. *fǫs*.

fondre 'to melt,' *confondre* 'to confound': weak. Pres. ind. *fon, font; fondoṇ*. Pres. subj. *fona, confonda*. Past part. *(con)fondut, confus* (adj.).

fránher (*fránger*) 'to break': *s/s*. Pres. ind. *franc, franh; franhs, franhes; franh; franhem*. Pres. subj. *franha*. Pret. *frais*. Past part. *frach, frait, franh, fraich*.

frire 'to roast, bake; shudder, shiver': no pret. system except past part. (*frezir* 'to become cold, shiver' is an I-*isc* verb). Pres. ind. 1 sg. *fri*. Pres. subj. 1 sg. *fria*. Pres. part. *frigen, frïen*. Past part. *frit, fregit, frih*.

fugir, fuire 'to flee': I non-*isc*. Pres. ind. *fug, fui; fuis, fuges; fui, fu(i)ch; fugem*. Pres. subj. *fuga, fuja; fujatz*.

gauzir 'to enjoy': I-*isc* and somewhat more often non-*isc*; we normalize with *g*- though *j*- is more common. Pres. ind. 1 sg. *gau, gauzisc*; 3 sg. *gau, gauzîs*. Pres. subj. 1 sg. *jauzisca, jauza, gauja*; 3 sg. *jauza*. Pres. part. *gauzen*.

gẹmer 'to groan': no pret. system. Pres. ind. *gem; gemem*. Pres. part. *gemen*.

iráisser (*irásser*) 'to become angry': weak. Pres. ind. *irasc, irais; iraisses; irais; iraissem*. Pret. *irasquęt*. Past part. *irascut, irat* (adj.).

jauzir: see *gauzir*.

jazer, jazir (*jacer*) 'to lie (down)': *c/g*. Pres. ind. *jatz; jas; jai, jatz; jazem*. Pres. subj. *jassa, jaia, jaga*. Fut. *jairá, jarrá*. Pret. *jac*. Past part. *jagut*.

jọnher 'to join': *s/s*. Pres. ind. *jonh*. Pres. subj. *jonha*. Pret. 1 sg. *jọis, joins, jons*; 3 sg. *jois, jons*. Past part. *joint, joinch, jonch, junt, jont, jonh, jon*.

legir, ligir, lęire, lęger, lire, lir 'to read,' *elegir*, etc. 'to choose,' etc.: I non-*isc* and E; pret. generally weak; *leg-* can become *lig-* especially when unstressed, and occasionally *lieg-* when stressed; final *-g* stands for /č/ or sometimes perhaps /k/. Pres. ind. *leg, lei; leges; leg, lig* (also *elegîs*); *legem; legętz; liegoṇ* (*leissoṇ*). Pres. subj. *leja*. Pret. *elesquęi, legí, elęc; legís, eleguist; legí, legic, elesquęt; legitz, elesquęsz; elegroṇ*. Impf. subj. *legís*. Cond. B 1 sg. *lesquęra*. Past part. *lescut, legit, ligit, -legut, elęch, elig, elęit, elest*.

lezer 'to be permitted' (impersonal): *c/g*. Pres. ind. *lẹtz, les, le*. Pres. subj. *leza, lega*. Impf. *lezia*. Pret. *lẹc, lic*. Past part. *legut*.

luzir 'to shine': I non-*isc*. Pres. ind. *lutz, lui, lus; luzoṇ*. Pres. subj. *luza*; 1 sg. and 3 sg. *luęia* (/i̯/? /ǧ/?). Fut. *luzerá*.

(re)maner, reman(d)re, remanir 'to remain': *s/z* (often with *ro-*). Pres. ind. *remanh, remanc; remas, remans; remaṇ* (*remanh*); *remanoṇ*. Pres. subj. *remanha, remanga*. Fut. *reman(d)rá*. Pret. *remas, remanguî; remazist; remas; remazoṇ, remazęroṇ, romaroṇ*. Impf. subj. *remazẹs*; 2 pl. *remansesẹs*;

remansẹssen. Cond. B *remazęran*. Past part. *remas*, *remasut*.

mędre, *meire* 'to harvest': weak. Pres. ind. *met*. Impf. *media*. Pret. *mezęt*.

mẹisser 'to pour (a drink)': weak. Pres. ind. 1 sg. *mesc*; 3 sg. *meis*. Pres. subj. *mesca*. Pret. *mesquęt*.

mentaure, *amentaver* 'to mention': *c/g*. Pres. ind. *mentau*; *mentavem*. Pres. subj. *mentava*. Pret. *mentac*, *mentauguî*. Past part. *mentaugut*, *mentagut*, *mentaubut*.

so-mergir, *somęrger* 'to submerge': I non-*isc* and E; no pret. attested. Pres. ind. 2 sg. *somęrtz* (or impv.). Pres. subj. *somerga*. Past part. *submergit*, *submęrs*.

merir 'to deserve': *c/g* and I non-*isc*; often tonic *mięr-*, *mieir-*, *meir-* in pres. system. Pres. ind. *mer*; *mers*; *mer*; *meroṇ*. Pres. subj. *mera*, *merga*. Fut. *merrá*, *merirá*. Pret. *meric*, *męrc* (and *mẹrc*?). Cond. B *meira*, *mera*. Past part. *merit*, *mergut*.

mẹtre 'to put': *s/z*. Pres. ind. *mẹt*, *meti*; *metz*, *metes*; *met*; *metem*. Pret. *mis*; *mezist*; *mẹs*, *mis*; *mezem*; *mezęroṇ*, *meiroṇ* (*mesdren*, *meroṇ*). Past part. *mes*, f. *messa*, *mesa*; *mis*, f. *misa*; *metut*.

mǫlre 'to grind': *c/g*. Pres. ind. *mǫl*. Pret. *mǫlc*. Past part. *mǫut*, *molut*, *molt*.

so-monre, *somondre*, *somonir*, *somoner* 'to summon,' *comonre*, *comonir* 'to exhort': *s/z* and I-*isc*; often *se-*. Pres. ind. *somoṇ*, *somonh*, *somonc* (*semonis*); *somons*; *somoṇ*, *somonis*. Pres. subj. *somona*, *somonha*, *somonga*, *comonesca*; *somonisco*. Fut. *comonrá*, *cominirá*. Pret. *comọs*. Impf. subj. *somosẹs*;

communissen. Past part. *somọs, somọst, somons, somonitz*.

mọlzer 'to milk': *s/s*. Pres. ind. *moutz*. Pret. *mọls*. Past part. *mols*.

mǫrdre 'to bite': *s/s*. Pres. ind. *mort; mordọn*. Pret. *mǫrs*. Past part. *mors*.

morir 'to die': I non-*isc*; frequently tonic *(u)ǫ(i), uę(i)* in pres. system; often *u*, usually when unstressed. Pres. ind. *mǫr, muir, mori; mors; mor; morem; morọn*. Pres. subj. *mora*; 3 sg. *mora, mura, muira; moriam; moriatz; mueiran*. Fut. *morrá, morá*. Past part. *mǫrt*.

mover, mǫure 'to move': *c/g*; can have tonic *uǫ* or *uę* in pres. ind. 1 sg. and 3 sg. and in pres. subj. Pres. ind. *mǫu, movi; mous, moves; mou; movem*. Pres. subj. *mova*. Fut. *mourá*. Pret. *mǫc, muęc, moguî*; 3 sg. *moc, muec*. Past part. *mogut*.

nâisser 'to be born': weak and *c/g*. Pres. ind. *nasc*; 3 sg. *nais; naissem*. Pres. subj. *nasca*. Pret. *nasquęi, nasquî; nasquęst, nacquist; nasquęt, nasquęc, nasc; nasquem; nasquẹs; nasquęrọn*. Impf. subj. *nasquęs, nasquẹs*. Cond. B *nassęra*. Past part. *nat, nascut*.

nozer, nǫzer, nǫire 'to harm': *c/g*. Pres. ind. *nǫtz, nos; nozem*. Pres. subj. *nǫja, noia, noza, noga*. Pret. *nǫc*. Past part. *nogut*.

obrir 'to open,' *cobrir* 'to cover,' etc.: I non-*isc* and *c/g*; *o* often becomes *u* when unstressed and *uę, uǫ* when stressed. Pres. ind. *ǫbri; obres; obre; ubrem; ubrẹtz; obrọn*. Pres. subj. *obra*. Pret. *obrî, obric* (*uberc*, with /ẹ/? /ę/?). Impf. subj. *ubrîs, ubriguẹs*. Past part. *obęrt, cubęrt, cobrit*.

ofrir 'to offer,' *sofrir, sofęrre* 'to suffer'; I-*isc* and non-*isc* or *c/g*; *o* can become *u* (/u/ and /ü/) and tonic *uę*; tonic *ę* can become *ię(i)*; *f* can be doubled. Pres. ind. *sofris(c), sǫfri, sofęri, sufer; sofers, sufres; sofrîs, sofre, sofer; sofrem; sofroṇ*. Pres. subj. *sofera, sofra; sofras; sofra, sofieira* (*sofrisca*). Fut. *sofrirá*. Impf. *sofria*. Pret. *sofrî, suffęrs; sofrîs, suffrist; sofrî, sofęrc* (*sofręc*); *sufrem; sofrîs*. Impf. subj. *sufrîs; soffrissẹtz*. Cond. B *sofrira* (*sofęrgra*). Past. part. *sofęrt, sofrit*.

ǫler (*oldre*) 'to smell': no pret. system. Pres. ind. *ǫl*.

ọnher, ọnger, perọnher 'to anoint': *s/s*. Pres. ind. *onh*. Pres. subj. *onga*. Pret. *ọis, peronhs*. Past part. *onh, ọint*.

páisser 'to feed': *c/g* and weak. Pres. ind. *pasc* (*pas*); *pais; pais; paissem*. Pres. subj. *pasca*. Pret. 1 sg. *pac, pasquẹi*. Impf. subj. *paguẹs*. Cond. B 1 sg. *pagra, paissęra*. Past part. *pagut, pascut, paissut*.

párcer 'to spare': *s/s*. Pres. *parc; pars; partz*. Pret. *pars*. Impf. subj. 1 sg. *parcẹs*. Past part. *pars*.

parẹisser 'to appear': pret. system supplied by *parẹr*. Pres. ind. *paresc*; 3 sg. *pareis; pareissem*. Pres. subj. *paresca*.

parẹr 'to appear': *ec/eg*. Pres. ind. *par*. Fut. *parrá*. Pret. *parẹc, paręc; pareguem*. Past part. *paregut*.

partir 'to leave': non-*isc* and *isc*. Pres. ind. *part, partis(c), parc*; 3 sg. *part; partis; parton, partissoṇ*. Pres. subj. 1 sg. *parta, parca, partisca*. Fut. *part(i)rai*.

penedir, pentir, penẹdre, pendir, repentir 'to repent': I non-*isc* and E. Pres. ind. *penẹt, penedis, repen(t), rependi; penet, pen, repen(t); pentoṇ*. Pres. subj. *peneda, repenta*. Pret. *repentí*. Impf. subj. *pentís, penedęs*. Past part. *penedit, pentit, penedut*.

pẹnher 'to paint,' *em-, es-* 'to push,' etc.: *s/s*. Pres. ind. *empenh, espenc; penhs, penhes; penh*. Pres. subj. *penga, penha*. Pret. *pẹis; empeiceroṇ*. Impf. subj. *empeissẹs; enpenhẹses; empeinssẹs*. Past part. *penh, peint, pench*.

penre, prendre, prenre, pendre 'to take': *s/z*. Pres. ind. *prenh, prenc, pren, prendi; prens, prendes; pren, prent; prendem, prenem*. Pres. subj. *prenda, prenha, prenga, prena*. Pret. *pris, prẹs, prezí, prenguí; prezist, presęst; prec, presęt; prezem; prezęroṇ, prezoṇ, preiroṇ, preisęroṇ, presdroṇ, preroṇ*. Impf. subj. *prezẹs* (*prenguẹs*). Cond. B *preira*. Past part. *prẹs, pris*.

pęrdre 'to lose': weak. Pres. ind. *pert, perc, perdi; pertz; pert; perdem*. Pres. subj. *perga, perda*.

plánher, plánger 'to lament': *s/s*. Pres. ind. *planc, planh; planhs, plans; planh; plangętz; planhoṇ*. Pres. subj. *planga, planha*. Impf. *planhia*. Pres. part. *planhen*. Pret. *plais; plaissoṇ*. Impf. subj. *plaissẹs, pla(i)nguẹs*. Past part. *plaint, planh*.

plazer 'to please': *c/g*. Pres. ind. *plai, platz; plazoṇ*. Pres. subj. *plaia, plassa*. Fut. *plairá, plazerá.* Pret. *plac; plagroṇ, plaissoṇ.* Cond. B *plagra.* Past part. *plagut.*

plevir, plęure, pliure 'to pledge': I non-*isc* and sometimes *isc*, also *c/g*; the base vowel, when unstressed, is usually *e* before stressed *i* and *i* before stressed *e*. Pres. ind. *pliu, plevisc; pliu, plevis, plęu, plięu; plevim; plivętz; plevoṇ.* Pres. subj. *pliva, pleva.* Fut. *pliurá.* Pret. *plevî, plevic, plẹc.* Impf. subj. *plevîs.* Cond. B *plevira.*

plǫure 'to rain': *c/g.* Pres. ind. *plou, pluou; plovoṇ.* Pres. subj. *plova, pluęva.* Pret. *plǫc.* Past part. *plogut.*

poder 'to be able': *c/g.* Pres. ind. *pǫsc, puęsc, pusc, puosc, podi, puecs; potz, podes; pot, po; podem.* Pres. subj. *posca, puesca, puosca, pusca.* Fut. *poirá, podrá, por(r)á.* Pret. *pǫc, puoc, puęc, pogui; poguist; poc, pot.* Impf. subj. *poguẹs; pocsem, poguessem.* Past part. *pogut.*

pọnher 'to prick': *s/s*; *o* can close to *u* even in base-stressed forms. Pres. ind. *ponh, ponc; ponh; ponhoṇ, pongoṇ.* Pres. subj. *ponga, ponha, ponja.* Pret. 1 sg. *pọis, poins.* Past part. *point, ponh.*

ponre, pondre 'to lay (eggs)': *s/z.* Pres. ind. *poṇ; ponem.* Pres. subj. *ponga, pona.* Pret. *pǫs.* Past part. *pǫst.*

prẹmer (premre) 'to press': *s/s.* Pres. *prem.* Pret. *prems.* Past part. *prems, preins, premut, premi.*

prendre: see *penre.*

provezir, pre-, per-, provezer, per- provir 'to provide (for), care for, furnish': I-*isc* and (in pres. system only) E; *pervezer, pervẹire* 'to foresee' is purely a compound of *vezer*. Pres. ind. *provẹi*, *proveg*, *provezisc*; *pervẹ*, *provezís*. Pres. subj. *perveias*; *provezisca*. Impv. *prevesís*. Pres. part. *perveen*. Fut. *provezirá*. Past part. *provezit*.

querre, *querer*, *querir* 'to seek,' *con-* 'to conquer,' etc.: *s/z* and I non-*isc* (rarely *ec/eg*); tonic *ie* is frequent. Pres. ind. *quęr*, *queri*; *quers*, *queres*; *quer*. Pres. subj. *quera*; *queiram*. Fut. *querrá*, *conquer(r)á*. Pret. *quis*, *quezî* (*quizî*, *querî*, *conquerrî*); *quezist*; *quẹs*, *quis*, *querî*, *queric* (*querec*, *querrec*, *querrî*, *quizî*); *quezem*; *queiroṇ*. Impf. subj. *quezẹs*, *quezîs* (also 1 sg. *querîs*). Cond. B *enquesira*. Past part. *quist*, *-quest*, *quis*, *ques*, *quesut*, *quezit*, *queregut*, *-querit*.

raire 'to shave': *s/z*. Pres. ind. *ra*, *rai*; *razem*. Pres. subj. *raza*. Impv. *ras*. Pret. *rais*. Past part. *ras*.

recire: see *au-cire*.

regir: 'to rule': non-*isc* (in general). Pres. ind. *rięg*, *rig*, *riech*; *riejoṇ*. Pres. subj. 2 pl. *rejhás*. Pres. part. *regen*. Impf. *regia*.

resplandir, *resplandre* 'to shine': I-*isc* and non-*isc*; E weak. Pres. ind. *resplan*, *resplandîs*. Pret. *resplandęt*. Past part. *resplandut*.

respondre 'to respond': *s/z*, weak. Pres. ind. *respon*, *respondi*; *respondes*; *respon*, *respont*; *respondoṇ*. Pres. subj. *responda* (*respona*). Pret. *respọs*, *respozî*; *respondęt*, *respos*; *respondęroṇ*. Impf. subj. *respondẹs*, *resposẹs*. Past part. *respọs*, *respondut*, *respǫst* (*respons*).

rezẹmer, *rezembre*, *rẹimer*, *redemir*, *rẹmer*, *rezemẹr* 'to redeem': *s/z* and weak; *-z-* can become *-d-* or rarely -*c*-, -Ø-. Pres. ind. *rezem*. Pret. *rezems*, *rezemȩi*; *rempsist*; *rezemȩt*, *rezems*, *rem(p)s*; *rezensoṇ*, *rezemȩroṇ*. Impf. subj. *re(d)emȩs* (*rezembȩs*). Past part. *rezemut*, *rezem(p)s*, *rezemut* (*rezemt*, *remps*).

rire, *rir* 'to laugh': *s/z*; -*z*- rarely becomes -*d*- or -*c*-, -*ç*-. Pres. ind. *ri*; *ris*; *ri*; *rizem*. Pres. subj. *ria*. Pret. *ris*. Past part. *ris*.

rọire 'to gnaw': *s/z*. Pres. ind. *rọ*; *rozem*, *roem*; *rozȩtz*; *roen*. Pres. subj. *roza*. Pres. part. *rozen*. Pret. *rọs*. Past part. *ros*, *rodut*.

saber 'to know': *up/ub*. Pres. ind. *sai* (*sȩi*); *saps*, *sabes*; *sap*; *sabem*. Pres. subj. *sapcha*, *sápia* (*sacha*). Impv. *sapchas*; *sapchatz* (*sapiatz*). Fut. *sabrá*. Pret. *saup*, *saubí*, *saupí*; *saubist* (*saubȩst*); *saup*; *saubroṇ*, *sauproṇ*, *sauboṇ*. Impf. subj. *saubẹs*, *saupẹs*. Cond. B *saupra*, *saubra*. Past part. *sauput*, *saubut*.

sȩgre, *seguir* 'to follow': weak E and I non-*isc*; often stressed *iȩ*. Pres. ind. *sec*; *seguem*. Pres. subj. *sega*; *segan*, *seguisco*. Fut. *segrá*; *segrán*, *seguirán*. Pret. *seguȩt*, *seguí*. Impf. subj. *seguẹs*, *seguís*. Past part. *seguit*, *segut*.

sezer, *sȩire*, *sezir* 'to sit,' *assire*, *assezer*, *assir* 'to set,' etc.: *s/z* and *c/g*; -*z*- can become -*d*- or rarely -Ø-. Pres. ind. *assȩt*; *se*, *sieu*; *sezem*. Fut. *seirá*. Pret. *sẹc*, *asís*; *sis*, *sec*, *assic*, *seguȩt*; *seguem*. Past part. *assís*, *segut*, *assẹs*.

sofrir: see *ofrir*.

soler 'to be accustomed': *c/g*; can have *uȩ* or *uǫ* before *lh*. Pres. ind. *solh* (*soli*); *sol*. Pres. subj. *suelha*. Pret. *solc*. No past part.?

sǫlvre, sǫlver 'to dissolve,' *as-, ab-* 'to absolve,' etc. Pres. ind. *solvi; sols; sol, solv; solvem.* Fut. *solverá* (*asolrá*). Pret. *sǫls; solsem; solsęro, absolvęro, solso.* Impf. subj. *solsęs, solvęs.* Cond. B *solvęra.* Past part. *solt* (*solut*).

sọrger, sọrzer, sorzir, sorgir, sordre 'to raise, rise,' *re-* 'to rise again,' etc.: *s/s.* Pres. ind. *sors;* 3 sg. *sortz; sorzoṇ* (*sorsoṇ*). Pres. subj. *sorja* (*resorgua*). Fut. *sorgerá, ressorzirá; resorserán.* Pret. *sọrs, sorzí; sorzist; sors, ressorzic* (*sorgí*); *ressorzís, sorsẹtz* . Impf. subj. *sorsẹssan.* Cond. B *ressorsęra.* Past part. *ressorzit, sors.*

e-stẹnher: see *tẹnher.*

e-strẹnher 'to squeeze,' *destrẹnher* 'to force,' etc. (rarely *-strẹnger*): *s/s.* Pres. ind. *estrenc, estrenh; estrens, estrenhes; destrenh.* Pres. subj. *estrenha, estrenga.* Pret. *estrẹis* (*estrenguí*); 3 sg. *estreis.* Impf. subj. *estreissẹs, destrenguęs.* Past part. *estrẹit, estrẹ(i)ch* (*estreinh, estreis*).

de-struire, destruir (*destruzir*) 'to destroy,' *coṇstruire* 'to construct,' etc.: *s/s.* Pres. ind. *destrui; costruizem, destruzem; destruizoṇ.* Pres. subj. *destruia, destruza* (*destrua*). Pres. part. *destrüen, destruzen.* Fut. *destrurai; destruirẹtz.* Pret. *destruis, costrus;* 3 sg. *destruis, costrus, destruic.* Past part. *destruch, destruit, destrut, destrusit.*

tánher 'to be fitting': *s/s.* Pres. ind. *tanc; tanh.* Pret. *tais.* Impf. subj. *taissęs* (*tainssẹs, taignẹs, tanguís*).

tazer, táisser, taizir, taire 'to be silent': *s/s.* Pres. ind. *tatz, tais; tai, tatz, tais; tazem.* Pres.

subj. *taissa, taia.* Fut. *tairá.* Pret. *tais.* Past part. *taizit.*

tęisser 'to weave': weak and *s/s*. Pres. ind. *teis*. Pres. subj. *teissa, tęsca*. Pret. *teissęi, tęis; teissęst; teissęt, tęsc*. Impf. subj. *teissęs*. Past part. *tescut, tẹs, teissut*.

temer 'to fear': *s/s*. Pres. ind. *tem*. Pres. subj. *tẹmias; tema*. Pret. *tems, tens, tims;* 3 sg. *tems; temsoṇ, tensoṇ*. Impf. subj. *tem(p)sẹs, tensẹs*. Cond. B *temsęra*. Past part. *temsut, temut*.

tendre 'to stretch,' *atendre* 'to wait,' etc.: weak, occasionally *s/z*. Pres. ind. *ten, atenc; tens, tendes; ten, atent; tendoṇ*. Fut. *aten(d)rá*. Pret. *atendęt, tẹs; tendęroṇ*. Impf. subj. *tendęs*. Past part. *tẹs, tendut*.

tener 'to hold': *c/g*. Pres. ind. *tenh, tenc* (*teni*); *teṇs, tenes; teṇ; tenem*. Pres. subj. *tenga, tenha* (*tena*). Fut. *ten(d)rá*. Pret. *tinc, tenc, tenguí; tenguist; tenc, tẹc; tengroṇ, tegroṇ* (*tengoṇ*). Impf. subj. *tenguẹs, teguẹs; tenguessẹtz, tencsẹtz*. Cond. B *tengra*. Past part. *tengut, -tegut*.

tẹnher 'to color, darken,' *atẹnher* 'to attain' (also *e-stẹnher, destẹnher* 'to extinguish,' even though of different origin): *s/s*; confused with *tendre* (and *estendre* 'to extend') and *tener* in some forms, for example, those ending in *-n* for *-nh*. Pres. ind. *estenc, estenh; estenhs, estenhes; tenh*. Pres. subj. *tenha, tenga* (*tinga*). Fut. *atendrá*. Pret. *tẹis*. Impf. subj. *esteissẹs*. Past part. *teint, tenh, tent, -tens, tench, tenhit*.

tęrger, tęrzer (*tęrser*), *ab-* 'to wipe,' etc.: *s/s*. Pres. ind. *tęrc, tierc; tiers; tertz, tiers*. Pres.

subj. *terga; abstergescas; terga.* Pret. *tęrs.* Past part. *ters.*

tǫl(d)re, toler, tolir 'to take away': *c/g;* can have *ųe* before *lh.* Pres. ind. *tolh, tol; tols, toles; tol, tolh; tolem.* Pres. subj. *tolha, tola.* Fut. *tolrá.* Pret. *tǫlc, tolguí; tolguist; tolc* (*tols*). Past part. *tǫlt, tolgut.*

tǫrser, es- 'to twist': *s/s.* Pres. ind. 2 sg. *estorses; tortz; torsem.* Pret. *tǫrs.* Past part. *tǫrt, tors.*

traire 'to draw,' *retraire* 'to withdraw,' etc.: *s/s.* Pres. ind. *trai, trac, trau* (*trauc*); *tras, trazes; trai, tra, tratz; trazem.* Pres. subj. *traia, traga* (*traissa*). Pret. *trais* (*traguí*); *traissist; trais; traissęroṇ, traistroṇ* (*traissen*). Impf. subj. *traissẹs, tragẹs.* Cond. B *retraissęra.* Past part. *trach, trait, traich.*

trazir, traïr 'to betray': I-*isc;* sometimes borrows forms from *traire.* Pres. ind. *traïs* (*trai*). Pres. subj. *traïsca, traia.* Pres. part. *trazen.* Pret. *traït, trais* (*trait*); *traistroṇ.* Impf. subj. *traís.* Past part. *traït, trait, trach.*

tremẹr, tremir, trẹmer 'to fear' (cf. *crẹmer*): E and I. Pres. ind. *tremi.* Fut. *tremerá, tremirá.* Pret. *tremic; tremiro.* Past part. *trem(p)s.*

valer 'to be worth': *c/g.* Pres. ind. *valh, val; vals, vales; val, valh; valem.* Pres. subj. *valha.* Fut. *val(d)rá.* Pret. *valguí; valguist; valc; valgroṇ.* Past part. *valgut.*

vẹncer, vẹnser, vẹnzer 'to conquer': weak (forms with *s* are the most common). Pres. ind. *vens, venz;*

vensem. Pres. subj. *vensa*, *venca*. Pret. *venquęt*. Impf. subj. *venquęs* (*vencęs*). Past part. *vencut*.

venir 'to come': E-verb (except inf.), *c/g*. Pres. ind. *venh*, *venc*; *veṇs*, *venes*; *veṇ*; *venem*. Pres. subj. *venha*, *venga*. Fut. *ven(d)rá*; (*vindretz*). Pret. *vinc*, *venc*, *venguî*; *venguist*, *venguęst*; *venc*, *venguęt*; *vengroṇ*, *vengoṇ*. Impf. subj. *venguẹs*; 2 pl. *vencsẹs*; *vencsoṇ*. Past part. *vengut*.

vezer, *vẹire* 'to see' (cf. *provezir*): *s/z*; -*z*- can become -*d*- or rarely -Ø-. Pres. ind. *vei*, *ve(i)ch*; *ves*, *vezes*; *ve* (*ves*); *vezem*. Pres. subj. *veia*. Impv. *ve*; *veiatz*. Fut. *veirá* (*verá*). Pret. *vi*, *vic*; *vist* (*vis*); *vi*, *vit*, *vic*; *vim*; *vitz*; *viroṇ*. Impf. subj. *vis*, *vezẹs*. Past part. *vist*, *vis* (*vegut*, *vezut*).

viure, *vięure* 'to live'; weak (and *c/g*). Pres. ind. *viu*; *vius*, *vives*; *viu*, *vięu*; *vivem*. Pres. subj. *viva*. Pret. *visquęt* (*visc*, *vesquęt*); *visquęroṇ*. Impf. subj. *visquęs*. Past part. *viscut*.

voler 'to want': *c/g*; can have *uę*, *uǫ* before *lh*. Pres. ind. *vǫlh*, *vulh*; *vols* (*voles*); *vol*; *volem*. Pres. subj. *volha*, *vulha*. Impv. uses subj. Fut. *vol(d)rá*. Pret. *vǫlc*, *volguî* (*vuęlc*); *volguist*; *volc*; *volgoṇ*, *volgroṇ*. Impf. subj. *volguẹs*; *volcsẹtz*, *volguessẹtz*, *volsẹtz*; *volguessoṇ*. Past part. *volgut*.

vǫlvre, *vǫlver* 'to turn': *c/g* and *s/s*. Pres. ind. *volf*, *vol*; *volvem*. Pret. *vǫls*, *volvc*; *volgroṇ*. Impf. subj. *volguẹs*. Past part. *vǫlt*.

12
VERBS: SYNTAX

12.1 Agreement in Number and Person

In general, verbs agree in number and person with their subject or its antecedent: "Altas ondas que venez suz la mar" 'High waves which come onto the sea' (113:1). But a grammatically singular collective noun, such as sometimes *totz om* 'everyone,' *usquẹcs* 'each one' and as a rule *gens* 'people' and *gran reṇ de* 'many of,' can take a plural verb: "Amor blasmen per no-saber, / Fola gens ..." 'Foolish people through ignorance blame love ...' (28:15-16).

Two or more subjects of similar nature--designating qualities, professions, people, places, etc.--in verse often take a singular verb when linked by the conjunctions *e*, *ni*, or *o*: "Luenh es lo castelhs e la tors / On elha jay e sos maritz" 'Far are the castle and the tower / Where she and her husband lie' (23:17-18). The 2 pl. in formal discourse often designates a single individual, particularly a lady or patron. The 3 pl. without an identifiable subject is equivalent to *om* 'one,' especially in *dizoṇ* 'people say.'

12.2 Commands and Wishes

Commands are generally expressed by the imperative: "Messatgers, vai e cor, / E di·m a la gensor ..." 'Messenger, go and run, and say for me to the most beautiful one ...' (29:73-74). When, as is obligatory with certain verbs and possible in others (10.11), the subjunctive is used in place of the imperative, it is sometimes introduced by *que*: "que fassatz ..., que honretz ..." 'do ..., honor ...' (40:28-29). This jussive subjunctive is usual in the negative with a grammatically plural verb: "no·l me vedetz" 'don't refuse it to me' (48:2). A negative command to one person or to people in general normally uses an infinitive: "non manjar" 'don't eat,' etc. The 1 pl. imperative is rendered by the subjunctive: "baizem nos" 'let's kiss each other' (178:9).

In the 1 sg., 3 sg., and 3 pl., the optative function, expressing a wish or desire, is likewise rendered by the subjunctive (sometimes introduced by *ar* 'now' or an untranslatable *si* or *car*): "Dieus m'o perdo" 'may God pardon it to me' (111:26); "e totas cridon: 'sia!'" 'and they all shout: "So be it!"' (109:90). The imperfect subjunctive can express a desire that is difficult or impossible to attain: "Ai! car me fos lai pelegris" 'Oh, if only I were a pilgrim there' (24:12); "Plagues a Dieu ja la neuitz no falhis" 'Might it have pleased God that the night not already end' (178:5).

12.3 The Present Indicative and Participle

The present indicative corresponds to several English constructions: *am* means "I love, I am loving, I do love.' In addition, it has a past meaning in two circumstances. It measures the time that a condition has been going on: "un an a qui sui ..." 'for a year I have been ...' And, particularly, in narrative texts, it can occur where one expects the preterit. When scattered in among past tenses, it seems merely to take on their connotations, thus: "pos la serps baissa lo ram / No foron tant enganairiz" 'since the serpent came down from the branch / There haven't been so many deceitful women' (10:7-8). But frequent uses in the biographies, chiefly in groups of three or more, suggest an evolution toward the "historical present," which renders a past narration more vivid or personal, thus: "venc s'en al leit de ma dona N'Alazais, et atroba la dormen, et aginoilla se davan ella e baiza li la boca" 'he came to the bed of Lady Alazais, and finds her sleeping, and kneels before her and kisses her mouth' (84:16-17). (There is, however, some contention that such forms are in fact morphologically preterit.)

The present participle, when it is seen as functioning adjectivally, substantivally, or sometimes verbally, is declined (10.14): "per los valenz homes e per los entendenz" 'by worthy men and by the wise [or: lovers]' (44:6-7). A few participles have a passive sense: "emperador prezan" 'praiseworthy emperor' (117:20), and similarly *conoissen* 'understandable,' *entenden* 'easily understood,' *trian* 'distinguished; recognizable' (27:33), etc. After *ęsser*, the participle often indicates a nonhabitual state or a condition of some duration: "A tot lo mon soi clamanz / De mi e de trop parlar" 'To everyone

I complain / Of myself and of speaking too much' (62:34-35). A similar meaning is rendered with *aver*: "ai mon cor jauzen" 'joy is in my heart' (117:5). The participle plus *ęsser* can also have a more or less substantival value: "Mortz es lo reys don em trastotz perdens" 'The king is dead, because of which we are all losers' (171:9). Very often, however, this construction seems roughly equivalent to the simple present tense, as in "siatz ... perdonans" 'may you pardon' or "esser recastenans" 'to reproach' (144:39, 43).

Whenever the participle retains full verbal value, it almost always remains invariable: "Qu'esta sobre l'arbre tremblan" 'That stays trembling on the tree' (7:15); "Que van las almornas queren" 'who go around begging alms' (54:60); "La ren per c'om vai meilluran" 'The person because of whom one gets better and better' (126:17); "tal se van d'amor gaban" 'some are accustomed to boast about love' (7:29).

This invariable participle, properly termed "gerund," can introduce clauses of means, manner, or circumstance; it is translated with forms in *-ing*, often preceded by *by*, *while*, or *in*: "si non pareis / Chivauchan sobre Serrazis" 'if he doesn't appear / Riding against the Saracens' (20:41-42); "Desirant, cre, morir se lais" 'By desiring, I believe, he is letting himself die' (57:19). Usually, as in these examples, the gerund describes an action by the subject of the associated conjugated verb. However, we also find what may strike us as a "dangling" participle referring to a direct or indirect object, as in: "que·m fos datz a rescos / En baisan guizardos," 'that there should be given to me in secret, / By kissing, a reward' (31:51-52). Even more loosely, the participle may be used with no grammatically related subject, in which case English must supply one: "Albertz, ges callan non enten / Qe·l respondres aja valor" 'Albert, I don't understand, by [the speaker's] being silent / How the answer can have any value' (130:19-20).

As in the second-to-last example just given, the gerund may be introduced by the preposition *en*, particularly in order to clarify its function in the sentence. When its subject appears in the subject case, it occasionally takes an *-s*. On the other hand, expressions like "en dormen" also apply to a direct object in constructions meaning 'to find someone sleeping' and the like.

Very characteristic of OP are two parallel gerunds indicating similar or contrasting actions, as in "jogan rizen" 'playing and laughing' (54:86), "cazen levan" 'falling and getting up' (145:45), and "durmen o velhan" 'sleeping or waking' (19:26). The gerund is sometimes accompanied by its own subject to form a self-contained subordinate clause: "Et aisi estan e duran lo lor amor, una dompna ..." 'And their love being and lasting thusly, a lady ...' (61:9); and similarly "a sol colgan" 'at sunset.' A related construction apparently started out with a participle and its subject both in the oblique case: "nos auzens" 'with us hearing.' But soon the invariable gerund took over: "auzen totz" 'in the hearing of all'; also, the gerund could become construed as a noun accompanied by a preposition ("auzen de totz") or possessive adjective ("mon vezen" 'with me looking on, in my presence').

The past gerund, with forms like *aven cantat* or *essen vengutz*, is rare.

12.4 Verbal Adjectives and Nouns in -dọr

Even though the various *-dọr* words are not properly verbs, we group them for convenience here because they often enter into verbal constructions.

The "verbal adjective" is formed by adding the suffix *-dọr/s* (f. *-dọira/s*) to a verb base plus the appropriate thematic vowel. With a transitive verb, it usually functions as a future passive participle indicating possibility or obligation, thus *blasmador* 'blameworthy,' *fazedor* 'to be done; suitable,' *devezidor* 'to be shared,' etc. Such adjectives, referring generally to non-permanent qualities, usually occur after the impersonal verb *ęsser* to form expressions like "ben es fazedor" 'it is very worthy of being done, suitable.' But one finds occasional personal constructions like: "Per Deu, Amors! be·m trobas vensedor" 'By God, Love! You certainly find me conquerable' (32:13). On the other hand, adjectives of this type can have an active meaning, functioning as future active participles, often with intransitive verb stems: *avenidor* 'to come, future.'

One must not confuse this verbal adjective with the active verbal noun whose masculine singular endings are *-aire*, *-ador*, etc. (5.4.3,B). The combination of this verbal noun with *ęsser* forms a periphrase that often describes the personal state of an "agent": "Ja mais no serai chantaire" 'I'll never be a singer [i.e., sing] again' (38:22).

This construction is equivalent to *ȩsser* plus the present participle used as noun or adjective; in fact, words like *chantaire* are occasionally used adjectivally: "eu sui gais e chantaire" 'I am merry and inclined to sing' (87:25). Thus both *ȩsser jauzire* and *ȩsser jauzens* mean 'to be an enjoyer, to be enjoying, to enjoy.' The problem is that many *-dor* words are ambiguous, capable of being both active and passive and formally identical in the m. obl. sg. and the neuter. For example, *vensedor*, passive in 32:13 (cited above), could also mean 'a conqueror,' an interpretation that would completely reverse the meaning of this passage.

12.5 The Preterit, Compound Past, and Imperfect

The three most frequent past tenses have, in principle, well-delimited uses. The one-word preterit or simple past, the narrative tense par excellence, generally recounts actions that occupy a circumscribed space in time and are not seen as directly related to the present. It naturally dominates in a context of historicity such as the *vidas* and *razos*: "el se crozet e mes·se en mar; e pres·lo malautia" 'he took the cross and took to sea; and sickness took him' (21:5-6).

The compound past, on the other hand, portrays actions or, more typically, states or conditions, as continuing in the present: "Quar senes lieys non puesc viure, / Tant ai pres de s'amor gran fam" 'For without her I can't live, / I have become so hungry for her love' (5:11-12). This usage is particularly clear with verbs which express change and movement, such as those conjugated with *ẹsser*: "per que·l dols m'es en cor intratz!" 'Because of which, grief has entered my heart!' (14:28); the speaker's heart remains in this state. The compound past can also suggest a past repetition or duration which continues or, less often, is terminated: "mout ai estat cuendes e gais, ... / eu ai avut joi e deport" 'I have been very jovial and merry, ... / 'I have had joy and sport' (8:29,39).

The frequent coexistence of the compound and simple past within one passage brings out their fundamental difference, as in: "Una domna·m det s'amor / C'ai amada lonjamen" 'A lady gave me her love, / Whom I have loved a long time' (34:3-4). Her gift of love is definitely passé since, as the poet goes on to explain, she now has another "intimate friend"; nevertheless, the poet still loves her, he says. As here, the compound past often implies an accompanying "still," whereas the preterit is often modified by temporally limiting adverbs like "once" or "last year."

In contrast to both these tenses, the imperfect primarily describes a totally past condition, state, or capacity, as in the first verb here: "la soa vida si era aitals que tot l'invern estava en escola et aprendia letras" 'his life was such that all winter he went to school and studied letters' (44:9-10). The other two verbs here illustrate the second important use of the imperfect: for repeated or habitual events.

The imperfect typically alternates and contrasts with the preterit: "amet longa sason una domna de

Proensa, que avia nom Madomna Maria de Vertfuoil, e l'appellava son ioglar e sas chiansos" 'he loved for a long time a lady from Provence, who was called Lady Maria de Vertifuoil, and he called her his jongleur in his songs' (39:5-7). The preterit "amet" designates a completed action (since Raimbaut d'Aurenga then went on to court another lady), while the imperfects indicate a condition (Lady Maria's name) and a habitual action (what Raimbaut called her). And similarly, with an action followed by a mental state: "cant anetz per crozar a Saysso, / Ieu non avia en cor ... / Que passes mar" 'when you want to take the cross in Soissons, / I didn't have it in my heart ... / To cross the sea' (111:25-27).

A phenomenon probably related to the "historical present" (12.3) is the periphrastic preterit composed of a present (or rarely preterit) form of *anar* plus an infinitive, used at least in postclassical prose and narrative, to emphasize vividness, intentionaltiy, intensity, or duration: "n'Arnautz la va tota arretener" 'Arnaut remembered it all' (66:24).

For other uses of these tenses, see 12.6 and 12.12. It should also be noted that the preterit of *ęsser* can mean 'went,' and that the preterit of *ęsser* and *poder* occasionally takes on a conditional hue, thus *fọ* 'he would have been,' *pọc* 'he could have.'

12.6 The Pluperfect, Past Anterior, and Future Anterior

These three tenses generally occur in subordinate clauses, including conditions (12.9).

The pluperfect generally designates an event that has been definitively completed before the time of a narrative that typically takes place in the preterit: "fetz maintas bonas cansos recordan lo baizar qu'el avia emblat; e dis ... que de leis non avia agut negun guizardo" 'he made many good songs recalling the kiss that he had stolen; and he said ... that he had never had any reward from her' (84:32-34).

The past anterior, with the same meaning as the pluperfect, occurs principally after conjunctions indicating temporal anteriority, such as *quan* 'when,' *tro (que)* 'until,' *pọ(i)s* and *de(i)s que* 'since,' *el temps que* or *en aquel temps que* 'in the time when,' etc.; the main verb again is typically in the preterit: "Aquel levet cant ac dormit" 'This man got up when he had slept' (145:9). The past anterior, which generally indicates a fairly close relation to the time of the narrative, is sometimes replaced by the preterit or rarely by the compound past, imperfect, and other tenses. Conversely the past anterior can occur where we might expect the pluperfect or preterit: "Tu fust nada de Suria" 'You were born in Syria' (146:21).

The future anterior (also called "future perfect") occurs in a temporal or relative clause to designate an action that will have happened before a second action takes place: "·l jorn que l'aurai viza, / Non aurai pezansa" 'the day during which I have seen her, / I'll feel no sadness' (29:31-32). The future anterior is also used to show that a condition has been going on for a considerable time: "estat n'aurai perdutz un an" 'because of this, I have been lost for a year' (106:26).

12.7 The Past Participle

The past participle agrees as follows:

1) always with the subject of verbs conjugated with *ęsser*, namely passives (12.10), pronominal verbs (8.10), and the group of "verbs of motion" and the like given in 10.22;

2) whenever it functions as an adjective, including when combined with a noun or pronoun, generally in the oblique case, to form an ablative absolute construction: "vela levada" 'with raised sail,' "sas iras perdonadas" 'his anger being pardoned,' "fach aquo" 'this having been done,' etc.

3) almost always with a preceding direct object. With a personal or relative pronoun, the normal word order is pronoun + auxiliary + past participle: "Auzels, a tort m'a 'nvazida" 'Bird, he has attacked me wrongly' (17:34). A fairly short nominal direct object can come before the compound verb or be interposed: "Tant ha sa votz esclarzida, / Qu'ela n'a auzit l'entensa" 'He made his voice so clear / That she perceived its meaning' (17:14-15);

4) often (though not in the second line just quoted) with a following direct object: "C'als mil drutz / Ha rendutz / Mil salutz" 'For to a thousand lovers / She has given / A thousand greetings' (17:71-73). The order participle + auxiliary is likewise possible, and is usual at the beginning of a statement: "Faih ai longa carantena" 'I have undergone a long fast' (36:40).

When the participle agrees with two or more objects, it is almost always with the nearest one only.

Just as some present participles have a passive meaning (12.3), a few past participles have an active sense: *aperceubut* 'perceptive' (from *apercẹbre* 'to perceive'), *cauzit* 'indulgent; wise' (*cauzir* 'to choose'), *membrat* 'prudent' (*membrar* 'to remember'), etc.

12.8 The Subjunctive in Subordinate Clauses

The subjunctive mood indicates that an action takes on, in the mind of the person whose point of view is represented, a coloring other than one of objective reality. Besides occurring in wishes and commands (12.2) and in conditions (12.9), the subjunctive is found in the following grammatical contexts.

A) The verbs and verbal locutions that take the subjunctive express nuances along a spectrum from personal reactions to denials of reality:

1) The mind envisages an event positively: *voler* 'to want,' *desirar, aver lo dezirię̧r, aver talẹn, aver envẹya* 'to desire,' *platz, plazen ẹs, bę̧l es, a sabor, agrada* 'it is pleasing,' *es lor tart* 'they are impatient,' *esperar* 'to hope,' *vẹn en cǫr* or *coratge* 'it comes into the heart,' etc.

2) The mind envisages an event negatively, as in *temer* and *aver paọr* 'to fear,' *enǫia·m, pẹsa·m* 'it annoys me,' and, usually with a following negative whether pleonastic (13.3) or of full force, *devedar* 'to forbid,' *se cauzir* 'to avoid,' *castiar* or *gardar* 'to prevent,' *se gardar* or *penre cura* 'to be careful,' *laissar* 'to give up,' also *nọn poder mudar, estar, se laissar* 'not to be able to avoid, keep oneself, stop oneself.'

3) One person attempts or accepts to influence positively another's actions: *demandar* 'to ask,' *pregar* 'to pray,' *dire* 'to tell' (i.e., 'to order'), *(co)mandar* 'to command,' *faire* or *aver mandamen* 'to give or receive an order,' *quęrre* 'to seek,' *lauzar* and *conselhar* 'to advise,' *clamar (mercẹ)* 'to beg (mercy),' *autrejar* and *donar* 'to grant,' *coṇsentir* 'to permit,' etc.

4) In impersonal expressions of judgment, appropriateness, or necessity: *está beṇ* 'it is good,' *mais val*, *męlhs es* 'it is better,' *mal sembla* 'it seems bad,' *drẹitz* or *razoṇs es* 'it is right,' *honors es* 'it is honorable,' *profęgz es* 'it is profitable,' *aver razoṇ* 'to be right,' *tanh*, *conveṇ*, *lǫcs* or *sazoṇs es* 'it is the right occasion,' *ǫps es* and *a mestiẹr* 'it is necessary,' *cal* 'it matters,' etc.

5) In expressions of nonreality, imagination, doubt: *si ęsser podia* 'if it could be,' *noṇ i a esperansa* 'there is no hope,' *noṇ dic* 'I don't say,' *noṇ poder far* 'not to be able to,' *far semblan* or *fẹnher* 'to pretend,' *gręu es* 'it is difficult,' etc.

6) In expressions of belief or opinion: *cręire* and *cujar* 'to believe,' *tener* 'to maintain,' etc.

7) In impersonal expressions of appearance: *par*, *parẹis*, *sembla*, *es semblan* or *vejaire* or *vis*, all 'it seems.'

Since the expression of nonreality is one of the subjunctive nuances, negating the above types of expressions increases the likelihood of a following subjunctive. On the other hand, almost any of them, and particularly those of the last two groups, can take the indicative (by which we here understand "nonsubjunctive") whenever the affirmation of objective reality prevails in the speaker's mind, as in "A cascun de lor es veiaire / Qu'il son savi" 'To each of them it seems / That they are sane' (145:36-37). The expressions given in this subsection normally take the conjunction *que*, but those expressing feelings (A1, 2, 4) can take *car* 'because,' occasionally with the subjunctive.

B) A certain number of conjunctions color as nonfactual a subordinated idea; these signify

1) purpose or intention: *per que*, *per tal que*, *per so̧ que*, *a so que*, *per amor que*, and simply *que*, all 'in order that';

2) result or manner: *enaissí ... que*, *si ... que*, *de tal guisa que* 'in such a way that, with the result that,' *com* and *consí* 'how,' *d'aitan com* 'in whatever way,' etc.;

3) anticipation or limitation of an envisaged event or state: *abans que*, *ancẹis que*, *(en)ans que* 'before,' *tant com* 'as long as,' *d'aitan que* 'to the extent that,' *(en)trọ que* 'until' (with this last, the indicative is more frequent), etc.;

4) a concession: *jassiaisso̧ que*, *ja sia so que*, *mal que* 'although,' *ab (so) que* 'although, even if,' *cossî que* 'however,' *can que* 'however long,' *com que* 'however much,' *cọra(s) que* 'whenever,' etc. (but not after *si bẹn* and *sitọt* 'although,' 13.4);

5) a supposition, restriction, or condition: *sọl (que)*, *ab sol que*, *ab que* 'provided that, if only,' *ab so* (or *aço*, *aiso̧*) *que*, *mas que* 'provided that,' *en (lo) cas que* 'in the case that,' *sinọn que* 'unless' (in later texts), *pauzat que* 'supposing

that,' *noṇ* ... *que* ... *noṇ* 'not ... without, not ... unless,' *quan* 'when' in a hypothetical sense bordering on 'if,' etc.

6) comparison: *qais que, com si* (often preceded by *tot, enaissî, eissamen, atressî*) 'as if' and comparative constructions of the type "mielhs onra·m ... / Qu'om puesca vezer ni auzir" 'she honors me better / Than one could see or hear' (6:5-6).

Again, such conjunctions govern the indicative wherever factuality prevails over eventuality in the mind; for conjunctions that take principally the indicative, see 13.4.

C) After a relative pronoun referring back to a noun or pronoun, the subjunctive expresses a certain subjectivism, particularly with

1) a negation of reality or of feasibility: "Qar un non troba on s'aiziu" 'For it does not find one in whom it may take shelter' (20:35);

2) something imagined, speculated about, possibly resulting, intended, searched for, doubtful, restricted, or to be avoided: "Dieus, donatz mi saber e sen ab qu'ieu aprenda" 'God, give me knowledge and wisdom with which I may learn' (97:40). A special type here is the "consecutive relative" *que*, which often can be interpreted not only as a relative pronoun but also as a conjunction, in either case meaning 'that, such that, with the result that': "Mandon tot lor esfortz, / Que joves lombarda / No rest" 'They summon up all their effort / That no young Lombard / Should remain' (109:64-66);

3) an indefinite antecedent, particularly *ren̩* 'nothing' or one qualified by *to̩t* 'all': "Si tuit li dol ... / Que om anc auzis ..." 'If all the sadnesses ... / That anyone ever heard of ...' (75:1-3).

4) a superlative: "E·l genser qu'el mon se mire" 'And the nicest one who can be seen in the world' (87:21).

In any of these relative constructions, the indicative shows a more objective perception.

D) After indefinite pronouns, adjectives, and adverbs, the subjunctive envisages something as eventual rather than real, notably with

1) a demonstrative plus a relative pronoun in the sense of 'whoever' and particularly 'what(ever)' (9.7): "E faitz de mi so que·us vulhatz" 'And do with me whatever you wish' (122:44);

2) indefinites of generalization (9.7), in concessive expressions like "cui que plassa o cui que pes" 'whomever it may please or displease';

3) *qui* and *que* used alone in an indefinite sense (9.8): "Deu ben pensar e gardar que retraia" 'Should think well and take care what he repeats' (169:4);

4) the adverb, adjective, or pronoun *(ai)tan* ... *que* 'so that, so many that; to the extent that' (9.8): "Aitans d'enfans que l'us puosch' esser pros" 'So many children that one will be worthy' (79:4);

5) the adjective *(ai)tal* ... *que* 'such (a) ... that' (9.8): "Vueilh far ... / Chanso tal qe sia / Plazens" 'I want to make ... / A song such that it will be / Pleasant' (162:6-8).

Except for the *qui que* type, any of these categories can use the indicative to show a factual outlook or a more definite sense, as in the examples of demonstrative plus relative and of *qui* alone given in 9.7.

E) After interrogative pronouns in indirect questions, the subjunctive stresses the speaker's doubt: "Ges non sai ab qual mi tengua ..." 'I don't know at all with which I should remain' (2:24).

F) In addition to the present, shown in all our examples so far except in C3, the subjunctive has three other tenses (ignoring supercompounds); besides in conditions (12.9), they are used as follows.

1) The perfect indicates an event envisaged as potentially happening before a non-past time of reference: "No·m par qu'en re lur descortz nogut n'aia" 'It doesn't seem to me that their discord has done harm in any way' (169:20).

2) The pluperfect indicates an event envisaged as potentially happening before a past time of reference: "nul plazer li faria s'ella non sabes qu'el s'en fos partitz" 'she would give him no pleasure if she didn't know that he had left her' (61:21-22).

3) The imperfect indicates an event simultaneous or posterior to the action of a main verb in a past or conditional tense: "s'esser podia / Que ja mais alba ni dia / nos fos" 'if it could be / That never dawn or day / Came ...' (94:10-12). In addition, particularly after a main verb in the present indicative or imperative, it can show a previous action:

"Ja non er mais ni no crezatz que fos" 'There never will be and don't believe that there was' (75:15). Or, it envisages a simultaneous or posterior action with even greater subjectivity than would be shown by the present subjunctive: "Ai Deus! car no sui ironda, / Que voles per l'aire ...?" 'Oh God! Why am I not a swallow / Who would fly through the air ...?' (29:49-50).

12.9 The Conditional and Conditions

Outside of conditions, the conditional A, referring to the present or occasionally future, moderates an assertion: "A chantar m'er de so qu'ieu no volria" 'I have to sing about something that I wouldn't want to' (64:1). As a "future in the past," the conditional A (and by the fourteenth century also B) indicates an action subsequent to the moment of a past narration, thus: "el dis que se alegraria e laissaria lo dol" 'he said he would be merry and would abandon mourning' (85:16-17).

The conditional B functions in present contexts like the conditional A: "ab tot lo nei / M'agr' ops us bais" 'with all the snow / I would need a kiss' (67:48-49). In addition, it indicates actions that could have taken place in the past but did not: "'aital ren i degra mais metre'" '"he should have put in more of such and such a thing"' (179:13).

Both compound conditionals, A and B, show an event that could have happened but did not: "... d'aitan qe il agra sufert ..." '... to the extent that she would have allowed him ...' (39:24-25).

Conditions normally consist of an "if-clause" introduced by *si*, *se*, or normally *s'* before a vowel except in an enclitic, plus a "result-clause." Among the considerable number of possible combinations of verb categories, the following are the most frequent:

if-clause	*result-clause*	*meaning*
si + *pres. ind.*	fut., pres. ind. (or cond. A, impv., etc.)	a realizable condition; pres. or fut. context
si + *impf. subj.*	cond. B (or A, comp. B, etc.)	unrealizable condition; past or pres. context
si + *impf. ind.*	cond A (rarely, pres. ind. or fut.)	realizable or not; pres. or fut. context

Si plus the present indicative can introduce a variety of tenses, most commonly the future: "Bos metges er si·m pot guerir" 'He will be a good doctor if he can cure me' (3:23). The great majority of "contrary-to-fact" conditions--those envisaging an event as impossible--have *si* + imperfect subjunctive ... conditional B: "s'eu pogues contrafar / Fenix ... / Eu m'arsera" 'If I could imitate / The Phoenix ... / I would burn myself' (62:36-39). Less often, the result-clause contains the conditional A or, stressing that realization would have already occurred by now or that all possibility thereof is in the past, the compound conditional B: "Si el visques ni Deu plagues, / El los agra dese conqes" 'If he had lived or it had pleased God, / He would have quickly conquered them' (20:45-46).

The occasional formula *si* + imperfect indicative ... conditional A envisages an eventuality as either no longer realizable or, as in the following example, extremely unlikely or undesirable: "car vendria / sa gelozia / Si aitals dos amans partia" 'he would sell dearly / His jealousy / If he separated two such lovers' (107:18-20). On the other hand, a present indicative or future in the result-clause puts the situation back in the realm of normal expectation: "si mos enemicx perdia / Mi platz" 'if my enemy were to lose / It pleases me' (100:23-24).

Another way to introduce conditions is through the relative pronoun *qui* used in a general sense with no antecedent and usually translatable as 'if someone ...' (or, in the negative, 'if no one ...')" "platz mi be qui m'aculhia" 'it pleases me well if someone welcomes me' (100:19). In such cases, which can be seen as a form of anacoluthon (13.7), one often hesitates between translating 'if someone' and 'someone who'; but when the subjects of the two clauses differ, 'if someone' becomes the only interpretation: "Qi, per Dieu gazaignar, / Pren d'aitals desconortz, / ... / Ben es dregz ..." 'If someone, to win God, / Undergoes such hardships, / .../ It is right ...' (92:37-40). Whether with the same or different subjects, tense combinations vary widely, with most often the present indicative and future, but also the imperfect indicative and subjunctive, conditional A, etc., in either clause. This *qui* can also render ideas like 'when, even if,' or 'provided that someone ...'; and we also find a "dangling" conditional *qui*-clause of the type "qui·s vol" 'as you wish' (180:62).

No introductory words are needed in concessive parenthetical statements of the type "volgues o non volgues" 'whether he wishes or not' and "e fos mia Alamanha" 'and even if Germany were mine.'

12.10 The Passive Voice and Supercompound Tenses

The passive voice shows action affecting the subject (with which the past participle normally agrees, as in all the examples given in 10.23). The agent, which would be the subject in the corresponding active construction, is introduced by the preposition *de* if a condition or state is described ("esser amatz, doptatz de" 'to be loved, feared by') but, and much more frequently, when an action is described, by the preposition *per*: "anc per lui no fo feritz / Bos colps" 'never by him was struck / A good blow' (54:70-71). A meaning similar to the passive is expressed by the impersonal subject *om* 'one' (9.8) and by the pronominal construction (8.10); thus "non fo crezut," "om no crezet," and "no se crezet" all mena 'people did not believe.'

Though both passive and supercompound forms have two past participles, they are distinguished by the fact that the passive affects only transitive verbs and always takes the auxiliary *ęsser*. Compare, for example, "es estatz cantatz" 'it (m.) was sung' with the supercompound "a agut cantat" 'he sang.' The meaning of the supercompound past is rather elusive: it sometimes gives a feeling of completion more definitive or distant than the compound past *a cantat*, or else a feeling of temporal indeterminacy in the past; but when used in place of the past anterior, it suggests a more immediate connection to the present: "e quan son estat arribat ..." 'and when they (had) arrived ...'

12.11 Impersonal Verbs

Impersonal verbs--those with an understood neuter 3 sg. subject--generally introduce *que* and a subjunctive clause (12.8A). Verbs meaning 'to remember' are impersonal with an indirect object designating the person who remembers and *de* or the equivalent showing the thing remembered: "Remembra·m d'un' amor de lonh" 'I remember a love from afar' (24:4). In compound forms, certain impersonal verbs take the auxiliary *ęsser*: "Manhtas vetz m'es pois membrat / De ..." 'Many times since, I have remembered ...' (34:53-54).

12.12 The Infinitive and Modal Periphrases

Any infinitive can be used as a noun, then taking on the attributes of number and case and the possibility of being qualified by articles and adjectives, for example, "lo parlar" 'speech' (4:50), "ab loncs plorars" 'with long sobbings' (40:46), "al departir" 'upon separating' (119:23). At the same time, the substantivized infinitive can, in its verbal role, be qualified by an adverb: "el trop cantars" 'singing too much.'

Frequently, an infinitive clause is the complement of another verb; for example, in "el crezia anar conquistar l'emperi" 'he thought that he would go and conquer the empire' (83:12-13), *conquistar* depends on *anar*, which in turn depends on *crezia*. As in this example, many verbs with an infinitive complement normally require no preposition, including verbs of motion, the impersonal expressions given in 12.8,A1 and A4, and also *amar* 'to love,' *ausar* 'to dare,' *(co)mandar* 'to command,' *esperar* 'to hope,' *laissar* 'to allow,' *quęrre* 'to seek,' *saber* 'to know (how),' *soler* 'to be accustomed,' *temer* 'to fear,' etc.

Before an infinitive, many other verbs normally take *de*, e.g., *cessar* 'to cease,' *dire* 'to tell (i.e., order),' *s'enardir* 'to dare,' *s'entremẹtre* 'to undertake,' *(s')esforsar* 'to make an effort,' *gardar* 'to protect,' *(se) giquir* 'to desist,' *pensar* 'to think about,' *tener* 'to restrain,' etc. Verbs taking *a* include *avenir* 'to happen,' *convenir* 'to be fitting,' *ensenhar* 'to teach,' and *tornar* 'to go back (to).' Verbs taking *en* include *s'empenre* 'to undertake,' *s'entendre* 'to turn one's thoughts (toward),' and *ponhar* 'to make an effort.' *Comensar* and *(se) penre* 'to begin' take *a* or, less often, *de* or no preposition; *(se) laissar* 'to desist' and a few others take *de* or *a* indifferently; *se pọnher* 'to hasten' takes *a* or *en*. Sometimes we find a double prepositional construction: "Per los murs a fendre" 'In order to breach the walls' (109:106); in this and combinations like *a* ... *a* and *en* ... *a*, the second preposition is inserted in order, as here, to separate two tonic syllables, or by analogy or for metrical reasons.

With verbs of perception, the thing perceived, in the oblique case, is subject of the infinitive: "Eras quan vey verdeyar / Pratz ..." 'Now when I see the fields grow green ...' (108:1-2). But a transitive infinitive having its own direct object takes on a passive meaning and its subject, if expressed, becomes an indirect object introduced by *a*: "Ara vei possezir / A clers la seinhoria" 'Now I see / Clerics have dominion' (140:17-18). With two objects, the object of the verb of perception is indirect and the object of the infinitive is direct: "... qu'ieu·l lor veia plumar" '... so that I see them pluck it' (78:9).

All the above examples are of the present infinitive; the much rarer past infinitive looks backward one "level" in time: "no vuelh autr' aver conquis" 'I don't want to have won another' (53:34).

The auxiliary verbs with an infinitive have special meanings. The present of *aver* can be part of a separable future (10.16); and *aver* + *a* + infinitive indicates necessity: "ab lieys ai a guerir" 'through her I have to be cured' (6:48). The same meaning is rendered by *ęsser* + *a* + infinitive: "A chantar m'er de so qu'ieu no volria" 'I have to sing about something I don't want to' (64:1).

Far plus an infinitive likewise has special meanings. *Far* + direct object + infinitive means 'to make (or have) someone (or something) do something': "'selh qui fai lo bosc fulhar'" '"he who makes the woods become leafy"' (14:34). After *far*, a transitive infinitive can have its own direct object: "Ma·l cors ferms fortz / Mi fai cobrir / Mains vers" 'But my firm strong heart / Makes me conceal / Many truths' (67:45-47). When transitive infinitives take on a passive meaning, the agent, if expressed, is an indirect object: "el se fetz cassar als pastors" 'he had himself hunted by the shepherds' (85:25). On the other hand, in this type of construction, *a* can also show the receiver of the action:

"a si et a totz los sieus servidors fetz raire los cabelhs" 'he had his and his servants' hair cut' (85:3-4). Another construction is "far a saber" 'to make known' (cf. "donar ad entendre" 'to give to understand'). In addition, impersonal *far* + *a* + an infinitive (with a passive sense) means 'to be worthy of being ...': "vos fai ad amar" 'you are worthy of being loved.' Finally, we find impersonal *far* in the sense of 'it is' + adjective + infinitive: "Mal amar fai vassal d'estran pais" 'It is bad to love a lord from a foreign land' (113:13).

The modals *dever*, *poder*, and *voler*, alongside their normal meanings indicating respectively obligation, ability, and desire, can with an infinitive form periphrases functioning as futures or futures in the past, thus "volrai dir" 'I will say' (132:2). This usage is particularly frequent in the subjunctive, which these two verb categories lack, thus: "non puosc aver / Ren qem puosca ad amor valer" 'I can't find / Anything that might help me in love' (112:29-30); "pregero la qu'ella li degues perdonar" 'they begged her to pardon him' (61:50). *Dever* and *no voler* can also form periphrases for commands and wishes: "que no vuelha ..." 'let him not ...' (180:17).

Chapter 12: Exercises

Explain and justify all verb usage in the following quotations

1. S'ieu mueir aman, per vos cug far mo pro (164:35)

2. ieu e vos levem gen del sablo / N'Albert marques qu'era ios de l'arso. / Et ai estat per vos en greu preyzo (111:11-13)
3. E quan venc un dia, Peire Vidals saup qu'En Barrals se era levatz e que la domna era tota sola ... (84:14-15)
4. E qui qu'en sia lauzaire, / De ben qu'en diga no·i men (87:18-19)
5. e cascuna li ... prometia tot so que ill plagues e qu'el demandava (84:11-12)
6. cuieriant se qe·lz en tengues hom per pecs, si dizion qe no l'entendesson (179:34-35)
7. Per la gensor qu'anc fos d'amor enquisa (90:32)
8. us cavaliers de San Gili li fetz talhar la lengua, per so qu'el dava ad entendre qu'el era drutz de sa molher; e N'Uc del Bauz si·l fetz garir (83:6-8)
9. Greu partir si fa d'amor qui la trob' a son talen (2:6)
10. e dis a Ricchautz que s'el li volgues lo ben qu'el dizia, qu'el non deuria voler qu'ella l'en disses plus ni plus li fezes con ella li fazia ni dizia (61:6-8)

13

OTHER PARTS OF SPEECH AND SYNTACTICAL OBSERVATIONS

13.1 Prepositions

Since prepositions are by nature proclitic, they tend to lose final *-e* before a following vowel. Thus, prevocalically, *de* becomes *d'* and we usually find *entr'*, *contr'*, *sobr'* 'between, against, above.' For combinations of preposition + article, like *al* or *pels*, see 6.4.

Most prepositions pose no problem in usage. We have already seen (12.12) constructions with verb + *de*, *a*, *en* + infinitive, as well as various meanings of *far* + *a*. Here we shall merely pass in review a few of the most common prepositions.

A (often prevocalically in the form *az* or *ad*, both probably pronounced /az/) has varied meanings besides indicating location or direction. It introduces the indirect object after many verbs like *dar* 'to give,' *perdonar* 'to pardon,' *plazer* 'to please,' and optionally after some others like *pregar* 'to beseech' and *servir* 'to serve'; thus we find "preguet al rey" 'he asked the king' (66:28) but "pregero la" 'they beseeched her' (61:50). When an indirect object is a noun designating a person, *a* is often omitted (5.11). *A* can indicate possession or relationship: "la filha al rei" 'the king's daughter.' *A* is used when an adjective is qualified by a verb: "un son leu a chantar" 'a tune to sing.' *A* appears in expressions like "voler a senhor" 'to want as lord' and "tenir s'o ad escarn, ad afan" 'to consider it a bad joke, a burden.' In its other functions indicating manner, circumstance, instrument, or time, *a* is usually translated as 'in,' 'with,' or sometimes 'against'; before an infinitive, *a* sometimes means 'in order to.' For *a* as a second preposition before an infinitive, see 12.12.

The instrumental meaning 'with,' usually conveyed by *a* or more aften *ab*, can also be shown by *de*: "vos cobri del blizo" 'I covered you with my shield' (111:16). The most frequent use of *de* indicates possession (8.12); though nouns designating people can stand without any preposition (5.11), *de* usually does occur with nouns that are in series or are qualified, thus "maire del rei jove e d'en Richart" 'the mother of the young king and of Sir Richard' (1:6-7). *De* also indicates origin ("de Briva" 'from Brive,' 54:25), cause ("de joi" 'because of joy,' 37:2), time ("de ser e de maiti" 'in the evening and in the morning,' 11:10; "d'un an" 'in one year,' 6:18; "d'aqui" 'from now on'), manner ("creisser de pretz" 'to grow in worth,' 89:29), and inclusion ("fo del[s] plus fols homes" 'he was among the craziest men,' 83:2).

De also means 'concerning, about' ("dis grans mals d'autrui" 'he said very bad things about others,' 83:5-6), and in this sense can proleptically introduce the true subject or object of the following verb: "eu sai de paraulas com van" 'I know how words go' (7:27). In addition, *de* plus an infinitive sometimes indicates purpose. Also, indefinite pronouns take *de* before a following adjective: "tot quan fauc d'avinen" 'everything agreeable that I do' (87:26); and *de* can link an adjective and a noun or pronoun ("paubre de mi" 'poor me') or else two nouns in apposition ("lo fols de Peire Vidal" 'that crazy Piere Vidal,' 84:19; "la ciutat de Tolosa" 'the city of Toulouse'). Finally, a number of verbs normally take *de*, with various meanings, before a following noun: *aprochar de* 'to approach,' *s'azautar de* 'to take pleasure in,' *consirar* and *pensar de* 'to think about,' *s'enardir de* 'to dare,' *se meravillar de* 'to wonder at,' *s'oblidar de* 'to forget,' etc. For *de* as a partitive article, see 5.6; introducing a term of comparison, 7.12 and 13.2; with superlatives, 7.14; in a periphrasis for possessive adjectives, 8.12; with passive verbs, 12.10.

The preposition *en* can take on the forms *em* before *b* or *p*, *e* before other consonants, and *'n* after a vowel. It generally means 'in' and sometimes 'on,' with spatial, temporal or circumstancial functions: "en Provensa" 'in Provence,' "en breu" 'quickly,' "en patz" 'in peace.' A special meaning is seen in expressions like "parlar en fol" 'to speak like a madman.'

The preposition *per*, besides introducing the agent in passive constructions (12.10), indicates location ("pels pratz" 'in the fields,' "pel cap" 'on the head'), cause ("per vos" 'because of you,' "pel dous termini" 'because of the sweet season'), means ("per lonc esperar" 'by long waiting'), result ("pe·l nostre marrimen" 'for our sorrow,' 75:33), time ("pel matin" 'in the morning'), characteristic, and purpose both seen in this example: "L'an quist a Deu per lo melhor de totz / E per cobrar lo Sepulcr'" 'They have chosen him as (being) the best of all / And in order to regain the Sepulcher' (110: 6-7).

Prepositions take the oblique case (5.11). The repetition of prepositions in parallel constructions is usual but optional: "mes se ... a servir et a venir et anar" 'he began ... to serve and to come and go' (95:3-4).

13.2 Adverbs and Adverbial Locutions

Adverbs can be formed by adding the suffix *-men(t)* to the feminine form of adjectives, thus "lonjamen" 'for a long time' (27:59), "fortmen" 'strongly' (145: 26), etc. Stress in such adverbs probably falls both on the root and the suffix (3.8). When two adverbs in *-men* occur in parallel constructions, usually only the first takes the suffix: "se parla naturalmenz et drecha" 'is spoken naturally and correctly' (179:88). Often, as here, the ending is modified to *-menz* or *-mens* by the addition of an "adverbial *-s*." This *-s* was etymological in many adverbs, and by analogy it became optional not only in *-men* adverbs but also in others such as *ensem(s)* 'together,' *ęra(s)* 'now,' *sempre(s)* 'always,' and *volontięr(s)* 'willingly.' This optional consonant can become a convenience in the rhyme, as in *alhọr(s)* 'elsewhere.' About a dozen adverbs show an *-as* ending, as in *cęrtas* 'certainly,' from *cęrt* 'certain.' Another adverbial suffix, *-tre*, is added to a small number of present participles, as in *vezentre* 'in the presence of,' from *vezen(t)* 'seeing.'

Another group of adverbs are formed from neuter adjectives, usually common, short ones. These can, when closely linked to a verb, form certain fixed locutions, thus *montar alt* 'to mount high'; *alt* and *bas* with verbs of speaking or singing; *ferir gręu* 'to wound severely'; *saber boṇ, mal* 'to please, displease'; *tener car* 'to hold dear,' *tener vil* 'to scorn'; *comprar, vendre car, vil* 'to sell, buy for a high price, cheaply'; etc. Other neuter adjectives that function adverbially in a variety of contexts are *bręu* 'fast,' *drẹch* 'straight,' *dur* 'hard,' *fǫrt* 'strongly; very,' *gen* 'sweetly,' *gręu* 'with difficulty,' *len* 'slowly,' *lęu* 'easily,' *plaṇ* 'clearly,' *preon* 'deeply,' *segur* 'surely,' *sǫl* 'only,' and *suau* 'softly.' Other adjectives act as adverbs more sporadically, for example: "a chantat molt avinen" 'he sang very nicely' (102:9).

Though in such cases the adjective functioning adverbially usually describes a quality inherent in a stated or implied noun, still the adjective normally remains invariable. Sometimes, however, it is attracted into the case of the related noun: "E fo ... gens parlans" 'And he was sweet talking' (39:2-3); "n'er encolpatz premiers" 'he will be accused first' (54:8). This is in fact the rule with adverbial *tọt* 'all': "tota sola" 'all alone' (84:15); "totz trassalh" 'I tremble all over' (19:25).

In addition, many adverbial locutions are formed from a preposition plus a neuter adjective (*a drech* 'justly,' *de novẹl* 'anew,' *en breu* 'quickly'), a feminine singular or plural adjective (*a saubuda* 'known publicly'; *a longas* 'for a long time,' *de primas* 'first'), or a noun (*a tapiṇ* 'on the sly,' *a genolhọns* 'kneeling'; *de bada(s)* 'in vain'; *en perdon(s)* 'without reward'). Some adverbial locutions are derived from an article plus a noun: *lo cọrs* '(in a) hurry, hastily,' *el saut* '(at a) jump, hastily,' *l'ambladura* '(at) an amble'; such expressions make use of the oblique case denoting complements of measure, time, etc. (5.11). In a few cases, a preposition that has taken on adverbial force follows the related noun ("e sauta li desus" 'and jumps on him,' 181:17).

Adverbs not in *-men(t)* can be divided into groups indicating place, time, manner, quantity, demonstration, affirmation, negation, etc. The important group of intensifying adverbs includes the neuter adjective forms *ẹis*, *neis*, *meteis*, all with many variant forms, and meaning 'even'; these readily combine with other words in expressions like *aquí eis* 'at once' and *sọtz eis* 'right under.' For indefinite adverbs, see 9.8, notably adverbs of quantity.

As with adjectives (7.12), a number of adverbs have synthetic comparatives: *ancẹ(i)s* 'earlier,' *forçe(i)s* 'stronger,' *gense(i)s* 'nicer,' *longe(i)s* 'longer,' *mais* and *plus* 'more,' *mełh(s)* 'better,' *men(h)s* 'less,' *pęitz* and *sorde(i)s* 'worse.' Several of these can function as neuter adjectives (7.9), as in "t'es mieills que·t trencs" 'it's better for you to stop' (67:41), and also as nouns: *lo melhs, lo peitz*, etc.

The term of comparison to another potential subject is introduced by *de* ("plus trac pena d'amor / De Tristan" 'I suffer the pain of love more / Than Tristan,' 29:45-46) or (with the subject case, 5.10) *que* ("melhs s'enten que vos en amor" 'he knows more than you about love,' 36:7). *Que* is used if direct objects are compared: "mais amaria seis deniers en mon punh que mil sols el cel" 'I'd rather have six deniers in my fist than a thousand sous in heaven' (41:14); and *que* is also used to compare two clauses. The adverbial comparison of equality uses *(ai)tan ... com* or *can*: "nulhs autres joys tan no·m play / Cum jauzimens d'amor de lonh" 'no other joy pleases me as much / As the enjoyment of love from afar' (24:45-46). But a factual result clause after *(ai)tan* is introduced by *que*: "la servi tant ... qu'ella fetz ..." 'he served her so much ... that she did ...' (33:1-2).

The construction "the more ... the more" is expressed by *on* (or *com*) *mais* (or *plus, mełhs*) ... (*e*) *mais* (or *plus, melhs*) ... (*e*), as in "on plus josti, plus me plai" 'the more I joust, the more it pleases me' (128:55); for 'less,' substitute *men(h)s*.

The adverbial superlative is accompanied by the definite article, which is however omitted after a relative pronoun: "la re que plus volia" 'the person he most wanted' (94:2).

Spelling usually distinguishes the intensifying adverb *si* from the reflexive pronoun *se*, whether pleonastic (8.10) or not; in fact, the two can occur together: "P. Vidals ... si se marri molt" 'Indeed, P. Vidal was very sad' (85:1-2). In the *vidas*, the frequent opening formula "si fo" 'was' hence uses the adverb, not the pronoun.

13.3 Negations

The basic negative adverb is *noṇ* 'not'; only very rarely is it reduced prevocalically to *n'*. Negations, often occurring in clusters, form a favorite stylistic device, for example, in William IX's famous "Farai un vers de dreyt nien" 'I will compose a poem about nothing at all' (No. 3).

In certain circumstances, *noṇ* has no negative force and is untranslatable in English. This pleonastic *noṇ* occurs 1) after expressions that envisage an event negatively and take the subjunctive (12.8, A2): "el no la'n poc castiar qu'ela no mezes gran rumor" 'he could not prevent her from making a great uproar' (84:26-27); 2) after conjunctions of anticipation that take the subjunctive (12,8,B3): "tro qu'el non trobes merce" 'until he found mercy' (61:42); 3) in comparisons: "Melhor conselh dera na Berengera / Que vos no me donatz" 'Lady Berengera would give me better advice / Than you give me' (48: 39-40); 4) in some other expressions of nonreality, including those taking the subjunctive (12.8,A5) and some adverbial locutions: "A per pauc de chantar no·m lais" 'I almost give up singing' (89:1).

Nọn is often reinforced by *gens*, *reṇ(s)*, or *nien(t)*: "autr' amor no volh nien" 'I don't at all want another love' (38:56). We also find *cap* in the Southwest, *pas* under French influence in later texts, and occasionally *mi(g)a*. Other negative intensifiers are appropriate to special circumstances, for example, *noṇ* ... *(un) dọrn*, literally 'not a hand's breadth'; and various objects serve as a reference of worthlessness: "No val sos chans un aguillen" 'His song is not worth an eglantine' (102:48). 'Never" is rendered by *noṇ* ... *ja*, *anc*, *jọrn* or by *noṇca*; and 'no more' by *noṇ* ... *plus* or ... *(ja) mais*. The word order in such formulas is quite free, thus: "ja mais en lor no·m fiarai" 'I'll never trust them again (37:26). Some related expressions are the restrictive formulas *noṇ* ... *gaire* and *a(b) pena(s)* 'hardly', *si* ... *noṇ* 'if not, only' and *noṇ* ... *que* or ... *mas* 'only': "No·n a mas l'ufana" 'Has only the appearance of it' (15:28).

The negative adjectives include *neguṇ*, *neün*, *deguṇ*; *nul*, *nulh*, *lunh*; *ne(i)suṇ*. These are declined like *bȩl* and normally occur with *noṇ*: "nulhs autres joys tan no·m play" 'no other joy pleases me so much' (24:45). However, in hypothetical, comparative, or already negative contexts, and in some other circumstances, these adjectives by themselves, without *noṇ*, take on the positive meaning of 'any,' thus: "Non es meravelha s'eu chan / Melhs de nul autre chantador" 'It isn't surprising if I sing / Better than any other singer' (27:1-2).

The negative pronouns include *neguna reṇ*, *nula reṇ*, *nonreṇ*, all declined like *reṇ* (9.8); and *nien(t)* declined like *mur*. These all mean 'nothing' and the first two also mean 'no one.'

13.4 *Conjunctions*

The basic coordinating conjunction is *e* 'and,' prevocalically often *ez* or *et*, both probably pronounced /ez/. *E* frequently appears, especially in prose, at the beginning of successive sentences, almost as if it were a mere punctuation mark, and also to avoid a verb's being the first element in a sentence. Less often *si*, prevocalically *s'*, also means 'and' and coordinates clauses; we even find *e si* together in this use.

E and *si* can both occur in situations where English would translate either with terms like 'then, so, therefore,' etc., or else not at all, namely 1) at the beginning of a main clause following a subordinate clause indicating time, cause, hypothesis, purpose, etc.: "E quand lo paire moric, si·l laisset molt ric" 'And when his father died, he left him very rich' (95:2-3); 2) before a main verb (and pronouns attached thereto), when preceded by a locative or temporal expression, a comparison, other prepositional locution, lengthy direct object, vocative, etc.: "Atressi com l'olifanz / ... / Et eu segrai aquel us" 'Just like the elephant / ... / I will follow that custom' (62:1-5); 3) to introduce a question or exclamation: "Domna, e per que ...?" 'Lady, why ...?'

E can also introduce an utterance in direct discourse following a verb of speaking: "So dis: 'Et ...'" 'He said: "...."' *Si* can introduce an exclamation (13.6); and very often it stands between a subject and verb, particularly in prose and with the verbs *ęsser*, *aver*, *far*, and *voler*: "Arnautz Daniels si fo d'aquella encontrada" 'Arnaut Daniel was from that region' (66:1). In such cases it is not easy to distinguish the conjunction from the adverb *si* meaning 'indeed, in truth' or the pleonastic reflexive pronoun *se*, *si* (8,10).

Both *e* and *si* occasionally have an adversative function: "Mi faitz orguoill ... / E si etz francs vas totas autras gens" 'You are arrogant towards me ... / And yet you are noble towards all others' (64:14). However, this meaning is more usually shown by the conjunctions and adverbs *mas*, *mais* 'but,' *perǫ* 'but, however,' and *ans* 'rather.'

Mas, which also takes on meanings like 'but rather, but only, except for,' could be considered also a preposition except that it retains the nominative case with a logical subject; "tuih amador / Son gai ... / Mas eu" 'all lovers / Are merry ... / Except for me' (31:5-7). (Similarly: "con il" 'like them,' 138:9.) The sequence *nọn* ... *mas* comes to mean 'only': "Fenix, don non es mas us" 'The Phoenix, of which there is only one' (62:37). Similar combinations are *mas que* 'but rather,' *mas can (de)* 'except for,' and *nọn* ... *mas can* 'not ... except for; only.'

The meaning 'or' is rendered by *o* and *ni* (sometimes *vo* and *ne*; prevocalically often *oz* and *n'*).

Ni links two items that are negated or two clauses of which at least the second is negated: "chans ni flors d'albespis / No·m platz plus" 'Song or hawthorn flower / Does not please me more' (24:6-7). *Ni* also can occur in dubitative or hypothetical contexts, but sometimes is a mere substitute for *e*: "Digh vos ay d'En Guillem qui fo ni don" 'I have told you who Sir Guillem was and where (he was) from' (56:1). The formula 'neither ... nor' is expressed by *noṇ ... ni ... ni*.

Many subordinating conjunctions normally take the subjunctive (12.8,B). Those that usually or always take the indicative show time (*can, lancan, com* 'when'; *(de)mentre(s) (que), de so que* 'while'; *pǫ(i)s (que)* 'since, after'; *des que, de(s)pǫis (que)* 'since') cause (*car, per (sǫ) que* 'because'), circumstance (*com* 'how; why; as'; *segon(s) que* 'according to how'), comparison (*si, atressí, (en)aissí ... com* 'just as'); etc.

Besides being used after *si* 'if' in certain constructions (12.9), the indicative follows *si (que) ... noṇ* 'if not,' *noṇ ... si ... noṇ* 'only,' *si noṇ que* in the sense 'except that, even if,' and *si beṇ, si tọt* 'although, even if.'

Before a vowel, the conjunction *que* usually either elides to *qu'* or else takes on the longer form *quez*. This ubiquitous term has meanings as varied as 'that; the fact that; than; since; because, for; when, as'; for example, in the temporal sense, "l'autra nueig qe·m dormia" 'the other night as I was sleeping' (158:2), and in a causal sense, "Qued una vetz me dis" 'For she once told me (35:18). Temporal *que* is also often considered a relative pronoun; see 9.5. For the consecutive relative pronoun *que* 'such that,' see 12.8,C2.

In complex sentences, declarative *que* is often pleonastically repeated for the sake of clarity: "Pero si·m retinc ieu tan de covenen / Que s'el lo teni' un an qu'ieu lo tengues mais de cen" 'But I retained this much by agreement, / That if he had him one year, I would have him more than a hundred' (2:20-21). However, *que* can often be omitted, particularly in adverbial comparisons (13.2), in clauses after *tal* 'such a', *si* and *(ai)tan* 'so (much)', and similar terms ("Tant ai mo cor ple de joya, / Tot me desnatura" 'My heart is so full of joy, / Everything changes nature for me,' 29:1-2; cf. 12.8,D4), and after certain expressions regularly taking the subjunctive, particularly those described in 12.8,A ("No·m puesc mudar no·m sovena" 'I can't help remembering,' 59:11).

13.5 Questions and Exclamations

One type of question, which cannot be answered by 'Yes' or 'No,' is formed with the aid of inherently interrogative terms. This type contains one of the interrogative adjectives or pronouns described in 9.6, or else a similar term like the adverbs *on* 'where,' *d'on* 'from where,' and *com*, *cum*, *co(n)sí* 'how' or the conjunctions *car*, *per que* 'why.' The word order is usually interrogative term + verb + subject, if any, thus: "morgue, quar venguis? / Ni cum estay Montaudos / ...?" 'monk, why did you come? / And how is Montaudo / ...?' (99:6-7). However, when a subject pronoun is expressed, it can also come first, both in order to give it emphasis and to avoid inversion, thus: "Aiso, que sera, domna?" 'What will this be, lady?' (41:28). Other elements like direct and indirect objects, prepositional locutions, vocatives, and the adverbs *doncs* 'so, hence' are readily inserted, for example, "Qual pro y auretz, dompna conja / ...?" 'What profit will you have in this, charming lady / ...?' (5:19). When the sense is clear, the verb can be omitted: "Et ieu com?" 'How (can) I?'

The second type of question has no properly interrogative term and expects a 'Yes' or 'No' answer: "Pot me bon' esser, senhors?" 'Can she be good to me, gentlemen?' (41:21). A subject pronoun again normally follows the verb: "Cujatz vos ...?" 'Do you believe ...?' (12:55). Sometimes a term like *doncs* (see above), *e*, or an intensifying *ja* (literally 'indeed; ever') helps clarify that we are in the presence of a question. Questions like "Eu per que?" 'Why (should) I?' show ellipsis of the verb, as is also common in answering questions with a pronoun subject and an affirmative or negative particle: "Oc eu" 'Yes, I am (will, etc.)'; "Dic trop? Eu non" 'Do I say too much? I don't' (69:40).

Indirect questions are introduced by verbs of saying or perception like *cujar* 'to believe,' *demandar* 'to ask,' *dir* 'to say,' *entendre* 'to hear; understand,' *saber* 'to know,' and *vezer* 'to see.' With an interrogative pronoun, adjective or adverb, we find, for example, "no say que s'es" 'I don't know what it is' (41:1) or, with ellipsis of the verb, "no sai cau" 'I don't know which' (3:22). Occasionally, the subordinate clause requires the subjunctive (12.8,E). The 'Yes/No' type of indirect question is introduced by *si* 'whether': "Cujatz vos qu'ieu non conosca / D'Amors s'es orba o losca?" 'Do you think I don't know / Whether Love is blind or cross-eyed?' (12:55-56).

Exclamations can be formed by any forceful utterance, particularly with imperatives ("Escoutatz!" 'Listen!', 12:4), wishes, the word *tan* 'so much, so many' (9.8), and the interrogatives *cal* and *can* (9.6): "Dieus! qual enueg ... !" 'God! What a vexation ... !' (124:9). Some exclamatory sentences are introduced by *si* 'and; indeed,' *ar* 'now,' or *can* and *com* (in rhetorical questions); particularly common are optative exclamations of the type "si m'aiut Dieus!" or "si Dieus mi valha!" 'God help me!' Other exclamations are expressed with interjections: "oy, fil!" 'oh, son!'; "ai mi!" 'oh me!'; "ai las!" 'alas!'; "eu las!" 'woe is me!' And some are based on other parts of speech, such as *(a la) via!* 'away!' and *sus!* 'up!'

13.6 Word Order

An affinity for parataxis (the parallel use of clauses without grammatical coordination), the infrequency of the use of logically distinctive subordinating conjunctions, and the ubiquity of imprecise connectors like *que*, *e*, and *si* all challenge the modern reader's ingenuity in assembling the various parts of a Provençal sentence to make overall sense. Even though the systems of declension and conjugation on the whole show adequately how each inflected word functions within its clause, nevertheless the elision of final unaccented vowels can suppress some of the very endings that define the relations among words. Yet no need was apparently felt to make word order "grammatical," that is, for it to differentiate the meanings of two otherwise identical utterances. In fact, the language can emphasize almost any desired element by putting it first in its clause or sometimes, in verse, at the very end of the line or stanza. In addition, the needs of meter, syllabification, and rhyme often impose a word order even farther from that of Provençal prose (and even more so, from English).

Still, we have already enunciated certain principles of word order: articles precede the corresponding noun (6.1), attributive adjectives almost always adjoin the noun and certain types generally precede it (7.10), object pronouns usually come right before the verb except in a number of specific circumstances (8.7), and the order of two object pronouns together is quite fixed (8.8).

In addition, the auxiliary of a compound verb usually precedes the past participle (12.7), unless the latter receives special emphasis or (8.7) occurs at the beginning of a verse: "Anat ai cum cauz' enversa" 'I have gone like a backwards thing' (43: 33). The auxiliary and participle can be separated by prepositional locutions, personal pronouns (8.7), a noun used as direct object, etc. ("el avia tot so sen perdut" 'he had lost all his reason,' 71.II,14); a conjugated verb and its dependent infinitive are likewise separable ("Dieus vol los arditz e·ls suaus / Assajar" 'God wants to test the brave and the meek,' 11:50-51) (such cases are mostly in verse).

One can say that the order subject + verb + direct object (except personal pronouns) is "normal"; but many special factors can change this. Questions, of course, usually invert subject and verb (13.5), and wishes do so to a lesser extent. Inversion is common in main clauses preceded by a subordinate clause introduced by a subordinating conjunction: "pus me mirei en te, / M'an mort li sospir" 'since I saw myself in you, / The sighs have killed me' (37:21-22). And similarly, in interpolated clauses after a quoted utterance: "Senher, dis elha" '"Sir," said she' (14:36), and in clauses introduced by a subordinating conjunction (other than *si* 'if,' *car* 'because,' and *que* meaning 'that'): "que non era adoncs negus chantars apellatz cansos" 'for then no composition was called "song"' (51:7-8).

As the above examples show, the verb tends to gravitate toward the second position; so, if preference or emphasis places some element other than the subject first, the verb generally comes next, except for a pronoun subject. The foregoing element can be an adverb or adverbial locution (except for negative particles): "Longa sazon lo mantengront siei paren" 'For a long time his relatives supported him' (81:6). Or, a prepositional locution: "per cui a om pretz" 'because of which one has worth' (36:45). Or, a direct object: "Eu dic de totz, que·l pretz n'a trach l'engans" 'I say from them all, for deceit has taken the prize' (50:40). Naturally such word order is also possible where no subject is expressed, as here, with a predicate adjective or noun: "Quar genser etz" 'For you are the most pleasing one' (90:44).

Despite the foregoing generalizations, in verse at least, word order has almost infinite possibilities; particularly elements like adverbs and prepositional locutions are placed according less to any grammatical principle than to rhythm, emphasis, and other stylistic factors, as when Bertran de Born juxtaposes lines like those starting "Joves es domna" and "Et es joves domna" '(And) a lady is young" (79:17,22). As another illustration of such freedom, the subject or other element of a subordinate clause is often placed before the conjunction or relative pronoun that introduces the subordinate clause, thus: "Que genser cors no crei qu'el mon se mire" 'For I don't believe that a more pleasing body can be seen in the world' (30:16).

13.7 General Syntactical Observations

Among other syntactical phenomena that permit stylistic effects, we have already seen ellipsis in the occasional omission of object pronouns (8.5), of *que* (9.5, 13.4), and of the verb in short questions, answers, and exclamations (13.5). Alongside the elliptical construction "Mans jonchas" '(with) hands joined' (12.7,2), we find "cap cli" '(with) head bent,' "cara rien" '(with) laughing face,' etc. Ellipsis of a noun or demonstrative pronoun is shown in "Vers Dieus, el vostre nom e de sancta Maria" 'True God, in your name and (in that) of Saint Mary'

(97:1). Ellipsis of the second verb in parallel structures such as comparisons is frequent: "ie·ls pretz aitan pauc quon ilh me" 'I esteem them as little as they (esteem) me' (154:42). On the other hand, in such cases the vicarious verb *far* can also prevent undesired repetition of the verb: "Car aissi tremble de paor / Com fa la folha contra·l ven" 'For I tremble from fear / Just as the leaf does in the wind' (27:43-44).

Asyndeton, the omission of conjunctions, permits the juxtaposition of parallel elements: "son cantar magre dolen" 'his thin, doleful singing' (54:15). This effective device shows an affinity for participles: "jauzens jauzitz" 'rejoicing and joyous' (23:12), etc. (for more examples, see 12.3).

Pleonasm, the contrary of ellipsis, has already been noted in some uses of pronominal verbs (8.10) and in the unnecessary repetition of the conjunction *que* (13.4). Pleonastic anticipation or restatement of a noun by a personal pronoun is also not rare, for example, "Dieus l'aon e·lh don poder e forsa / Al comte" 'May God aid him and give him power and strength, / To the count' (148:78-79). Another type involves a personal pronoun restating a relative pronoun: "un drap que foc no·l pot cremar" 'a cloth that fire cannot burn' (181:49-50). And similarly, we find a possessive adjective reiterated by *a* plus a possessor or by an indirect object pronoun: "lor orgolh lor an doblat" 'they [the kings] have doubled their [the Moors'] pride' (89:37). Other pleonasms include a subject pronoun restating a prior noun or pronoun subject, usually after an intervening locution or clause; and the pronoun *en* anticipating a subordinate clause.

Anacoluthon is an abrupt change in construction that leaves the beginning uncompleted: "E, li dui siei fraire, l'uns avia nom n'Ebles e l'autres Peire" 'And, his two brothers, one was called Lord Eble and the other Peire' (125:2-3). A related syntactical peculiarity is the occasional use of "dangling" prepositional locutions--those without reference to their grammatical subject--, with the result that expressions like "ses vezer" or "per cobrir" must then be translated passively, as 'without being seen' or 'by being covered' (cf. with participles, 12.3).

Finally, zeugma, in which a single word governs two grammatically or logically different terms, is not infrequent after verbs of feeling and saying: "el se crezia drutz de totas e que cascuna moris per el" 'he believed himself the lover of them all and that each one was dying for him' (83:16-17).

Such constructions as all the above help give Provençal syntax the characteristic flexibility and expressiveness whose possibilities the troubadours so masterfully exploit.

13.8 Word Formation

One sometimes has the impression that the OP language must comprise chiefly words specialized in analyzing nuances of feeling. In fact, though its total lexicon is not large by modern standards, OP has its share of terms referring to daily life and a fairly complete array of largely Latinate words describing religion, law, medicine, and the other ideas and sciences of the time.

The vast majority of OP words and roots are inherited or borrowed from Latin; the rest are derived directly or indirectly from the following, in approximate order of importance: the Germanic idioms, Celtic, Greek, Arabic, French, Italian, a small pre-Indo-European stock, and a scattering of other or unknown sources: also, there are some onomatopoeic terms, often international, such as *miular* 'to meow.' The above elements also served to create numerous new words by prefixation, suffixation, composition, or a combination of these. Since it is not always easy to tell whether a particular juxtaposition of elements first arose in Provençal or in a sister language or Latin, we will merely give examples that show words whose component elements are recognizable in OP, whatever the chronology of their creation.

The major "living" prefixes--those which served to form new words in OP--are *a-* 'to, towards,' *contra-* 'against,' *denan(t)-* 'before,' *de(s)-* 'from, out of' or negative or intensifying, *en-*, *em-* 'in, inside,' *entre-* 'between,' *for(s)-* 'out of' or negative, *mes-*, *men(h)s-* 'badly' or negative, *non-* 'non-,' *oltra-* 'excessively,' *re-* 'again,' *reire-* 'behind,' *sobre-* 'very, very great' (for *sobre-* in absolute superlatives, see 7.14), and *sotz-* 'under.' Also used as prefixes are the preposition *sen(s)* 'without' and adverbs like *ben* 'well' and *mal* 'badly.'

A few representative examples of prefixation are *desamat* 'unloved,' *forsenar* 'to lose one's reason,' *me(n)scrẹire* 'not to believe,' *reiregarda* 'rear guard,' and *sobrafan* 'excessive suffering.'

While most prefixes apply to various parts of speech, suffixes can determine not only part of speech--like *-men(t)* used to turn adjectives into adverbs (13.2)--but also conjugation, declension, and even gender. Verbs can be formed from other parts of speech by adding the "living" infinitives *-ar* and, less often, *-ir*: (thus, *enansar* 'to advance'; (cf. *enans* 'forward'); *bailir* 'to govern' (cf. *baile* 'governor'). Also, we find more complex suffixes like *-ejar*, its learnèd variant *-izar*, and, especially with colors, *-(e)zir*, thus *domnejar* 'to court' (cf. *domna* 'lady'), *evangelizar* 'to evangelize' (cf. *evangęli* 'gospel'), and *negrezir* 'to blacken' (cf. *nẹgre* 'black').

Suffixes forming nouns, along with the resulting gender and connotations, are indicated in the following chart; the thematic vowel of the corresponding verb normally precedes those suffixes indicated as beginning with a consonant.

persons	*abstractions*	*concrete things*
		-al (m.)
		-alh (m.)
	-alha (f.)	-alha: collective, etc.
-aṇ, -ana		
	-aria (f.)	-aria
		-art, -arda: pejorative
		-as/sa: quantity, size
	-at (m.): domains, etc.	-at: young animals, etc.
	-atge (m.)	-atge: collective, etc.
		-aut, -auda: pejorative
	-da (f.): contents, extent, etc.	
-dọr (nom. -aire, -ẹire, -ire), -airitz, -eiritz: agents (cf. 5.4.3,B)		-dor, -doira: places, tools; verbal nouns and adjectives (12.4)
	-dura (f.)	
-ȩl/la, -ẹl/la		-ȩl/la, -ẹl/la: often diminutive
		-ẹlh/a
		-ẹnc/a
-ẹs/a: inhabitants	-ẹs/a	
-ẹssa (f.)		
-ẹt/a: generally diminutive		-ẹt/a: generally diminutive
	-ẹza (f.)	
	-ia (f.)	-ia: collective, etc.
-iȩr, -(i)e(i)ra: professions, etc.	:-ier, -(i)e(i)ra	-ier, (i)e(i)ra: trees, places, clothing, instruments, etc.

persons	*abstractions*	*concrete things*
		-il (m.) -ilha (f.)
	-ioṇ (f.): learned words	
		-is/sa
	-men(t) (m.) -nsa (f.)	-men(t)
		-ǫl/a: diminutive
-oṇ, -ona: mostly diminutive		-ǫ̣n, -ona: diminutive, including animals
	-ọr (f.) (but cf. -dọr)	-or (m.): holidays, lineage, rank, ethnicity, etc.
-ǫt/a: diminutive		-ot/a: diminutive
	-tat (f.)	
		-tǫri: use, place, etc.
	-ura (f.) -zoṇ (f.)	

Wherever the above chart gives different masculine and feminine variants, that suffix also generally serves to form adjectives, thus *ausart* 'daring.' Other adjectival suffixes include -*able*, -*ible* (possibility), -*al* (connection), -*at*, -*it*, *ut*, f. -*ada*, -*ida*, -*uda* (mostly past participles), -*iṇ*, *ina* (resemblance, composition), -*iu*, -*iva*, and -*ọs/a* (quality, quantity).

In addition, "deverbal" adjectives and nouns consist of the verb stem alone (hence with a "zero suffix") or with a thematic or supporting vowel: *plọr* 'weeping,' *espẹr(a)* 'waiting,' *cambi* 'change,' *paga* 'pay,' *consir(e)* 'care,' *dọpte* 'doubt.'

Some parts of speech are readily turned into others. Participles of course can be used as adjectives, and present participles can form nouns indicating persons who perform an action, such as *claman* 'one who cries out' or *entenden* 'lover' (for *ęsser* + present participles and -*dọr* words, see 12.3-4). Past participles can become nouns referring to persons acted upon (*plevit*, *plevida* 'promised one') or, less often, abstractions (*blasmat* 'blame,' *saubuda* 'knowledge'). And other adjectives can become nouns indicating personal characteristics ("gilos brau" 'cruel, jealous ones,' 23:45) or abstractions (*lo vẹr* 'the truth'). We find another change of grammatical category in infinitives used as nouns (12.12). A more unusual shift is the use of the preposition *pẹr* as an intensifying adverb: "molt per fon genta sa fis" 'his end was very, very noble' (20:18).

The other means of word formation is composition: two words with independent existences are joined, whether first in Provençal or previously, to create a new word. A noun can be formed from a noun accompanied by an adjective (*malcǫr* 'anger,' *ormię̨r* 'pure gold'), or from an adverb plus a noun or infinitive (*benvenguda* 'welcome,' *nonsaber* 'ignorance'). Or, we find two nouns juxtaposed (*aigarǫsa* 'rose water,' *terratrẹmol* 'earthquake'), or a verb plus a noun, usually a direct object (*cobricap* 'veil covering the head'). Adjectives can be formed from a noun plus an adjective (*capdescubę̨rt* 'bare-headed') or from an adjective accompanied by an adverb (*malastruc* 'unfortunate'). Finally, an adverb or noun can be joined to an extant verb to form a new one: *maldire* 'to curse,' *capvirar* 'to turn one's head.'

The processes of derivation and composition produce some rich word families, for example, the root *am-* gives us not only the familiar *amor* 'love,' *amar* 'to love,' and *aman(t)* or *amador* 'lover,' but also more complex formations like *sobrenamoramen(t)* 'excessive love,' with its two prefixes and two suffixes.

Word creation is a resource open not only to the language as a whole but to individual speakers as well. Thus Marcabru apparently creates *corna-vi* "wine-guzzler,' *coita-disnar* 'food-snatcher,' *bufa-tizọ* 'fire-blower,' and, from a verb plus a prepositional locution, *crup-en-cami* 'stick-in-the-mud' (11:46-48). And Arnaut Daniel, the champion in this domain, introduces an average of two neologisms, such as the striking *s'enonglar* 'to cling with the nail' (70:31), in each of his poems. Onomatopeia also offers creative possibilities, as in William IX's nonsense words "Babariol, babariol, / Babarian" (4:29-30).

In sum, a rich lexical stock and varied modes of word creation join a flexible and expressive grammatical system to make the subtle and expressive language that permitted the great achievements of the troubadours and other writers in a broad spectrum of literary and didactic domains.

Chapter 13: Exercises

Comment on the outstanding syntactical features of the following quotations, drawing upon our discussions in Chapter 13 and others, particularly 12.

1. C'anc non estei / Jorn d'Aragon qu'el saut / No·i volgues ir (67:99-101)
2. Del rey d'Arago vuelh del cor deia manjar (154:25)
3. Per una joja m'esbaudis / Fina (19:13-14)
4. Anz vol guerra mais que qualha esparviers (77:8)
5. Mais la vol non ditz la boca·l cors (69:11)
6. Qe neis li pastor de la montagna, lo maior solsatz qe ill aiant, an de chantar (179:26-27)
7. E las charcers en que m'a mes, / No pot claus obrir mas merces (27:21-23)
8. Que pus es ponhens qu'espina / La dolors que ab joi sana (22:26-27)
9. Quar molt castiava la follia d'aquest mon, e los fals clergues reprendia molt (137:9-10)
10. E, pus no·ns val arditz, valgues nos gens! (32:48)

ANSWERS TO EXERCISES

(Chapters 1 and 11 have no exercises.)

Chapter 2

A.1. dọ́ussa: Latin dŭlcem, French douce, Spanish dolce, Italian dolce, etc.

2. estǫ́ria: histŏria, histoire, historia, storia, etc.
3. sǫ́zer, sŏcerum, suegro, suocero, etc.
4. cortẹ́s: French courtois, cortés, cortese, etc.

B.1. Cánti, cántas, cánta, cantám, cantátz, cántan

2. Guilhém Cómte de Peitę́us, Bernárt de Ventadọ́rn, Raïmbáut d'Aurénga, Folquẹ́t de Marsę́lha, Lanfránc Cigála, Cerveríṇ de Giróna
3. Álba, cansóṇ, dánsa, descǫ́rt, pastorę́la, tensóṇ

C.1. fer'; estranhez': 11 (2:14)

2. s'; teni'; qu': 14 (2:21)
3. Qu'; l': 8 (19:6)
4. coind': 7 + (68:1)

D.1. 10 + (70:27)

2. 8 (73:24)
3. 10 (78:18)

Chapter 3

A.1. /gan/ (3.6)
2. /ọrgu̯ǫ́l̯/ (3.6)
3. /nadáu̯s/ (3.6)
4. /dọu̯s/ (3.6)
5. /fu̯ǫk/ (3.8)
6. /trü̯ęp/ (3.8)
7. /agí/ (3.6)
8. /pọǧár/ (3.7)
9. /maǧọ́r/ (3.7)
10. /süi̯/ (3.7)
11. /kai̯tíu̯/ (3.6)
12. /mau̯vái̯s/ (3.6)
13. /li̯ęi̯s/ (3.11)
14. /ü̯ęi̯t/ (3.11)
15. /mu̯ǫu̯/ (3.11)
16. /vaki̯ę́ra/ (3.6, 3.18)

B.1. ca-dię́-ra (3.8)
2. to-a-lhǫ́-la (3.10)
3. su-áu (3.6, 3.10)
4. es-ci-én (3.10)
5. fi-án-sa (3.10)
6. pa-ráo-la (3.6, 3.10)
7. jau-zi-on-da (3.6, 3.10)
8. cam-po-lię́it (3.11)

C.1. Di·m; qu'el; 8 (76:50)
2. autr'; 10 (78:13)
3. enueia·m; 8+ (101:46-47)
4. N'Elias; s'ieu; 8 (126:33)
5. maïstria; 8+ (138:45)

Chapter 4

A.1. /dẹ sai gárda dẹ lai̯ gín̯a/
2. /ę sü̯i̯ bẹ fǫls kar mẹn rẹgárt/
3. /dẹ tal gíza kẹ nọm pü̯ǫsc aǧüdár/
4. /kü̯ídọn káǧa pẹrdüt sọn sẹn/

B.1. abat (4.4)
2. amiga (4.8)
3. belazor (4.13)
4. domna (4.4)
5. frejamen (4.7, 4.11)
6. guerra (4.8, 4.12)
7. umil (4.5)
8. lancan (4.7, 4.8)
9. locs (4.8)
10. loncs (4.8)

11. molher (4.13)
12. nuts (4.7)
13. ops (4.6)
14. catre (4.8)
15. semblar (4.14)
16. senhor (4.14)
17. setmana (4.5)
18. serf (4.9)
19. vert (4.7)
20. vida (4.7)

C.1. canto (4.10,A; 4.11,B; 4.14)
2. cenc (4.7)
3. dotz (4.10,A, 4.13)
4. fas (4.11,B)
5. fil (4.10)
6. placa (4.10,A)
7. placa (4.11,A)
8. renha (4.11,A)

Chapter 5

A.1. F. 2.F. 3.M. 4.F. 5.F. 6.M. 7.M. 8.M. 9.M. 10.F.

B.1. emperaire, emperador, -Ø, -s
2. fabre, -Ø, -Ø, -s
3. jauzire, jauzidor, -Ø, -s
4. gat/z, -Ø, -Ø, -z
5. invariable
6. evangelista, -Ø, -Ø, -s
7. poch(s), -Ø, -Ø, poch(s)
8. om, ome, ome, omes

C.1. sazoṇ/s, -Ø, -s, -s
2. esperansa, -Ø, -s, -s
3. part/z, -Ø, -z, -z
4. verge, -Ø, -s, -s
5. mọlher, molhȩr, -s, -s
6. invariable

D.1. (18:1) Cercamons (5.10, 5.4.1), joglars (5.10, 5.4.1)
2. (28:1-2) Chantars (5.10, 5.4.1), cor (5.11, 5.4.4), chans (5.10, 5.4.1)
3. (4.75) Sor (5.10, 5.5.3), banh (5.11, 5.4.1)
4. (20:13-14) comte (5.11; 5.4.3,A), Proeza (5.11, 5.5.1), compaing (5.10; 5.4.3,C)
5. (20:31-32) Gasco (or *-on*; 5.10, 5.4.1), segnoriu (5.11, 5.4.1)

6. (23:1-2) chan (5.11, 5.4.1), essenhadors (5.11, 5.4.3,B) ensenhairitz (5.11, 5.5.4)
7. (24:6-7) Flors (5.10, 5.5.2), albespis (or -*ns*; 5.11, 5.4.1), yverns (5.10, 5.4.1)
8. (4.77-78) jorns (5.11, 5.4.1), forn (5.11, 5.4.1)
9. (116:5-6) Amix (Amics; 5.10, 5.4.1, 5.6), Peirols (5.10, 5.4.1)
10. (20:53-54) baro (or -*on*; 5.11, 5.4.3,C), pelegris (or -*ns*; 5.10, 5.4.1)

Chapter 6

A.1. ·l; l' (54:23-24)
2. li; ·lh, etc.; ·lh, etc.; las (75:1-2)
3. La; ·l; l' (97:12-14)

B.1. Ø (*lo* would be emphatic); d'un, d'una (both could be Ø, but the indefinite articles here mark his parents as individuals rather than class symbols) (26:1-2)
2. Ø; Ø (23:34)
3. pel (or *per lo*); De (4:23-24)
4. Ø; d'; la; ·ls; ·l; ·l (28:6-7)
5. d'; del; Ø (83:1-2)
6. Ø; la; de (1:5)
7. us (here with particularizing force; or Ø); de l'; de; Ø; d'un (or *del*); Ø; Ø (71.I;1-2)
8. Ø; de; d'; d'; del; de las (the last two are limited) (60:16-18)
9. Ø; de; Ø; Ø (88:1)
10. Ø; Ø (22:29)
11. d' (25:21)

12. li (particularized); ∅; ∅ (general); d' (24:1-2)
13. ∅; ∅ (37:15-16)
14. ∅ (a generality; or *La*); lo (here more clearly specified) (64:22-23)

Chapter 7

A.1. M. sg. and nom. pl. paubre, obl. pl. paubres; f. sg. paubra, pl. paubras
2. M. cortes; f. sg. cortesa, pl. cortesas
3. M. nom. sg. and obl. pl. gentils, obl. sg. and nom. pl. gentil; f. nom. sg. and pl. gentils, obl. sg. gentil

B.1. longa (33:3)
2. freja (29:15-16)
3. sals; sas (or -*ns*) (38:44)
4. bona; jauzionda (29:53)

C.1. fis (or -*ns*); naturaus (28:50)
2. tris; dolens (33:4-5)
3. joves (or -*ns*); gaia; gran (26:38)
4. Bela; pros (31:50)
5. Fer; esqiu (20:33-35)
6. mort (89:2-3; agrees with nearer noun)

D.1. majors (1:1)
2. gensor; plus avinen (34:51-52)
3. menor (34:26-27)
4. belaire (15:33)
5. męlher (28:52)
6. lonhor, pejor (36:41-42)

E.1. Nom. sg. lo májer om, obl. sg. lo major ome, nom. pl. li major ome
2. lo męlher senher, lo melhor senhor, li melhor senhor
3. la gẹnser sor(re), la gensor seror, las gensors serors

Chapter 8

A.1. mi (me) (4:39)
 2. me (mi) (4:41)
 3. s' (3:25)
 4. li (lhi) (8:15)
 5. li (lhi); ·m; si (se) (8:36)
 6. vos; ·us (62:55)
 7. me (mi); lui (el, elh) (64:2)
 8. liei (lei, leis, lieis, ela, elha) (68:6)
 9. nos (93:23)
 10. lor (lur) (109:13)

B.1. o (8:22)
 2. ·n (m'en): n' (38:58-59)
 3. ·y (·i) (111:35-36)
 4. o, en (143:37)

C.1. nostre (5:27)
 2. mas (mias); so (son, seu) (7:24)
 3. vostra (62:54)
 4. mon (mo, meu); m' (mi'); mon (mo, meu); mos (meus); ma (mia) (65:15-16)
 5. sieus (seus); mieu (meu) (68:25-26)
 6. lor (99:13)

Chapter 9

A.1. sest' (24:39)
 2. aicist (31:11)
 3. aquestz (-sts, -tz) (54:1)

B.1. selha (sela, sil, silh) (14:6-7)
 2. aicel (aicelh) (28:46)
 3. aquilh (aquil) (84:8-9)

C.1. So c' (qu') (37:35)
  2. Aco; que (139:29)
  3. la quals (la cals; more usual is *que*) (58:12-13)
  4. cela (celha, cil, cilh); cui (45:10)
  5. que (10:20)

D.1. Que (48:6)
  2. Cals (43:3)
  3. cals (4:3-4)

E.1. quecx (-cs) (59:8)
  2. Mout (81:11-12)
  3. ren; quan (3:20)
  4. tanta; aital (tal) (15:20-21)

F.1. onzeṇ
  2. quatre vint e nou
  3. cinc cens e detz e set

Chapter 10

A.1. 2 sg. pres. ind.
  2. 3 pl. pres. ind.
  3. 1 and 3 sg. pres. ind.
  4. 2 sg. pres. ind.
  5. 2 sg. pres. subj.
  6. 3 pl. pres. subj.
  7. 2 sg. pres. subj.
  8. 1 pl. impf. ind.
  9. 2 pl. impf. ind.
  10. pres. part.
  11. 2 pl. fut. ind.
  12. 2 sg. cond. A.

B.1. bẹc, beguem
  2. cazẹc, cazeguem
  3. ceis, ceissem
  4. aucís, aucizem
  5. recẹup, receubem
  6. vi, vim

C.1. 1 and 3 sg. impf. subj.
  2. 2 pl. cond. B
  3. 2 sg. plupf. subj.
  4. 1 pl. past cond. B
  5. 1 sg. compound past, f.
  6. 3 pl. compound past, passive

D.1. 122:23: fortz (10.12), destrenc (10.11,B; could be *destrenh*)

2. 116:30: prec, guit (both 10.12)
3. 145:21-24: menasset, maldis (10.18,A3), juret, ris (10.18,A4), parlet, saup (10.18,A5), fes (10.18,A6)

E.1. contẹn, 1 sg. pres. ind. (10.9)
2. morí, 3 sg. pret. (10.17)
3. tesquẹt, 3 sg. pret. (10.18,A1)
4. deguessẹtz, 2 pl. impf. subj. (10.19)

Chapter 12

1. Condition: *si* + pres. ind. ... pres. ind. (12.9). *Aman*: gerund, 'by or while loving' (12.3). *Far*: inf. complement of *cuidar* (12.12).
2. *Levem*: 1 pl. pret. indicating an event (12.5); comp. 1 sg. and 2 sg. subject. *Era*: impf., describing a state (12.5). *Ai estat*: comp. past, a repeated action still pertinent to the present (12.5).
3. *Venc*, *saup*: pret. for completed events (12.5); *saup* therefore means 'learned' rather than 'was aware.' *Se era levatz*: an earlier event in the plupf. (12.6); a pronominal verb whose past part. agrees with its subject (12.7,1). *Era*: impf. describing a state (12.5).
4. *Sia*: subj. with an indefinite of generalization (12.8,D2); *ęsser* plus active verbal noun (12.4). *Diga*: subj. after relative pron. (perhaps best 12.8,C3: the lack of article makes *ben* speculative, as if preceded by *tot lo*). *Men*: pres. ind.
5. *Prometia*: impf., habitual action (12.5). *Plagues*: impf. subj., posterior to action of main verb (12.8,F3), after an indefinite (12.8,D1). The

impf. ind. *demandava* envisages his requests as fact, not eventuality.

6. *Cuieriant se*: impf. ind. with a mental state (12.5). Condition: *si* + impf. ind. ... cond. A (12.9); for the rare *-t* see 10.6. *Tengues* : impf. subj. posterior to action of main verb (12.8,F3) of believing (12.8,A6). *Entendesson*: impf. subj. simultancous to *dizion* (12.8,F3), which denies reality (12.8,A5).
7. Passive (12.10) impf. subj. for a previous action (12.8,F3) after superlative plus relative pron. (12.8,C4).
8. *Fetz*: pret. for events (12.5), twice in *far* plus inf. with passive sense (12.12). *Dava*: impf. ind., habitual action (12.5); takes *a(d)* with following inf. (12.12). *Era*: impf. ind., since he affirmed a state.
9. Impersonal *fa(i) greu* 'it is difficult' (12.12) cond. *qui* 'if someone ...' (12.9)
10. *Dis*: pret., an event (12.5), with *que* pleonastically repeated (13.4). Condition: *si* + impf. subj. *volgues* ... cond. A. *deuria* (12.9), with dependent inf. *voler* (12.12). *Dizia* and *fazia*: impf. for a past habit (12.5). *Disses*, *fezes*: impf. subj. simultaneous or posterior (12.8,F3) to verb of desiring (12.8,A1).

Chapter 13

1. *Anc non* ... *jorn* 'never' (13.3); *de* 'away from' (cf. 13.1); subjunctive after a negative expression (12.8.A5); noun-derived adverb (13.2); the second *non* is not pleonastic!

2. *De* introducing the true subject (13.1); omission of *que* (13.4); *dever* in a modal periphrasis (12.12).
3. Rare separation of attributive adjective from the noun (13.6).
4. Adverbial comparison (13.2) with ellipsis of verb (13.6); inflection shows *esparviers* is nom. sg., hence the subject, following the object *qualha* (the contrary is grammatically possible but doesn't make sense in the context).
5. Ellipsis of *que* in a comparison (13.4); quite recherché word order, since *cors* can only be the subject of *vol*; both verbs precede their subject (13.6).
6. Expressive word order (13.6); subject + object (including pleonastic restatement of subject, 13.6) + verb (one also expects restatement of the object: *l'an* ...).
7. Object + verb + subject (13.6); *mas* in comparison introducing nominative (13.4).
8. Unusual separation of *p(l)us* (7.11) and the corresponding adjective (derived from a present participle, 13.7); if we ignore *pus*, both verbs are second in their clauses (this word order achieves heptasyllabic lines and spaces out the three alliterating *p*'s in the first line).
9. Artful word order (13.6) produces triple chiasmus: adverb + verb + object; object + verb + (repeated) adverb.
10. Verb before subject, then first in a main clause after a subordinate (13.6); noun derived from a past participle (13.7); optative imperfect subjunctive (12.2); note also root repetition in two forms of *valer*.

READING SELECTIONS

The following selections provide easier reading than is afforded by the troubadours' lyric poetry. We have respected the texts and spellings of the various editors, except as mentioned; and have corrected obvious typographical errors without mention. Selections are arranged not in chronological order but approximately in order of increasing difficulty.

A. *AISO SON LAS NATURAS D'ALCUS AUZELS E D'ALCUNAS BESTIAS*

This late thirteenth-century bestiary, which belongs to a tradition stretching back to the second-century Greek *Physiologus*, exemplifies the postclassical language with its breakdown of the case system and certain phonetic developments. Our text is from Carl Appel, ed., *Provenzalische Chrestomathie*, 6th ed. (Leipzig: O.R. Reisland, 1930), 201-4.

Del pol. La natura del pol es que canta lo vespre, can sent venir la nuech, pus soven, e·l mati, can sen venir lo iorn, canta pus soven; e vas la mieia nueg engrueissa sa vot, e canta pus tart e pus clar.

Del aze. La natura del aze es que canta cant a fam et om mais se trebalha.

Del lop. La natura del lop es que, can ve hom' enans c'om lo veya, el li tol lo parlar; e si l'ome lo ve enans, l'ome li tol la forsa. Et a·l col tan rot que no'l pot plegar. E so que cassa, va fort luenh de sa lobeyra; e cant vol intrar en cortal, va fort suau, e can mena segle ab sos pes, el pren son pe a mors fort e rege, et aysi s'en venia.

Del grilh. Lo grilh a tal natura que tant ama son cantar e tan s'en delecha que no·s percassa de vianda e mor cantan.

Del signe. Lo signes a tal natura que, can deu morir, canta tan clar, que si hom li ve denan ab esturmens, el si acordara ab los esturmens; adonx conoys hom que deu morir.

Del ca. Lo ca, cant a maniat et es sadol e ples, el geta so que a maniat, e cant a fam, o torn' a maniar.

De la vibra. La vibra, can ve home nut, ela non l'auza regardar de paor; e cant lo ve vestit, no·l preza re e sauta li desus.

Del simi. Lo simi vol contrafar tot cant ve far. E cant hom lo vol penre, hom se met en loc que lo veya e caussa ·I· sabatas ab corregas e pueys laissa las sabatas e va's metre a ·I· part. E·l simi va e fay aital; e cant es caussatz, hom lo pren.

Del corp. Lo corp, cant a sos corbatos, que son ses pluma e no semblan paire ni mayre, ia non lur donara clam ni cosselh, tro que an pluma e que·ls semblo. E cant troba home mort, primieiramen li mania los huelhs e per los huelhs lo servel.

Del leon: Can lo leon a preza e home li passa denan, ia no·l tocara, que passar y pot ·VII· vetz, sol que·l home no·l regarde. Mas si l'home lo garda, el es tan senhorilh que cui' esser deceubutz, car esgart d'ome es tan senhoril, e per so el laissa la cassa e cor vas hom e·l cofon. E cant hom lo cassa, que ve que no·s pot defendre e l'aven a fugir, el cobri sas pezadas ab la coa dereire per so c'om no veya son esclau. E can la leonessa a leonat, el nais mort, e ·III· iorns lo paire crida e rugis sobre el e fay lo vieure.

De la mostela. Can la mostela a son mostelon qu'es natz, ela·l muda per paor c'om no loy emble; e si hom loy men' a mort, ab c'om loy rendes, ela·l revieu.

Del calandri. Si·l calandri porta hom denan ·I· malaute et hom lo geta sul lieg e lo calandri gara lo malaute en la cara, senhal es de guerir, e si·l gira la coa, es senhal de mort.

Serena canta tan dossamen que tot hom que l'auia ven vas luy, e non pot estar que no s'adorma, e cant es adormit, ela·l met mort.

De aspis. Aspis es la serp que garda lo basme; e cant hom vol aver del basme, hom lo adormis ab esturmens e pren hom del basme; e can ve que es enganatz el se clau la ·I^{a}· aurelha ab la coa e freta tan l'autra per terra, tro que tota l'a clauza per so que non auia los esturmens, e velha.

Del merle. Merles noiris hom volontiers; e non canta mas ·III· mes del an, e fa·l pus plazen can que auzel que sia.

Del huelh de veire. Huelh de veire es ·I· petit auzel blanc e vert et a la pus sotil vista que res que sia, que be veiria tras ·I· paret.

De la talpa. Talpa no ve, ans a los huelhs desotz lo cuer; e sen pus fort d'autra bestia; e vieu de pura terra.

Del pluvier. Pluvier vieu de pur aire del cel.

De la salamandra. Salamandra vieu de pur foc; e de son pel fa hom un drap que foc no·l pot cremar.

De l'eranh. Eranh vieu de pur' aiga.

De la trida. Can la trida a sos cadels e·ls cassadors la casson, que·l volon emblar sos tridos, els meton miralhs per aqui que els van, e prendo sos tridos. E cant la trida a perdutz sos cadels, ela torna forssenada e sec per esclau los cassadors e troba los miralhs e mira se, et a tal gaug, can se ve, que tota sa dolor pert, et aisi s'oblida de sos tridos.

Del unicorn. Hunicorn es la pus salvatia bestia que sia, que non es res que l'auzes esperar, ab ·I· corn que a sul cap. Et a ta gran plazer de flairor de pieuzela e de verginitat, que, cant los cassadors lo volo penre, els li meton el pas ·I· pieussela; e can la ve, el s'adorm e sa fauda et adoncx es pres.

De la pantera. La pantera a tan dous ale e tan be flairan, que tot' autra bestia, pueys que l'a vista, no·s vol d'ela partir, tro qu'es morta, per la flairor del ale.

De las gruas. Gruas an tal natura que s'aiuston en grans tropels. E lur natura fa las trop dormir, e la una fay la garda, can las autras dormo; e per tal que la garda no s'adorma, ela met a sos pes de petitas peiretas, per tal que non puesca estar ferma, car lur natura es que dormon en pes.

Del paon. Paon, tota la garda que a, es en regardar sa coa.

Del argus. Argus es homs que a cen huelhs, e dorm de dos en dos huelhs, et enaissi velha tostemps.

De la randola. Randola, qui trazia los huelhs a sos randolos e·ls y tornava, la maire los fay revezer. E no mania ni pais mas en volans, e non a paor d'auzel de cassa.

Del pellica. Pellican es us auzel que ama mot sos poletz; e cant sos pols lo senton venir, els baton lurs alas e donon ne al pellican per los huelhs, e·l pellican es tan ergulhos e de tal natura que totz los aussi. E cant ve que son mortz, el a gran dol, e leva l'ala et ab lo bec obri son costat et arroza·ls de son sanc, e tornon vieus.

Del castor. Lo castor es una bestia que a un membre que porta medecina e per aco lo cassa hom. E can ve c'om lo cassa, a gran paor de mort, e sap que per lo membr' es cassatz, c'aital es sa natura; et el lo pren ab las dens et arraba lo·s e laissa·l cazer el sol; e·ls cassadors venon aprop, e can vezon lo membre prenon lo e laisso·l anar; empero d'an en an remet lo menbre.

Del pic. Pic a aital natura que fai son nis en albre cavat, e cant hom li tapa son nis ab que que sia, el va per una erba e toca lo·n, e tantost es hubert.

Del erisso. Erisso a tal natura que se met en las grans rodas d'espinas, que no·l puesca hom penre, que per totas partz ponh; e garda que sia en loc pres de pomier, que dins de la barta puesca maniar.

De la cocodrilla. Cocodrilha es una bestia mala e can ve hom, ela·l devora; e cant lo a maniat, ela lo plora totz lo temps que vieu. Et estalva sse que una serp que a nom idre, ven vas la cocodrilla e fa sse adormitz; e can la cocodrilla ve que·l idres dorm, ela·l devora en un morcel; e can lo ydre ve qu'es el ventre de cocodrilla, el li trauca los costatz e va fora gauzens, e la cocodrilla mor.

Del idre. Idre es una serp que, can hom li talha una testa, el ne met doas; e d'aquel idre s'a paor la cocodrilla.

De la vibra. Can la vibra vol aver paria de sa par, el li met son cap en la boca bayan de la femela, e la femela estrenh li tan fort lo bec e·l cap al mascle que mantenen mor; e la femela reman prenhs de dos vibros, mascle e feme, e can devon naisser, els salhon per l'esquina e la mayre mor; et enaissi el mon no·n son mas dos.

De la simia. La simia fay dos simios; e cant hom la cassa, ela met sel que mens ama, sul col, e tenga se, si·s vol; e cel que mays ama, lo maior, met entre sos bras, e fug ab dos pes. E cant ve que non li val re, per tal que puesca mielhs fugir ab catre pes, ela laissa sel que mays ama, e fug s'en ab lo menor.

La serra. La serra es un peys ab alas; e can ve nau en la mar, ela met alas e va contra la nau per meravilhas a un' alenada; e tan cant l'ale li dura, ela cor, e ten o be a contrast ·lx· legas. E can l'alena li falh, el se dona tanta d'anta que tot essems se laissa anar al fons de mar.

La tortre. La tortre es d'aquela natura que, cant a perduda sa par, ia mays no s'apariara ab autra.

De la perditz. Can la perdis a postz sos huous, lo ven autra perditz, que·ls li pana e·ls cobri, e·ls coa e·ls noiris, tro que son grans, que van per tot. E can los perdigos auzon lo can de la mayre que·ls pos, tantost la entendon e segon la e laisso la falsa maire que·ls a coatz.

Del estrus. Cant l'estrus a post son huou, el lo laissa estar, que negun cosselh no·l dona; e apres lo solelh lo coa el sablon e l'espelis.

De la ganta. La ganta noiris sos gantos, e can son grans, els renoirisson la maire, aitan cant ela los a noiritz.

La upa. Cant la upa es mal empenada, ia may no se mudara co fay autr' auzel; e venon los upels et arabon li las vielhas plumas, e pueys la cobron e noirisson la tan que tota es renovelada de pluma, e noyrisson la aitan can ela los a noiritz.

Del drago. Lo drago, cant troba ren dormen, el ab lo bec de la lenga enverina hom, qu'estiers no mort mas lepan.

Del orifan. Can l'orifan vol enfantar, ela vay al flum de Tigre sobeira de India et a la riba enfanta per la paor del drago que·l li enverinaria; et aco es sa natura de totz, car lo drago a sobeirana cremor, per que ela se met en l'aiga enfantar.

Del colom. Lo colom set trop voluntier sobre aiga* per paor d'auzel de cassa, que sia leu a gandida.

De la balena. De la balena s'estalva que s'esquina par sobre mar, e venon los mariniers e pesson se que sia ilha, e meton se sus ab lur barca e fan sus lor foc per cozer lur vianda, car els se pesson sertamens que sia ilha, car ela a lo cuer de la color del sablon; e cant ela sen lo foc ela·s mou e met o tot als fons de mar.

De la volp. La volp se fa morta en cami e cobri se de terra roia, per tal que semble sancnoza, e ten la lenga tracha et esta enversa; e venon las pigas e cuion se sia morta, e picon li la lengua; et ela gieta sas dens e sas arpas e pren las pigas e las devora.

Del voutor. Voutor sent de tres legas carronhada, e sec las ostz, quar sap que cavals y morran et homes.

* "set ... aiga": we have adopted an emendation suggested by Appel (p. 204, note to line 113), whose text reads "sec ... son agre."

B. *AISO ES LA REVELATIO QUE DIEU FE A SANT PAUL ET A SANT MIQUEL DE LAS PENAS DELS YFERNS*

This is probably a fourteenth-century version of the popular legend of the descent into hell of St. Paul, guided by St. Michael. Our text is from Appel (see selection A, above), pp. 177-79, with additional paragraph demarcations introduced.

Lo dia del dimenge es elegutz, del cal s'alegron tug li angel et li archangel e li sant, car maior es de totz los autres dias.

Demandador es: cal fo que premier pregues de las animas que aguesson repaus en yfern? So fo lo bonauzat Sant Paul apostol et San Miquel archangel, que volc Dieu que visson las penas d'yfern.

E San Paul vi denan las penas d'ifern albres de foc, on vi los peccadors tormentatz e pendutz. En aquels albres li ·I· pendian per los pes e·ls autres per las mas e·ls autres per los cabels e·ls autres per las lengas e·ls autres per las aurelhas e·ls autres per los brasses. Et entorn los albres avia ·VII· flamas ardens en diversas colors, que puiavon per aquels albres. E vi en autre loc apres los albres ·VII· tormens: lo premier gran torbessalh, lo segon glatz, ...* lo ·VI· fouzers.... E ... li peccador ... cridon e queron mort e non la podon aver, car las animas no podon morir. En autra part vi lo foc d'ifern, el cal es tristeza ses alegransa, el cal es dolor durabla e gememen de cor et aondansa de lagremas e cruciamen d'animas. En autre loc vi ·I· flum mot espaventable, el cal a motas bestias diablessas, que y eron enaissi com peysos el mieg de mar. Et era totz ples d'animas peccairitz. E sobre aquel flum avia ·I· pon, per lo cal passavon totas las animas drechurieiras ses dopte, et motas animas peccairitz cuiavon passar per lo pon e trabucavon en aquel flum. E segon que fag avian, ressebian en aquel flum. E en aquel flum ac motas animas cabussadas, las unas tro als ginhols, las autras tro las aurelhas, las autras tro las lavias, las autras tro als sobresilhs, e per tostemps seran cruciadas. E Sant Paul ploret e sospiret e demandet al angel

* The text is fragmentary here; we omit some disconnected words.

que eran sels qui eran cabussatz entrols ginhols. E·l angel dis: "Aquels son que semenan estranhas paraulas. Li autre, que so cabussatz tro l'emborigol, aquels son fornicadors et otracuiadors, que non prezon penitencia. Aquels que son tro las lavias, aquels son que fan tensos en las glieyzas e non auzon la paraula de Dieu. Aquels que son tro als sobresilhs so selhs que s'alegro de la maleza de lur pruesme." E Sant Paul ploret e dis: "Ta mala es ad aquels als cals son aparelhadas estas penas!"

Apres vi ·I· autre loc tenebros qu'era ples de baros e de femnas que maniavan lurs lengas, dels cals dis l'angel: "Aquels son li renoviers dels avers, que prendon las ezuras e non an misericordia e per so son en esta pena." E pueys vi ·I· autre loc, en que eran totas las penas d'ifern; et aqui avia massipas negras que vestion vestimens negres que pudion a pega et a solpre e tenian en lors cols serpens e dragos e foc. E demandet Sant Paul qui eran aquels. E l'angel dis: "Aquestas son aquelas que non agron verginitat entro las nupcias e aussiron lurs effans e davo·ls efans a cas e·ls gitavon els flums o ad autres perdemens." E Sant Paul ploret, e·l angel li dis: "Per que·t ploras? encaras non as vistas las maiors penas d'iffern." E mostret li ·I· potz sagelat ab ·VII· sagels, e dis li l'angel: "Estaitz luenh, que puscatz sostener la pudor." Et obric lo potz, e la pudor issic mala e grans, que s'estendet sobre totas las penas d'iffern. Dis l'angel: "Aquels que son mes en aquest potz non aura desmembramen d'elh."

E Sant Paul li dis: "Cals son aquels que seran mes en aquest potz?" E l'angel li dis: "So seran aquels que non creyran Ihesu Crist que vengues en la verge Sancta Maria, ni son bateiatz ni comergat per lo cors ni per lo sanc del Senhor. Et estara l'una anima sobre l'autra aisi com estan los anhels sobre las ovelhas."

E pueys agardet el cel et en la terra e vi ·I^{a}· anima pecairitz entre ·VII· colpables ploran et udolan, e menavon la·n, car aquel iorn era issida del cors. E li angel de Dieu crideron contra aquela dizens: "Mesquina anima, car obriest en terra tan malamen?" E disseron entre els: "Veiatz d'aquesta anima, en cal manieyra mensprezet los comandamens de Dieu." Et aqui meteys aquela anima legic una carta, en que eran escritz totz sos peccatz, e si meteissa's iutiet. Et adoncx prezeron la li diable e mezeron la en las tenebras exterioras, aqui ón es dol e plor e gememen de dens. E dis l'angel: "Crezes e conoisses qu'enaissi co hom fara enaisi recebra?"

E pueyssas vi una anima qu'en menavon li angel, que era iusta, e portavon la en lo cel; et auzi la votz de ·M· milia angels alegrans e dizens: "Oy, anima bonauzada, be·t deus alegrar car tu fezist los comandamens de Dieu." Pueys aquest'anima legic una carta en que eran escrichas totas sas obras. Apres Sant Miquel la colquet en paradies, aqui on son tug li gaug, e fon faitz grans critz per els, can viron aquela anima. E li peccador que eran en yfern crideron, dizen: "Merce aias de nos, bonauzat Sant Miquel, angel de Dieu, e Sant Paul, amat de Dieu; anatz e pregatz Dieu per nos." E l'angel lur dis: "Aras ploratz, e yeu e Paul plorarem per vos, e per aventura Dieus aura merce de vos, que·us donara calque repaus."

Can auziron aiso sels que eran en las penas d'ifern, crideron ab tan gran votz et ab ·M· miliers d'angels. Adonc fon auzitz lo so de totz els dizens: "Merce, Crist!" E vi Sant Paul soptamen lo cel moure, e·l filh de Dieu dissendet del cel, e crideron sels qu'eran en yfern, dizen: "Merce, filh de Dieu altisme!" Et aqui meteys fon auzida la votz de Dieu per totas las penas: "E com podetz a mi querer repaus? qu'ieu fuy crucificatz per vos et ab lansa feritz et ab clavels clavelatz et ab fel abeuratz. Et yeu meteys me doney per vos, que vos ab mi venguessetz. Mas vos fos messongiers e cobes et enveyos d'avers et ergulhos et maldizedors et anc nulh be ni almoinas ni penidencia no fezes; fos messongiers e felos en vostra vida!"

Apres aquestas cauzas Sant Miquel e Sant Paul ab ·M· miliers d'angels s'aginolheron denan lo filh de Dieu, requeren repaus que aguesson lo dia del dimergue tug silh d'ifern. E·l filh de Dieu, per los precx de Sant Miquel e de Sant Paul e dels angels e ... men per la sua bontat, donet ad els repaus de la ora nona del dissapte entro la prima del dilus ... lo portier de ifern, lo cal es dig Cherubus, levet son cap sobre totas las penas d'ifern e fo mot trist; et adoncx foron mot alongatz totz sels que eran tormentatz aqui e cridavan dizen: "Benezectes sias, filh de Dieu altisme, que doniest a nos repaus de ·I· dia e ·II· nueitz; car pus es a nos de repaus que tot sel que prezem en l'autre segle." Demandet Sant Paul al angel: "Cantas penas son en yfern?" E·l angel dis: "Las penas son ·LIIII·M·, e si eran ·C· baros parlans del comensamen del mon tro aras, e cascus avia ·V·C· lengas de fer, non poirian nomnar las penas totas d'ifern".

E per aiso, cars fraires, gardem lo dimerge, que puscam renhar ab nostre senhor Ihesu Crist, nostre redemptor e salvador, le cal vieu e renha ab lo paire et ab lo sant esperit *per omnia secula seculorum. Amen.*

C. BARLAAM ET JOSAPHAT

Our selection is from an early fourteenth-century novel that reaches back via a Latin translation to an eighth-century Greek text. The beginning of this popular legend of Islamic origin introduces us to King Avenis, a persecutor of Christians who is eventually converted by his son Josaphat (ultimately derived from Buddha), after the prince's own conversion by the holy man Barlaam. Our text is from Karl Bartsch, ed., *Chrestomathie provençale*, 6th ed., rev. by Eduard Koschwitz (Marburg: N.G. Elwert, 1904; rpt. New York: AMS, 1983), columns 381-88.

En aquel temps que hom comenset los monestiers edificar, e·ls monegues e·ls hermitans comenseron a creyser la renomada de la crestiandat, fon luenh saupuda que venc tro en la terra d'India. Motz hy ac d'omes que desampareron lurs possessions e tornavan a conversion. Esdevenc si que en aquella terra ac un rey que avia nom Avenis; aquel era de mot gran poder e de mot gran riqueza, e gentil hom e poderos contra sos enemix, e de la riqueza d'aquest mont ben azondos; mays encar segon l'arma era mot mal azornatz, car el crezia las ydolas. E domens qu'el vivia aysi dousament el joy et el delich d'aquest mont, que avia aquo que si volia, veieyre li fon que una cauza tant solament li falhia, que mot l'agreuiava e mot li mermava sa gloria, so es a ssaber que non podia aver enfant.

Lo glorios linage dels crestians e las mayzons dels monegues e dels hermitans mesprezavon lo coutivament del rey, e per menassas ni per paor de mort non laysavan a prezicar la ley de Jesu Crist ardidament e ses paor. Et aco que a la ley s'apertenia, estudiozament fazian, e prezicavan lo nom de Jesu Crist. Cant lo rey Avenis auzi aquesta paraula que aytals gens s'eran levadas que mesprezavan las ydolas e prezicavan lo nom de Jesu Crist e que non doptavan morir, mot fon plen de gran yra e de gran tristor, e comanda per tota sa terra a sos baylons et a ssos senescals que totz sels que poyrian trobar que creyrian el nom de Jesu Crist, que per diversas mortz los fezessan morir. E sertas li benahurat amic de Nostre Senhor s'en annavan davant lo rey e reprenon li la soa fellonia e la soa mescrezensa. E cant lo rey o auzi, de gran yra era plens e fazia los morir per diverses martiris.

Cant la terra d'India era en aytal error, un prebost del rey que mot era de gran poder e de gran gentileza e de gran pres en la cort del rey, cant el auzi aytal fellon comandament, mesprezet la vanetat d'aquest mont tan fortmens que prezent si mezeys l'abit de religion pres e mes si en un dezert, e la soa vida era en dejunis et en vigilias. Lo rey Avenis amava lo mot e mot li portava d'onor gran. E cant lo rey auzi aytal cauza de luy, non vos pot hom dir lo gran dol que el ac en son cor, car aytal amic avia perdut, e de tot en tot crec adonx la soa yra contra los morgues. Adoncx trames sos sirvens per los puetz e per los dezertz e per motz luox que·l quezessan amablamens e que li amanessan. E cant venc a cap de pessa, aquil que l'anavan querent, serqueron tant que troberon lo; preron lo e meneron lo davant lo rey. Garda le rey e vi lo pauramens vestit, seluy que tant resplandens vestirs solia vestir e tant delicadamens solia viure, e vi lo lag e mesprezat e vestit a guiza d'ermitan. De la tristor e de la yra que avia lo rey parlava e dizia a seluy: "Oy, tu fol' arma perduda; per qual cauza tu as mudada ta gloria ni ta honor que solias aver en mon regne; car tu eras premiers en ma cort, onratz davant totz los autres; en aytal dezonor et en aytal viltat as mudada ta gloria, e que cuias gazanhar? Car totz nostres dieus e tot lo joy d'aquest mont as laysat per un home que es apellat Jesu Crist - per que as ayso fag?" Cant le bons homs auzi ayso, alegrament e sanament respondet e dis: "Reys, si tu vols de mi auzir razon, gieta de ton palays tos enemix, et adonx respondray ti d'aquo que tu volras demandar, que, tant com aquilh y seran, neguna paraula tu non poyras recebre en pas que yeu ti diyses; per razon vuelh que m'aucias, o fay de mi que ti volras." Lo rey respondet e dis: "E qui son aquist enemix que mandas hostar?" E·l benahurat li respont: "So es yra e cobeeza. Aquestas doas cauzas tollon ad home que non pot entendre razon; mas si tu hostas aquestas desobre tu, e per aquestas doas cauzas tu as en tu saviza e lialtat, verayament tota cauza diray a tu." E·l rey respont: "Hyeu ti autrey que yra e cobeeza giete de mon cor que·y fassa aver saviza e lialtat. Digas mi, don t'es venguda aytal error que aquo que vezem et auzem, aias laysat per nulla esperansa." Respont l'ermitans e dis: "Reys, si tu vols auzir lo comensament, escouta.

Els jorns de mon jovent, cant eu era joves, auzi una paraula que mot es bona e de profiech e de gran salut e que mot mi intra el cor aytant fort que hanc pueys no·n parti. La paraula es aquesta: so es a veieyre als fols que aquellas cauzas que son divinas, que hom non pot vezer, deu hom mesprezar atressi com si non eran, et aquellas que son d'aquest mont, deu hom amar e car tener atressi com si eran durablas. Non conoyses per qual cauza hyeu ay dezamparat aquest mont? Car la sobeyrana apellation m'a apellat a vida durabla; e cant plac a la benignitat de Nostre Senhor Jesu Crist que·m volc desliurar del poder del dyable, el mi fes mesprezar la vanetat d'aquest mont, et adonx yeu mi consiriey que aquest mont non era mays cant nient e vanetat, e perpensiey mi per que yeu era fatz e que·m covenia ad annar davant mon Senhor per rendre razon; et adonx dezempariey tot cant avia e segui lo, e fas li gracias; car li plac que·m desliures del poder del dyable e de las tenebras d'aquest segle e car mi demostret via per on podia annar a luy. E dic ti que neguns autres bens ni neguna autra via non es bona mays cant aquella don tu, caytieus reys, yest partitz e desesperatz, per que nos em partitz de la toa conpanhia; car nos ti vezem a Dieu dezagradable per so car tu mesprezas Nostre Senhor Jesu Crist que es senher de tot cant es et es egals a Dieu lo payre que·l sel e la terra establi e de sas proprias mans formet home e·l mes en paradis; e·l dyable per sa enveia decep lo, mas lo benigne Senher que nos formet, regardet si a las obras que avia fachas de sas mans e volc per nos sufertar mort e passion, per la qual nos desliuret de la poestat del dyable. E tu, caytiu rey, offendes en la cort de celuy que nos a fach dignes d'aytals bens ad aver, e tu yest el delieg de ton cors totz entendutz e de las ydolas que yeu veg que apellas dieus. Oy, e tu tant solament non tolles als crestians ben, que abans o fas a totz aquels que als tieus comandamens obeziyson. E sapjas en ver que hyeu non ti creyray ni non consentiray als tieus comandamens d'aquesta maniera ni encontra Dieu non faray fellonia ni mon bonfaytor ni mon bon salvador non renegaray, si tu a bestias salvagas mi liuravas per devorar o a glazi o a fuoc mi fazias morir. Non temi ni non am la prezent vida, que plena es de vanetat o d'enfermetat tant fortment que longa cauza seria a dire. Mays per bona paraula ensenha mo senher sant Johan que tot lo mont es pauzatz en malignitat, e que non vuelha hom lo mont ni las cauzas que·y son, que tot cant es el mont es cobeeza de la carn et enveia dels huelhs, e lo mont traspassa en la cobeeza de luy, et aquel que faza la volontat de Dieu permanra en durabletat. E per far la volontat de Dieu ay dezanparat totas cauzas, e de totz aquels que crezon Dieu Nostre Senhor en ay fag mos amix e mos frayres e mos parens, e d'aquels que ja foron mieu amic e mieu frayre, et yeu m'en soy lunhatz e permane en la soleza et esperi Nostre Senhor que·m fassa venir salut."

Totas aquestas paraulas e mays d'autras ganren dis le bons homs al rey. E cant lo rey l'auzi, fon mot sosmogutz en yra e volc lo ferir; mays per honor e per reverencia de si mezeys et el s'en retenc e comenset li a dire: "Caytiu, e don t'es moguda aytal perdicion que tant as aguda ta lenga a recontar aquesta fablazon? Sertas, si al comensament de tas paraulas non ti agues promes que partis yra de mi, a fuoc liurera ta carn; mas car al comensament de tas paraulas mi conjuriest e per l'amor que solia aver an tu, sufre ta vida; leva ti e fug denant los mieus huelhs que ja mays non ti veion e que non ti destrua." Adonx le bons homs s'en tornet el desert mot corrossatz, car lo martiri non avia sufert; ans sertas cascun jorn suffertava martire en sa consciencia contra las temptaciones del dyable. E cant le bons homs s'en fon annatz, lo rey fon mot yratz e consiret si de diverses turmens encontra los monegues et honorava plus largamens que non solia sos dieus e sas ydolas.

Domens que·l rey era en aytal error et en aytal pensier, un filhs li nasquet a meravilhas bels, e la gran beutat de luy figurava aquo que de luy era a esdevenir. E dizian que en tota la terra non era vist tant bel enfant ni tant agradable. Le rey ac a meravilhas gran gaug de la nativitat de luy, et apelleron l'enfant Jozaphat. E lo rey si com autre fol annet s'en al temple de sas ydolas far gracias e lauzor, e le caytiu non conoysia a qual senhor covenia rendre lauzor per lo gaug de la nativitat de son filh. E lo rey fes far festa et ajustet ganren dels coutivadors de cels que azoravan las ydolas, e de l'autre pobol ajustet ganren, et a celebrar la festa el fes ausir ganren de taurs al sacrifizi far, e donava sos dons als grans et als paucx et als rix et als paubres en la sollempnitat de la festa que·l rey fazia. Et esdevenc si que aquil cinq barons que si fazian savis de l'art de la estrolomia, aquels lo reys fazia estar e prop de si e demandava a cascun d'aquels que dizessan d'aquel enfant cals devia esser. Et ac n'i motz que dizian que l'enfant seria de gran riqueza e de gran poder e sobre totz los autres reys que enans hy avian estat. Un dels estrolomiayres que fon plus savi dels autres dis al rey: "Si con sels que m'ensenheron d'estrolomia, en tant com yeu puesc conoyser, trobi que aquest enfant non sera en ton regne, mas en autre regne melhor ses compte, et es mi a veieyre que la religion dels crestians que tu persegues el recebra, e que el mezeys y aura sa esperansa." Cant le reys o auzi, mot o receup greu, e tornet sa leticia en tristor.

En aquella ciutat on el era, basti un palays a meravilhas bel, et en aquel fes cambras mot bellas e mot resplandens; e cant l'enfant ac la etat d'enfanteza, el lo mes el palays et establi li sirvens e ministres, e aquilh eran joves mot e de gran beutat, e comandet ad aquels que negun home de lains non intres e que neguna cauza d'aquesta vida que pogues engenrar yra non li manifestes hom, ni mort ni vilheza ni enfermetat ni pauretat ni neguna autra cauza, si non era joyoza e delichable, non li aportes hom denant per so que non pogues consirar neguna cauza ad esdevenir. E comandet que neguna cauza pauca ni gran de Jesu Crist non li deches hom; et aquo que l'estrolomiayre li avia dig, mandava que sobre totas cauzas fos celat. E cant neguns dels ministres era malautes, el rey lo comandava gitar foras.

D. VIDA DE LA BENAURADA SANCTA DOUCELINA

This beautifully written early fourteenth-century life of a saint from Provence who died in 1274 is filled with asceticism and mysticism. Our excerpt is from Appel (see selection A, above), pp. 182-84.

Partia las nuetz en tres partz; e la maior partida de la nueg illi metia en legir e en orar; l'autra illi pauzava; pueis illi si levava e dizia sas matinas; e negun temps apres non tornava en lieg, mais aquel temps d'apres despendia en obras de pietat ho en oration. E cant lo iorn per lo trebaill non podia orar, la nueg apres ill esmendava, cant si degra pausar, so que lo iorn non avia pogut dire. Lo iorn et illi trebaillava en servir los malautes et en obras de pietat; la nueg illi vellava en la oracion. Era tan grans li sieua honestatz que sobre homes non gircra sos huols; et en la sieua cara, quez era sobre-bella, conoissia hom temensa, vergonha et honestat; e sobre totas cauzas fugia tota amistansa d'omes e totas lurs paraulas. Mortification de carn comenset a penre tantost et a seguir tan afortidamens que a son cors en ren non perdonava. Illi portava selici secretamens, c'om non sabia, de cuer de truega tondut, que era fers e durs e ss'encarnava en son cors que motas ves no·l podia despullar, e, cant l'avia mogut, remania son cors esquintatz e plagatz. Una ves li esdevenc que si fon tant fort encarnatz en son cors que per ren que fezes non lo poc despullar; et adonc illi, per gran necessitat costrecha, apellet la serventa, quez era femena en qui si confizava, e despullet lo li per forsa esquintant am lo cuer, e tantost illi li fes iurar qu'a res non ho disses. E tenia sench son cors destrechamens d'una corda nozada, qu'en la luogua dels nos que s'eran encarnat, eran soven li verme. Ab tot aquo portava continuamens celcle de ferre, que res non sabia per mais afligir lo cors; e desus illi portava vestirs bels e paratz, iassiaisso que draps de lur propria color amava e portava. E cant s'estalvava que li serventa trobessa ren d'aspreza de penedencia qu'illi fezes, tantost qu'illi ho pogues saber, li fazia iurar qu'a rres non o disses. Iassia atressi per penetencia en un petit de palla a l'angle de la cambra. E per so que non si repauzes en dormir, ill estacava una corda sus desobre son lieg, e de l'autre som de la corda ill si senhia, et era en maniera que, cantost si movia, li corda la tirava, e despereissia si; e tantost si levava per dire sas matinas am reverencia e metia si legir; et enaissi fortmens son propri cors ab cilicis domptava, enaissi cant fazia Sancta Cezilia verge benaurada, et atressi las nuegz aissi cant aquist verge vellava en oracion et en sanctas vegilias. Aquesta vida tenc estant en abiti seglar.

Le novens capitols es de l'estudi e de la fervor de sa oracion e de sos autz raubimens.

Gracia d'oracion avia aconsegut li sancta per lo meravillos exercici que n'avia agut, car tostemps deus sa enfansa en aquesta vertut meravillozamens s'era acostumada. E non li semblava ni crezia que res pogues ben far lo servizi de Dieu ses ella, e en totas manieras que podia, movia e envidava las autras az acostumar si en ella. Motas ves lur dizia: "Per cert sapias que tant cant continuares oracion, vostre estamens durara e perseverares en totz bens, mais pus s'envanezira entre vos autres, que dezemparares oracion, tot ho tenc per perdut, car aquisti, sa dizia, es estaqua e fermeza de tot nostre estament."

Era oracion en totas cauzas sos refugz, que semblava en ella agues adordenat tot son temps e totas sas obras. En tan gran auteza de pensa era vengutz sos esperitz que neis maniars e beures li era oracion. Mot soven neis maniant era tirada en Dieu, que cais si desnembrava, que non sabia maniar; car en totas bontatz e doussors que sentissa, contemplava e rennembrava la sobeirana dousor e boneza de Dieu, per que totas cauzas e neis si mezeusa desnembrava per la renembransa ques avia de son Seinnhor. Car aquist sancta femena fon tan resplandens en excercici d'autas vertutz, aissi con le santz amics de Dieu, sos fraires, fraire Hugo de Dinnha, avia davant dich d'ella e profetizat, dizent que non podia estar le sieus entendemens afectuos que a grans cauzas non vengues sos esperitz, tan fervens era en Nostre Senhor Dieu; car iassiaisso qu'illi fos simpla femena e ses letras, a las sobeiranas autezas de contemplacion la levet Nostre Seinnhers, car per motz cors e espazis de temps continuamens entenduda els celestials fagz, tan soven era ab Dieu en los autz raubimens, aissi cant presentmens estant ab ell, que mais semblava menes vida d'angel entre las gens que non fazia de femena.

Amava e queria luechs solitaris, per so que plus entendudamens pogues estar ab Dieu; e per aisso avia ·I· oratori mot secret, on si metia pregar Nostre Seinnhor e esser i ab Dieu plus familiarmens en sa oracion. E aquel luoc illh arozava de sanctas lagremas, e estava aqui en continua contemplacion, e d'aqui seguia si que l'amor qu'illi avia a Ihesu Crist, engenrava en ella novels deziriers, e per los cobes deziriers ill s'enbevia de novellas ardors, en tan que totas cauzas e neis si mezeussa traspassava e sobremontava. Non podia auzir parlar de Dieu ni de Nostra Donna ni neis de Sant Frances ni de sans ni de sanctas, qu'illi non fos moguda az alcun tirament. Motas ves era sospenduda en tan gran levament de contemplacion qu'estava raubida per l'espazi d'un iorn, e sentent en aquel estament sobrehuman sentiment, non connoissia ni sentia ren c'on li fezes entorn. Motas ves ho proheron alcunas personas per motz proamens que li fazian adoncs cant la vezian tan tirada en aquel raubiment, que la tiravan e la soissidavan mot fort e neis li fazian motas aficcions, que no·n la podian moure. Alcuna ves estava sospenduda en aut, que non si sufria a ren, ni tocava de pe en terra mai sol dels ·II· artels maiors, si que tan fort era eslevada en aut, sus en l'aer suferta per forsa de meravillos raubiment, que entr'ella e la terra avia d'espazi ben ·I· palm, e tan que motas ves estant en aquel raubiment li baizavan las solas desotz los pes.

Una ves, en la gleiza, illi era raubida, e ·I· noble cavalier, ques avia nom monseinnh'en Iacme Vivaut, seinnhers ques era del castell de Cuia, era en la gleiza mezeussa am son fil, lo vespre d'una festa as hora que·ll sermons era dichz. E auzi per sa moller, ques era nobla donna e devota a tot ben, per nom madonna Sansa, que·l sancta maire avia estat raubida deus lo matin entro az aquella hora, la qual illi avia acompainnhat en una capella dels fraires, on illi aquell iorn avia cumenegat. E cant le nobles homs auzi per la devota donna ques ancars era en aquell raubiment, per gran devocion e ell l'annet vezer; e vi la eslevada sus en l'aer tant aut qu'estava sospenduda per forsa d'aquell meravillos tirament ques avia sus a Dieu, qu'a ren non si sufria ni s'apilava, ans estava sobre terra tant aut que·ll nobles homs e son fill, a mot gran reverencia aginollat, li baizeron per gran devocion las solas desotz los pes, amdui lurs capions baissatz. E foron plens de meravillos gauch e d'alegrier esperitall per so que viron d'ella; e ho comteron pueis a ganres, a motas de sertezas afermant qu'enaissi de lurs huels ho avian vist e de lur bocas baisat.

Autra ves per semblant fon d'en Raimon del Puei, de la cieutat mezeussa de Massella, que la vi raubida en la glieza dels fraires davant l'autar ques avie cumeneguat; e estava en aquella maniera sobre terra que l'autres avia vist. Adoncs e aquel cieutadans am gran devocion va si aginollar, e mezuret am sa man propria l'espazi qu'estava sobre terra, e atrobet largamens un palm que non tocava en terra; e am gran fe e ell mes tot son cap, ques avia malanans, desotz los sieus santz pes e los li baizet am gran devocion. Anc pueis non ac malannansa el cap, ans ac bona e sana e sobrefort la testa per azenant lonc temps. Atressi ell avia en l'un de sos huels festola que li avia durat alcun temps e non podia garir; e anc pueis d'aquell' hora enant non senti negun toc d'aquella malautia, ans fon del tot garit denfra fort pauc de temps. Comptava atressi aquel mez[e]us que Dieus li avia fach una gran gracia per los sieus meritis: ques enans ques aisso fos ques avem dich desus, ell avia dezacordi mot gran ab sa moller, si que em pas non podian estar, tan gran doll si fazian. Car alcuna persona per malvais esperit avia fach alcunas malas obras per nozer lur que non aguessan pas, per tal que si lunnhessan. E apres, cant aisso fon agut qu'ell ac vist la sancta en aquel raubiment, en breu de temps li avenc qu'ell ac gran pas ab ella, ques aquilla persona que lur avia nogut, soptamens si reconnoc, apres cant ell s'en fon annatz, le cals venc de la gleiza a mot gran pas de cor per so ques avia vist; e aquilli persona revelet si az els e desfes so que lur avia fach; de que li persona mezesma si meravillava com ni per que li era venguda tant sopta convercion d'aquella cauza, que negun temps non crezia desfar. E adoncs ill ac tal conciencia que non pauzet tro qu'en fon confessada e que ho ac desfach. E pueis d'aqui enant non lur estalvet semblant cauza, ans visqueron ben e em pas lonc temps; e per devocion le prozoms mes pueis una filha a Robaut....

En motas de manieras si prohet li certeza del[s] sieus vers raubimens; car alcunas personas per plus fort a prohar li plantavan alenas e la poinnhian amb agullas, que ren non en sentia ni sol non s'en movia. Una ves illi era raubida en la gleiza dels fraires, e una persona aprobenquet si d'ella, e car doptava la vertat d'aquell raubiment, trais un grafi que portava e plantet lo li malamens; e anc li sancta maire non s'en moc ni ren non en senti. E trobava hom apres los blavairols e las ponchuras feras que li avian fach, en tant que·ll sancta, cant era retornada, en sentia apres motas ves gran dolor e gran afligiment, iassiaisso qu'illi non s'en plaisses. La premiera ves que le reis Karlle la vi raubida, ell volc prohar s'era ver raubiment. So fon el temps qu'era comps de Prohensa. E prohet en aquesta maniera qu'ell fes legar ganren de plomb, e davant si fes lo li gitar tot bollhent sus los pes totz descaus, e anc ren no·n senti; de que le reis la pres en tant d'amor ques en fes sa comaire. Mais apres, cant fon retornada d'aquell sant raubiment, senti mot gran dolor dels pes e tan fera engoissa que non si poc sufrir, e ganren en malaveiet, que non podia annar.

E, F, G. VIDAS and RAZOS

The *vidas*, or biographies of the troubadours, and *razos*, or attempts at explaining the circumstances of individual poems' composition, were written in the thirteenth and early fourteenth centuries by authors of whom one was Uc de Saint Circ (see E, below). Jongleurs apparently recited a troubadour's *vida* and the appropriate *razo* before performing a given song. The data on the troubadours' lives have some historical basis but the information on their loves and individual poems is either derived from the poems themselves or often entirely imagined. Our three selections are taken from Guido Favati, ed., *Le biografie trovadoriche* (Bologna: Libreria Antiquaria Palmaverde, 1961), 313-15, 184-88, and 324, respectively. For the *razos*, we give the standard "Pillet-Carstens" number of the corresponding poem.

E. UC DE SAINT CIRC

N'Ucs de Saint Circ si fo de Caersin, d'un borc qui a nom Tegra. Fills fo d'un paubre vavassor, qe ac nom n'Arcman de Sain Circ per so qe·l castels don el fo a nom Saint Circ, q'es a pe de Sainta Maria de Rocamador, qe fo destruitz per gerra e derrocatz.

Aqest n'Ucs si ac gran ren de fraires majors de si; e volgron·lo far clerc e manderon·lo a scola a Monpeslier; e qand ill cuideron q'el apreses letras, et el apres chanssons e vers e sirventes e tensons e coblas e·ls faitz e·ls ditz dels valens homes que eron adoncs ni que eron estat denan; et ab aqest saber el s'enjoglaric.

E·l coms de Rodes e·l vescoms de Torena si·l leveron mout a la joglaria ab las coblas et ab las tenssons qe ill feiron ab lui.

Lonc temps estet ab la comtessa de Benauges e per lieis gazaignet l'amistat d'en Savaric de Malleon, lo cals lo mes en arnes et en raubas, et estet lonc temps ab el en Peitieus et en las soas encontradas; e pois en Cataloigna et en Aragon et en Espaigna ab lo bon rei Amfos de Lion et ab lo rei Peire d'Aragon, e pois en Proenssa ab totz los barons, e pois en Lombardia et en la Marca Tervisana; e pres moiller en Tervisana, gentil e bella.

Gran ren apres de l'autrui saber, e volontiers l'enseignet ad autrui.

Chanssos fetz de fort bonas et de bons sons, e bonas coblas; mas anc non fo fort enamoratz: mas ben se saup feigner enamoratz, e ben saup levar las soas dompnas, e ben decazer.

Razo to 457.4

N'Uc de Sain Circ, qi fo ni don, ben l'avez auzit.

E si amava una do[m]pna d'Andutz, qe avea nom madompna Clara. Mout fo adrecha et ensenhada et avinenz e bella, e auc gran volontat de pretz e [d]'esser auzida loing e pres, e d'aver l'amistat e la domestighessa de las bonas do[m]pnas e dels valenz homes; e n'Uc conoc la volontat d'ella e saup·li ben servir d'aiso q'ella plus volia: qe non ac bonas dompnas en totas aqellas encontradas con qal[s] ell non fezes q'el' agues amor e domestigessa e no·ill fezes mandar letras e salutz e joias per acordansa e per honor; e n'Uc le' fasia las lettras de la[s] responsions qe convenian a faire a las dompnas, dels plasers q'ellas li mandavan.

Et ella soufria a n'Uc los precs e lo 'ntendimen e·ll promes de far plaser en dreit d'amor; e n'Ucs fetz mantas bonas chansos d'ella, pregan leis e lausan sa valor e sa beutat, et ella si s'abelli mout de las chansos qe n'Uc fasia de leis.

Loncs temps duret lors amors e mantas guerras e mantas patz feron entre lor, si com s'ave d'amors en amadors.

Et ella avia una vizina mout bella, qe avia nom madompna Ponsa. Mout era cortesa et ensegnada, et ac gran enveja a madompna Clara del pretz e de l'honor qe n'Uc li avia facha gasagnar; si se penset e penet con pogues faire q'ella tolgues n'Uc de la soa amistat e traes·lo a si. E mandet per n'Uc e det·li a entendre qe madompna Clara avia autre amador a cui ella volia miel qe a lui; e promes·li de far e de dir so qe a n'Uc plagues.

N'Uc, si com sel qe non fo ferms ni lials a neguna, qe vas autra part volontier non s'en procases, e per so qe gran mal l'avia dit de madompna Clara, e per bel semblant q'ella li fasia e per lo gran plazer q'ella li prometia, si se parti malemen de madompna Clara e comenset a mal dir d'ella e lausar madompna Ponsa. Mado[m]pna Clara fo mout irada et ac gran desdeng, qe non s'en clamet ni rancuret d'el.

Longa sason estet n'Uc amics de madompna Ponsa, attenden lo ben e·l[s] plagers q'ella li avia promes; et ella no·ll fetz negun, anz l'amermet chascun dia los bels acuillimenz q'ella solia far. E n'Uc, qant vi qe aisi era engannatz, mout fo dolenz et iratz, et anet·s'en a una amiga de mado[m]pna Clara e moustret·li touta la caison per q'el s'era loignatz de madompna Clara e preget·la aisi caramen com el poc, q'ella degues cercar la patz entre madona Clara e lui, e far si q'ella li degues rendre grazia e bona volontat; et ell[a] li promes de far tot so q'ell' en poria far de bon; et ella dis tant a madompna Clara e la preget, q'ella promes de far la patz con n'Uc e si ordeneren que n'Uc fos a parlamen con lor doas.

E si fo el, e fetz la patz mout amorousamen; e [d']aqesta[s] raisos si fo facha aquesta chanson que dis:

Anc mais non vi temps ni sason
ni noig ne jor ni an [ni] mes
qe tan, com er fai, mi plagues,
ni on tan fezes de mon pron:
qar soi estortz a mal' amor
ou merzes valer non poria.
e soi tornat sa[i] ou deuria
hom trobar franchessa et honor
e leal cor d'una color.

F. RAÏMBAUT DE VAQUEIRAS

Razo to 392.2

Ben aves entendut qui fo Raimbautz de Vaqueiras ni com venc az onor, ni per qui; mas si vos vueill dire que, qan l'ac fait cavalier lo bons marques de Monferrat, Raimbautz si s'enamoret de madona Beatritz, sa seror e seror de madona n'Azalais de Salutz.

Molt l'amet e la deziret, gardan·se qu'ella no·l saubes, ni autre; e molt l'enanset son pretz e sa valor, e mantz amicx li guazanhet e maintas amiguas, de luenh e de pres; et ella si·ll fazia gran honor d'acuillimen, et el moria de dezirier e de temensa, qu'el no l'auzava preguar d'amor ni far semblan q'el entendes en ella.

Mas, com hom destreitz d'amor, si venc un dia devan sella com hom amaestratz d'amor, e si·ll dis com el amava una dona gentil e jove e valen et avia gran privadansa ab ella e no l'auzava dir lo ben qu'el li volia, ni mostrar, ni preguar d'amor; tan temia sa gran ricor e sa onrada valensa; e preguet·la per Dieu e per merce qu'ela li degues dar conseill: si·l dizia son cor ni sa volontat ni la pregava d'amor, ho si morria selan e temen et aman.

Aquela gentil dona madona Beatritz quant auzit so que Raimbaut dizia e conoc l'amoroza volontat q'el avia--e denan era ben aperceubuda qu'el moria languen e deziran per ella--si la toca piatatz et amors, e si·ll dis:

"Raimbaut, ben cove que totz fis amicx, si ama una dona gentil, que·ill port honor e temensa a mostrar l'amor q'el ha az ela; mas, enans qu'el mueira, si·ll don conseill qu'el li digua l'amor e la volontat qu'el li porta, e qu'el la prec que·l prenda per servidor e per amic. Et asegur·vos be, si la dona es savia ni corteza, qu'ill non ho penra en mal ni en dezonor, ans l'en prezara mais e l'en tenra per meillor home. Et a vos don conseill que vos a la dona que amas dejatz dire lo cor e la volontat que vos li aves, e que vos la dejatz preguar que vos retengua per servidor e per cavalier: que vos es aitals cavaliers que non es dona el mon que no·us deja retener volonteira per cavalier e per servidor: qu'ieu vi que madona n'Azalais comtessa de Salutz sofria Peire Vidal per entendedor; e la comtessa de Burlatz, Arnaut de Marueill, e madona Maria, Gauselm Faidit, e la dona de Marceilla, Folquet de Marceilla; per qu'ieu vos do conseill et austorgui que vos, per la mia paraula e per la mia segurtat, la pregues e l'enqueiras d'amor".

En Raimbautz, quant auzit lo conseill qu'ela li dava e l'aseguramen qu'ela li fazia e l'autorc qu'ela li promezia, si li dis q'ela era eisa aquela qu'el amava e de la cal el avia quis con-seill; e madona Beatris si dis qu'el fos ben vengutz e ben trobatz, e qu'el s'esforses de far ben e de dire e de valer; e se anc fo gai ni amoros, q'el se deges esforzar d'esser mais; et enaisi lo retenc per cavalier: don Raimbautz fetz mantas bonas cansons d'ella, e fes adonx aquesta que dis:

Era·m requer sa costum' e son us.

Razo to 392.9

Ben avetz auzit de Rambaut qi el fo ni don, e si com el fo fait cavalier de[l] marqes de Monferrat, e com el s'entendia en madompna Biatrix e vivia jausen per lo so amor.

Et aujatz com el ac um pauc de temps gran tristessa: et aiso fon per la falsa jen envejosa a cui non plasia amors ni do[m]pneis, qe dizion paraolas a madompna Biatrix et encontra las autras dompnas, disen aisi:

"Qi es aqest Rambaut de Vaqera[s], sitot lo marqes l'a fait cavalier? E si va entendre en tan auta dompna con vos o ez, sapchatz qe non vos es onor: ni a vos ni al marqes".

E tan disseron mal, qe d'una part qe d'autra (si con fan las avols genz), qe madompna Biatrix s'en corecet contra Raimbaut de Vaqera[s]: qe qant Rambaut la pregava d'amor e·l clamava merce, ella non entendea sos precs; anzi li dis q'el se degues entendre en autra dompna qe fos per ell, et als non entendria ni auziria d'ella.

Et aqest' es la tristessa qe Rambautz ac un pauc de temps, si com eu dis al comenzamen d'aqesta rason: dont el se laisset de chantar e de rire e [de] toz autres faitz qe·l deguesson plager; et aiso era gran danz. Et atot aqest ac per la lenga dels lausengiers, si com el dis en una cobla de la stampida qe vos ausiret[z].

En aqest temps vengron dos joglars de Franza en la cort del marqes, qe sabion ben violar, et un jorn violaven una stampida qe plazia fort al marqes et als cavaliers et a las dompnas; et en Rambaut non s'allegrava nien, si q'el marqes s'en [a]percepet e dis:

"Senher Rambaut, qe es aiso, qe vos non chantatz ni·us alegratz, c'ausi[tz] aisi bel son de viola e veïtz aiqi tan bella dompna com es mia seror, qe vos a retengut per servidor et es la plus valen dompna del mon?"

Et en Rambautz respondi qe non faria rien.

E·l marqes saubia ben la caison, e dis a sa seror:

"Mado[m]pna Biatrix, per amor de mi e de totas aqestas genz, vol qe vos deignat[z] pregar Rambaut q'el per lo vostro amor e per la vostra grazia se deges alegrar e chantar e star legre, si com el fazia denan".

E mado[m]pna Biatrix fu tan cortes[a] e de bona merce, q'ella lo preget e·l confortet q'el se deges per lo so amor rallegrar, e q'el feses de nou una chanson; dont Rambaut, per aqesta raison qe vos avez ausit, fet[z] la stampida e dis aisi:

Kalenda maia
ni foll de faia
ni cant d'ausell   ni flor de glaia
non cre qe·m plaia,
pro dompna gaia,
tro c'un isnel   messagier n'aia
del vostre bel   cors qe·m retraia
[plazer novel   qu'amors m'atraia]
q'eu ai[a]
e·m trai[a]
vas vos,   dompna veraia;
e chaia
de plaia
gelos,   anz qe me traia.

Aqesta stampida fu facta a las notas de la stampida qe·l jo[g]lars fasion en las violas.

Razo to 364.47

Et esdevenc·se qe la dona se colqet dormir ab el; e·l marqes, qe tan l'amava, atrobet·los dormen e fon iratz; e, com homs savi[s], no·ls volc tocar, mas pres son mantel e cubri·los·ne, e pres sel d'en Raymbaut et anet·s'en. E cant en Raymbaut se levet, conoc tot com era; e pres lo mantel al col et anet·s'en al marqes dreg cami, et aginolhet·se denan el, e clamet·li merce.

E·l marqes vi qe saviamens era vengutz, e membret·li los plazers qe li avia fatz en mans locs; e car li dis cubertamens (per qe no fos entendutz al qerre del perdo) qe·l perdones car s'era tornatz a sa rauba, selh qe o auziron se cujeron qe o disses per lo mantel car l'avia pres; e·l marqes perdonet·li e dis·li qe mays no·s tornes a sa rauba; e no fo sauput mas per abdos.

Apres esdevenc·se qe·l marqes ab son poder passet en Romania, et ab gran aiuda de la Gleyza, on conquis lo regisme de Salonic; et adonc fon cavayers en Raymbaut per los bos fatz qe fes; e lay ly donet gran terra e gran renda; e lay mury.

E per los fatz de sa sor fetz ·I· canso qe trames a·n P[eire] Vidal, qe di:

Tant ay ben dig del marqes.

G. GUILLEM DE LA TOR

Guillems de La Tor si fon joglars e fon de Peiregorc, d'un castel qu'om ditz "La Tor", e venc en Lombardia.

E sabia cansos assatz, e s'entendia, e chantava e ben e gen, e trobava; mas, qant volia dire sas cansos, el fazia plus lonc sermon de la rason, que non era la cansos.

E tolc moiller a Milan, la moiller d'un barbier bella e jove, la qual envolet, e la menet a Com; a volia·le meilz qu'a tot lo mon.

Et avenc si que ella mori: don el se det si gran ira, qe·n venc mat, e crezet qu'ella se fezes morta per partir·se de lui: don el la laisset detz dias e detz nuoitz sobre·l monumen, e chascun ser el levava lo monumen e trasia·la fora, e gardava·la per lo vis baisan et abrasan e pregan q'ella li parles e·ill dises se ella era morta o viva; e, si era viva, qu'ella tornes ad el; e, si morta era, qu'ella li dises quals penas avia: qu'el li faria tantas messas dire, e tantas elimosinas faria per ella, qu'el la traria d'aquellas penas.

Saubut fon en la ciutat per los bons homes, si que li omne de la terra lo feron anar via de la terra; et el anet cerquant per totas partz devins e devinas, si ela mais poiria tornar viva. Et uns escarniers si·l det a creire que, si el legia chascun dia lo salteri e disia ·C· e ·L· "Patres nostres" e dava a ·VII· paubres elemosinas anz qe manges, et aissi fesses tot un an que non faillis dia, ella venria viva, mas non manjaria ni beuria ni parlaria.

El fo molt alegres quant el so auzi, e comenset ades a far so que aquest li avia enseignat, et enaisi o fez tot l'an entier, que anc non failli dia. E quant el vit qe ren no·ill valia so que a lui era enseignat, el se desperet e laisset·se morir.

H. RAIMON VIDAL DE BESALÚ, *LAS RAZOS DE TROBAR*

This Catalan troubadour (fl. 1190-1220), author also of three octosyllabic rhymed *novas*, or stories, wrote this early grammatical treatise, as he explains, for the benefit both of poets and their audiences. Our excerpt is from Appel (see selection A, above), pp. 193-97.

Per so qar ieu, Raimonz Vidals, ai vist et conegut qe pauc d'omes sabon ni an saubuda la dreicha maniera de trobar, voill eu far aqest libre per far conoisser et saber qal dels trobadors an mielz trobat et mielz ensenhat ad aqelz qe·l volran aprenre con devon segre la dreicha maniera de trobar. Pero, s'ieu i alongi en causas qe porria plus breumens dir, no·us en deves meravellar, car eu vei et conosc qe mant saber en son tornat en error et en tenso, qar erant tant breumens dig; per q'ieu alongerai en tal luec qe porria ben leu plus breumenz dir. Et si ren i lais o i fas errada, pot si ben avenir per oblit, o qar ieu non ai ges vistas ni auzidas totas las causas del mon, o per faillimentz de pensar; per qe totz hom prims m'en deu rasonar, pois conoissera la causa. Ieu sai ben qe mant home i blasmeran o diran: "aital ren i degra mais metre", qe sol lo qart no·n sabrian far ni conoisser, si non o trobessen tan ben assesmat. Autressi vos dig qe homes prims i aura de cui enten, si tot s'estai ben, qe i sabrian meilhorar o mais metre, qar greu trobares negun saber tan fort ni tan primamenz dig qe uns hom fort no i pogues melhurar o mais metre; per q'ieu vos dig qe en neguna ren, pos basta ni ben ista, non devon ren ostar ni mais metre.

Totas genz, cristianas, iusieuas e sarazinas, emperador, rei, princep, duc, conte, vesconte, contor, valvasor, cavalier, clergue, borgues, vilan, pauc et gran, meton totz iorns lor entendiment en trobar et en chantar, o q'en volon trobar, o q'en volon entendre, o q'en volon dire, o q'en volon auzir, qe greu seres en loc negun tan privat ni tant sol, pos gens i a paucas o moutas, qe ades non auias cantar un o autre o totz ensems, qe neis li pastor de la montagna, lo maior sollatz qe ill aiant, an de chantar, e tuit li mal e·l ben del mont son mes en remembransa per trobadors, et ia non trobares mot be dich ni mal dich, pos trobaires l'a mes en rima, qe totz iorns non sia en remembranza, e trobars et chantars son movemenz de totas galliardias

En aqest saber de trobar son enganat li trobador e li auzidor egalment motas vetz; e dirai vos com ni per qe: Li auzidor qe ren non intendon, qant auziran un bon chantar, faran senblant qe for ben l'intendon (et ges no l'entendran), qe cuieriant se qe·lz en tengues hom per pecs, si dizion qe no l'entendesson. Enaisi enganan lor mezeis, qe uns dels maiors sens del mont es, qi domanda ni vol apenre so qe non sap, et assatz deu aver maior vergogna cel qi non sap, qe aicel qi demanda e vol apenre. E sil qe entendon, qant auziran un malvais trobador, per ensegnament li lauzaran son chantar; o si no lo volon lauzar, al menz no·l volran blasmar. Et enaisi son enganat li trobador et li auzidor n'an lo blasme, car una de las maiors valors del mont es, qui sap lauzar so qe fa a lauzar et blasmar so qe fai a blasmar. Sill qe cuion entendre et non entendon, per otracuiament non aprendon, et enaisi remanon enganat.

Ieu non dic ges qe toz los homes del mon puesca far prims ni entendenz, ni qe·ls fassa tornar de lor enueitz ni de lor vicis per la mia paraola; pero hanc Dieus non fes tan grant error, per qe ben i sia escoutatz ni ben puesca parlar, que no·n traga alcun home qe o entendra; per qe, si tot ieu non entent qe totz los puesca far entendentz, si vueill far aqest libre per l'una partida.

Aqest saber de trobar non fon anc mes ni aiostatz tan ben en un sol luec, mais qe cascuns s'en ac en son cor, segon que fon prims ni entendenz. Ni non crezas que neguns hom n'aia istat maistres ni perfaig, car tant es cars et fins le sabers qe hanc nuls homs non se donet garda del tot. So conoissera totz homs prims et entendenz qe ben esgard' aqest libre. Ni eu non dic ges qe sia maistres ni perfaitz, mas tan dirai, segon mon sen, en aqest libre qe totz homs qi be l'entendra ni aia bon cor de trobar, poira far sos chantars ses tota vergoigna.

Totz hom que vol trobar ni entendre, deu primierament saber qe neguna parladura non es naturals ni drecha del nostre lengage mais acella de Franza e de Lemozi, o de Proenza o d'Alvergna o de Caersin; per qe ieu vos dic qe, quant ieu parlarai de Lemosy, qe totas estas terras entendas et totas lor vezinas et totas cellas qe son entre ellas. Et tuit l'ome qe en aqellas terras son nat ni norit, an la parladura natural et drecha. Mas cant uns d'els es eiciz de la parladura, per una rima qe i aura mestier, o per autra causa, miels lo conois cels qe a la parladura reconeguda qe sil qe non la sabon; et aquil non cuian tan mal far con fan, cant la iettan de sa natura, anz se cuian qe lors lengages sia, per q'ieu vuell far aquest libre per far conoiser la parladura a cels qe la parlon drecha et per ensennar a cels qe non la sabon.

La parladura francesca val mais et es plus avinenz a far romanz, retronsas et pasturellas, mas cella de Lemosin val mais per far vers et cansons et serventes, et per totas las terras de nostre lengage son de maior autoritat li cantar de la lenga lemosina que de neguna autra parladura, per q'ieu vos en parlarai primeramen.

(Mant home son qe dizon qe *porta* ni *pan* ni *vin* non son paraolas de Lemosin, per so car hom las ditz autresi en autras terras com en Lemosin; et sol non sabon qe dizon, car totas aqellas paraolas q'om ditz en Lemosin atressi com en autras terras, son aitan be de Lemosin com de las autras terras, mas aqellas q'om ditz en Lemosin d'autras gisas qe en autras terras, aqellas son propriamenz de Lemosin.)

Per q'ieu vos dic qe totz hom qi vuella trobar ni entendre, deu aver fort privada la parladura de Lemosin, et apres deu saber alqes de la natura de gramatica, si fort primamenz vol trobar ni entendre, car tota la parladura de Lemosyn se parla naturalmenz et drecha per cas e per nombres et per genres et per temps et per motz, aisi com poretz auzir aissi, si ben o escoutas.

I. SORDELLO, *ENSENHAMEN D'ONOR*

This great figure, who flourished ca. 1225-70 and spent much of his career outside his native Italy yet was later ennobled by Dante, left about forty poems or fragments in Provençal as well as a lengthy *ensenhamen*, or didactic work, from which we give a passage concerning feminine conduct. Our selection is from Marco Boni, ed., *Sordello, Le poesie* (Bologna: Libreria Antiquaria Palmaverde, 1954), 231-33.

Tota dompna, que be·s volria
far azautar als pros, deuria
esgardar las autras que·s fan
adaut per aver pretz prezan
e qu'en saupes lo mal giquir,
e·l be apenre et retenir:
qu'en quatre maneras d'azaut
son totas e de desazaut.
L'una es azauta et adautada,
e l'autra es desazautada,
e non azauta en nul endreg;
la terza adaut'als pros per dreg
e non es en si eis' adauta;
pero la quarta desazauta
a totz ab gran azautamen
de cors e de captenemen.
Cil, qu'es azauta et azautar
si fai per be dir e per far,
deu esser pels pros coronada;
e l'autr' als malvatz comandada,

que no es adauta de re,
ni fai ni dis azaut nul be,
per qu'om bos azautar s'en deia;
la terza, qu'a de pretz enveia,
que gran adautamen non a
en si, pero a la gen fa
tan quan pot amor e plazer,
deu om amar e car tener;
la quarta, de cors e de cara
azauta, que toz jornz si gara
de far e de dir azauteza
per pretz ni per avinenteza,
laiss om com malastrug' estar,
quar totz om deu dopn' azirar
azauta, pos li faill talenz
d'esser grazid' entre·ls valenz.

Pros dopna, que vol gen regnar,
cove que sia e·s deia far
orba, sorda, muda a sazo,
e dirai vos per qual razo:
que dopna non deu esgardar
zo que es laig per remirar,
qu'en l'esgardar qu'ell i esgarda
la te totz om bos per musarda;
ni deu auzir per son grat re
que no l'esteia gen e be,
e s'a l'auzir no·s pot escondre,
mal ni be no i deu respondre;
e faill trop s'a parlar s'affraign
m[as] del parlar qu'a dopna taign,
q'us calars val trop melz de taill
q'us parlars que razo trassaill;
per que dopna ses retenenza
no pot be far, quar la suffrenza
es mout bona de desplazer
que adus onor e plazer.
Mas ja be non o gardara
dopna, si noble cor non a,
quar lo nobles cors l'acompagna
a totz bes, e del mal l'estraigna.
Pero de dopna·us faz saber
que non pot noble cor aver,
si non es estraigna als privatz
e privad' als estraignz; qu'assatz
en vc om, qui que plaz' o tire,
joga[r] e solazar e rire

ab privada masnada gen,
que pos apres, quan li valen
estraign per solazar lai van,
a penas n'an un bel semblan.
D'aquestas non pot om bos vers
chantar, car regnan a revers,
quar fan zo que degran laissar
e laissan zo que degran far.
Non o dic per mal de neguna,
anz o dic per be de cascuna,
que d'ar enanz i pregnon garda,
qu'estiers nulla son pretz non garda.

Bona dopna non taign qu'esgart
d'oillz ni de cor vas nulla part
tan coralmen, qu'el mieg non sia
sos pretz per miraill tota via,
en que·s mir; qu'aitan tost perdra
son pretz com faillimen fara,
don no·ill puesca razonamenz
tener pro entre·ls conossenz.

J. MATFRE ERMENGAUD, *LO BREVIARI D'AMORS*

At the very end of the thirteenth century, a Franciscan from Béziers wrote this work of some 35,000 lines comprising an "encyclopedia" organized around the theme of the different kinds of love: for God, fellow man, the goods of this world, and woman. Our selection, from a chapter entitled "De la corruptio d'umana natura pel peccat original e quo Dieus las gitec de paradis terrenal pueys quels a formatz," is from Gabriel Azaïs, ed., *Le Breviari d'amor de Matfre Ermengaud* 1 (Béziers: Société Archéologique, Scientifique et Littéraire de Béziers, 1862), 273-82.

Dig vos ai que per natura
Homs es mortals creatura,
Pero no mortals fo creatz
De premier, quar per cert sapchatz
Que totz temps vieure podia
Si no fos per sa folia,
Quar manjet del pom elegut
Que Dieus avia deffendut.

Quar Dieus quant ac creat lo mon
E las creaturas quei son,
El pueis formet tot en derrier
De la terra l'ome premier,
E l'espeiret d'arma viven,
La qual el creet de nien,
E no fos ges creatz effans
Ans fo be d'etat de ·XXX· ans.
Apres mes lo per son cabal
Ins en paradis terrenal,
Qu'era garnitz d'albres fruchans
Delechables et hodorans
Don las fuelhas no cazian
Ni las flors nos marfezian,
Entrels quals albres avia
Un bel albre d'aital guia
Que nulhs homs que del frug manjes,
Domentre que d'aquel uzes,
Ja nulh temps malvat no fora,
Ans visquera be tota hora
Joves e fortz e vigoros
E sas e sals e delechos:
So era l'albres de vida.
Pero de l'autra partida
N'ac un autre que fon assis
Ins el mieg luoc de paradis,
Que fo nomnat de nom aital:
Albre de saber be e mal.
Adoncx det son autreiamen
Dieus a home generalmen
Que manjes assatz e culhis
De totz los frugz de paradis,
Mas per res non manges d'aital
Nomnat de saber ben e mal;
Quar saubes que si o fazia
A morir l'en covenria.
Apres Dieus ta fort l'endormi
Quel trais, quez anc re non sent,
Del costat la cost'antieira,
De quelh fetz sa companhieira,
Que lh'ajudes ad engenrar
Et autras cauzas de be far;
E si tot Dieus premieiramen
A l'home fetz comandamen,
Abans que la femna formes,
Quez el del dig frug non manges;
A femna fo fag atressi

Segon que l'escriptura di,
Quar l'oms apres loi revelet
Et ela pueis o cofesset,
Que respondet a la serpen
Segon qu'auziretz mantenen.
Femna doncx d'ome tracha fo
Per senhal de dilecxio;
E per senhal d'ajustamen
A pres Dieus d'ome solamen
Lo cors, mas l'arma, so crezatz,
Fetz de nien la Deitatz;
E las autras quascun dia
Fai Dieus cert en semblan guia;
Quar tan tost quant es semenatz
Lo cors d'ome et es formatz
Dieus creet l'arma mantenen
Ins el cors d'ome de nien.
Apres Dieus quant los ac formatz
Dis: creissetz e multiplicatz,
E quar vos ai sen e saber
Donat, auretz planier poder
Sobr'aucels, bestias e peissos,
Quar totz los ai creatz per vos,
E tot' autra creatura
Qu'en terra nais e s'atura.
Dieus doncx lor det bes terrenals
Prometen los celestials
Ab quelh fosson obedien,
Esquivan mal e be fazen.
Quan lo diables o auzi
E per cert conoc e senti
Quez om, si fos de crezensa
E gardes obediencia,
Paradis aver podia
Lo qual el perdut avia
Per son orguelh, ac mot gran mal
E cosseup eveia mortal;
Comenset tantost [a] pessar
Que pogues far home peccar,
E quar vi qu'en lunha guia
Home forsar no podia,
El cossiret de mantenen
Quel venques ab galiamen;
E quar conoc que l'oms ac pro
Mais que la femna de razo
E d'entendemen e de sen,
E que mot plus leugieiramen
La femna temptar podia,

Quar petit de sen avia,
Venc a la femna demanes;
E per so qu'elh nol conogues
E que no l'agues en azir,
Volc en autra forma venir,
Mas Dieus no sostec issamen
Qu'elh vengues amagadamen
Ni en tan bela figura
Quez umana creatura
Pogues son peccat excusar
Per la manieira del temptar;
Per que sostenc qu'el solamen
Vengues en forma de serpen;
Quar sitot de nozer a nos
Lo diables es volontos
Nons pot per cert nozer en re
Mas aitan quan Dieus en soste.
Don quant lo diables malvatz
Sobre aquo se fo pessatz
E conoc que n'ac aizina,
Venc en forma serpentina
A la femna que vic estar
Sola e nolh volc comandar
Quez fezes lo peccat per so
Que nol conogues ad aquo,
Mas en forma de demanda
Tot per falsia mot granda
Que conogues son cor tantost
Ad aquo que lh'agra respost,
Li demandet de mantenen:
Per que a fag comandamen
Dieus que vos en nulha guia
No manges de frug que sia
En lunh albre de paradis?
Respon la femna: qui o dis?
Sapchatz per cert que non es vers
Ans nos es ben donatz poders
Per lo creator, ses dubtar,
De totas las fruchas manjar
Exceptat la frucha bela
D'aquel albre qu'om apela
Albre de saber mal e be.
Dis lo diables: E per que?
--Que per aventura moriam
Dis la femna, si o faziam.
E quar dis per aventura
Parec que no fos segura,
El diables conoc o be

E dis li tantost: Sobre me
Manjat[z] del frug quar no morretz,
Ans sapchatz cert que vos seretz
Semblans al rei celestial
E conoisseretz be e mal.
Doncx la femna de mantenen
Cum fola crezet la serpen,
E manget del frug, quelh fo bos
E mout plazens e saboros.
Pueis portet del frug atressi
Al prumier home e dis li
Qu'el del frug manjar podia,
Quar ela manjat n'avia;
E quar l'oms vi que la fada
Era de mort escapada,
Crezet que disses veritat
E manjet del frug devedat.
Tantost cascus se reconoc,
Et ac vergonha quar conoc
Sa lageza, e van culhir
Fuelhas d'albres per se cobrir,
E sentiro nostre senhor
Em paradis venir vas lor,
E van s'amagar temeros
En ·I· luoc cubert e rescos
Mantenen ses autra ponha
De paor e de vergonha.
Apres aquo Dieus demandet:
On iest Adam? El respondet:
Senher aissim soy rescondutz
De vergonha quar era nutz.
Dis Dieus: Sabes que t'a mostrat
Que fosses nutz, quar as manjat
Coma fol del pom elegut
U quez ieu t'avia defendut.
Adams mantenen respondet:
Senher, la femna m'en donet
Quem donest per companhona.
Dieus! e qu'a mal se razona
De so que no pot escondir!
Quar semblava que volgues dir
Que d'aquo Dieus mal meria
Quar femna dada lh'avia.
Apres en semblan manieira
Ditz Dieus a la companhieira
Digas, femna, per qual raso
As tu facha la falhiso
Contra lo mieu comandamen?

Ela respos de mantenen:
Quar la serpen me galiet.
Quascus son peccat escuzet,
E dobleron lur falhizo
Quar non demanderon perdo,
Quar d'orguelh mou e de no sen
Qui a dig o fag falhimen,
E vai son peccat excuzan,
Excusacios prepauzan
Fadas, defenden sa error,
Qu'en aquo dobla so folor,
Quar non apar ges que sia
Penedens de sa folia.
Dieus doncx per aquesta raso
Lur det sa maledictio
E dieis adoncx a la serpen:
Quar as fag aquest falimen,
Seras tostemps mesprezada,
Maldicha et azirada
E ton ventre resegaras,
La terra tostemps manjaras,
E la femna e siei effan
Tan quan viu[r]as mal te volran,
E femnat fara tempesta
Tal quet brizara la testa.
A la femna dieis atretal:
Tu sofriras dolor e mal
Et ab dolor effantaras
E sotz poder d'ome seras.
Apres aquo dis ad Adam:
Quar as manjat del frug del ram
Quez ieu t'avia defendut
Et as mais lo cosselh crezut
De femna quel comandamen
De me que t'ai fag de nien
Per ta folor davan dicha
Er cert la terra maldicha,
Quar espinas i creisseran
E malas herbas a ton dan,
Et ab trebailh d'ela trairas
Ton vieure aitan quan vieuras
Et ab maltrag et ab suor,
Quar anc fezis tan de folor,
Tro que sias en pols tornatz
Qu'eissamen fust de pols formatz.

K. *BOECIS*

Our selection comprises most of the surviving 258-line fragment from an Old Provençal paraphrase, written in the third person, of the fifth-century Latin philosopher Boethius's *De consolatione*. This early eleventh-century text is in epic style, with decasyllables divided 4/6 and arranged in stanzas having masculine assonance. It uses acute accents on occasion to show tonic stress or intonational rhythm. Our source is Vincenzo Crescini, *Manuale per l'avviamento agli studi provenzali*, 3d ed. (Milan: Ulrico Hoepli, 1926), 150-57.

Nos, jove omne quandius que nos estam,
de gran follia per folledat parllam;
quar no nos membra per cui viuri esperam,
qui nos soste tan quan per terra annam,
e qui nos pais que no murem de fam,
per cui salv esmes per pur tan que·ll clamam.

Nos jove omne menam ta mal jovent,
que us non o preza si·s trada son parent,
senor ni par si·ll mena mala ment,
ni l'us ves l'aitre si·s fai fals sacrament.
quant o a fait, miia no s'én repent,
e ni vers Deu no·n fai emendament.
pro non es gaigre si penedenza·n pren:
dis que l'a presa, miia nonqua la te,
que epslor forfaiz sempre fai epsa men,
e laisa·n Deu, lo grant omnipotent,
ki·l mort et viu tot a in jutjamen.
eps li satan son en so mandamen:
ses Deu licencia ja non faran torment.

Enanz en dies foren ome felló:
mal ome foren, aora sunt peior.
volg i Boecis metre quastiazo:
auvent la gent, fazia en so sermo
creessen Deu, qui sostenc passio:
per lui auríen trastút redemcio.
molt s'en penét, quar non i mes foiso,
anz per eveia lo mesdren e preiso.

Donz fo Boecis, e corps ag bo e pró,
cui tan amet Torquator Mallios.
de sapiencia no fo trop nuallos:
tant en retenc que de tót no·n fo blos,

tan bo essemple en laiset entre nos.
no cuid qu'e Roma om de so saber fos.

Cóms fo de Roma, e ac ta gran valor
aprob Mallio, lo rei emperador:
el era·l meler de tota la onor;
de tót l'emperi·l tenien per senor.
mas d'una causa nom avia genzor:
de sapiencia l'apellaven doctor.

Quan veng la fis Mallio Torquator,
donc venc Boeci ta granz dolors al cor,
no cuid aprob altre dols li demor.

Morz fo Mallios Torquator, dunt eu dig:
ecvos e Roma l'emperador Teiric.
del fiel Deu no volg aver amig.

No credét Deu, lo nostre creator;
per zo no·l volg Boecis a senor,
ni gens de lui no volg tener s'onor.

Eu lo chastia ta bé ab so sermo,
e Teiríx col tot e mal sa razó.
per grant evea de lui volg far fello:
fez u breu faire per grán decepcio,
e de Boeci escriure fez lo nóm;
e si·l tramét e Grecia la regio.
de part Boeci lor manda tal raizó,
que passen mar, guarnit de contençó:
eu lor redra Roma per traazo.
lo sénz Teiric miga no fo de bo:
fez sos mes segre, si·lz fez metre e preso.

El capitoli, l'endema al di clar,
lai o solíen las altres leis jutjar,
lai veng lo reis sa felnia menár:
lai fo Boecis, e foren i soi par.
lo reis lo pres de felni' a reptar,
qu'el trametía los breus ultra la mar,
Roma volia a óbs los Gréx tradár:
pero Boeci anc no venc e pesat.
sál en estánt e cuidet s'en salvar;
l'om no·l laiset a salvament annár.
cil li falíren qu'el soli' ajudar:
fez lo lo reis e sa charcer gitar.

Ecvos Boeci cadegut en afán,
e granz kadenas, qui l'están a pesant.
reclama Deu de cél, lo rei, lo grant:
"*domine pater*, e te·m fiav' eu tant,

e cui marce tuit peccador estánt.
las mias musas, qui ant perdut lor cánt,
de sapiencia anava eu ditan.
plor tota dia, faz cosdumna d'efant:
tuit a plorár repairen mei talant."

* * *

Cum jáz Boecis e péna charceral
plan se sos dols e sos menuz pecaz.
d'úna donzella fo lainz visitaz:
filla 's al rei, qui a gran poestat.
ella 's ta bella reluz ént lo palaz.
lo mas, o íntra, inz es granz claritaz:
ja no es óbs fox issia alumnaz:
veder ent pót l'om quaranta ciptáz.
qual ora·s vol, petita·s fai asáz:
cum ella s'auça, cel a del cap polsát:
quant be se dreça lo cel a pertusat,
é ve lainz tota la maiestat.

Bella 's la domna, e·l vís a tant preclár:
davan so vís nulz om no·s pot celar:
ne éps li omne, que sunt ultra la mar,
no potden tánt e lor cors cobeetár
qu'ella de tot no vea lor pessar:
qui e leis se fia, morz no l'es a doptar.

Bella 's la domna, mas molt es de longs dis.
no·s pot rascúndre nulz om denant so vis:
hanc no vist omne ta grant onor agues,
si·l forfez tan dont ella·s rangurés,
sos corps ni s'anma miga per rén guaris.
quoras que·s vol, s'en á lo corps aucís,
e pois met l'arma en efférn el somsís.
tal l'i cománda, qui tot dia la brís.
ella·s mét éssma tén cláus de paradis:
quoras que·s vol, laínz cól sos amigs.

Bél sun si drap: no sai nomnar lo fíl;
mas molt perforen di bón e de sobtíl.
ella se féz, avía anz plus de mil:
tán no son vél míga lór préz avíl.
Ella medesma teiset so vestimént,
que negus óm no pót desfar neienz.
pur l'una fremna, que vers la terra pent,
no comprari' om ab míl livras d'argént
ella ab Boeci parlét ta dolzament:
"molt me derramen donzellét de jovent,

que zo esperen que faza a lor talén.
primas me ámen, pois me van aissent:
la mi' amor ta mal van deperdén".

Bél sun li drap que la domna vestít:
de caritat e de fe sun bastít.
il sun ta bél, ta blánc e ta quandi,
tant a Boecis lo vis esvanuit,
que el zo pensa, uél sien amosit.

El vestiment, en l'or qui es représ,
de sóz avia escript ú pei ·Π· grezésc:
zo signifiga la vita qui en ter' es.
sobre la schápla avia ú tei ·Θ· grezesc:
zo signifiga de cél la dreita léi.

Antr' ellas doas depent sun l'eschaló:
d'aur no sun gés, mas nuallor no son.
per aqui monten cent miri' auzello.
alquant s'en tórnen aval arreuso.
mas cil, qui poden montar al ·Θ· alçor,
en epsa l'ora se sun d'altra color.
ab la donzella pois an molt gran amor.

Cals es la schala, de que sun li degra?
fait sun d'almósna e fé e caritát:
contra felnia sunt fait de gran bontat,
contra perjúri de bona feeltat,
contr' avaricia sun fait de largetát,
contra tristicia sun fait d'alegretat,
contra menzónga sun fait de veritat,
contra lucxuria sun fait de castitat,
contra superbia sun fait d'umilitat.
quascus bos óm si fái lo so degra.
cal sun li auzil, qui sun al tei montat,
quí e la scála ta ben án lor degras?
zó sun bon ómne, que an redems lor peccaz,
qui tan se fien e sancta trinitat:
d'onór terrestri non an grán cobeetat.

GLOSSARY TO THE READING SELECTIONS

This glossary is designed for maximum utility and convenience. It includes duplicate forms that are distinguished only by spelling, irregular verb forms, and many cross-references. The only omissions are of articles, possessives, personal pronouns, and the regularly inflected forms of verbs. In head terms, but not in cross-references, diacritical marks are used as in the body of the book. Optional letters are shown in head terms and listed variants. Where variant spellings coexist, words are usually alphabetized under the form closest to our normalized spelling system; however, cross-references are always given. Proper names appear in the same listings as common nouns, but only when useful and non-obvious information can be conveyed.

A, ad, as, az: to, at, on, with
ab, an: with; ... que: provided that
abanz, -ans: before, formerly, first; rather; ... que: before
abdọs, amdui: both
abelir: to charm, please; vr. to delight in
abit, abiti: clothing, dress
abras(s)ar: to embrace
ac, ag: 3 sg. pret. aver
acel, acest: see aic-
aco, aquo: see aiso
acompanhar, -ainhar: to accompany
aconseguir: to achieve, accomplish
acordansa: resolution, decision, agreement, harmony
acordar: to consent, agree with, match, rhyme
acostumar: to accustom; vr. : to become accustomed, habituated
acoutar: see ascoltar
actor: author

acullimẹn: welcome, reception, greeting
ad: see a
adaut, adautar: see azaut, azautar
adęs: always, at once
adonc(s), adoncx: therefore, then, so
adordenar: to order, dispose
adormir: to put to sleep; vr.: to fall asleep
adrẹch, adreit: able, skilled, clever, proper
aduire: to cause, bring about, produce
adus: 3 sg. pret. aduire
aer: air
afan: trouble, distress
afectuọs: affectionate, devoted
afermar: to affirm, assure
afliccioṇ: affliction, torment
afligimen(t): pain, affliction
afligir: to afflict, mortify
afortidamen(s): vigorously
afráigner: to turn towards, begin
ag: see ac
agardar: to look at
aginolhar, -llar, vr.: to kneel
agra: 3 sg. cond. B aver
agradable: pleasing
agreviar: to weigh upon
agroṇ: 3 sg. pret. aver
aguẹssoṇ: 3 pl. impf. subj. aver
agulha, -lla: needle
aia: 1 and 3 sg. pres. subj. aver
aiant: 3 pl. pres. subj. aver
aias: 2 pres. subj. and impv. aver
aicẹl, pl. aicil: this (one), that (one)
aiga: water
aiqi: see aqui
aïr: to hate
aire: air
aïssent: pres. part. aïr
ais(s)í, aicí: so, thus, as; here, in this or that place
ais(s)ǫ: this, that
aital: such (a), like; likewise
aitant: so much, so many, as much; ... que: as long as
aitre: see altre
aizina: occasion, opportunity
ajostamẹn, -ustamẹn: union, company
ajostar, -ustar: to collect, assemble, organize; vr.: to gather
ajuda: aid, help
ajudar: to aid, help
al, als: something else, anything else

ala: wing
albespiṇ: hawthorn
albre: see arbre
alçor: height
alcuṇ: some (one), any (one)
algramen(t): cheerfully, happily
alegrans: rejoicing
alegranza: happiness, joy
alegrar, all-: to make happy; vr.: to rejoice
alęgre, legre: happy, gay
alegretat: joy, happiness
alegrięr: happiness, joy
aleṇ, alena: breath
alena: awl
alenada: breath; intake of breath
allegrar: see alegrar
almoinar: to give alms
almǫsna, almoina: alms
alongar, -jar: to prolong, delay, linger
alongat: given respite
alonhar: to send away; vr.: to go away, depart
alquant: some, somewhat
alques: something
als: see al
altre, autre, aitre: other, another
altisme: all highest
alumnar: to brighten, light up
Alvergna: Auvergne
am, amb: see ab
amablamẹn: kindly
amador: lover
amaestrar: to teach, train
amagadamẹn: secretly, covertly
amagar: to hide, conceal
amanar, -enar: to bring, lead
amar: to love
amdọi, -dọs, -dui: both
amermar: to diminish, lessen
ami, amic, amig, f. amiga: friend, lover
amistanza: friendship, love
amistat: friendship, love
amor: love
amorọs: loving, affectionate; -amẹn -ousamẹn, adv.: affectionately, tenderly
amosit: weakened
an: see ab
an: year; d' ... en ... : from year to year
anar, -nnar: to go, walk; vr.: to go away

anc: ever; ... non, ... mais: never
ancara, -(a)s: still, yet
anęl: ring
ángel: angel
angle: angle, corner
anhęl: lamb
ánima, anma, arma: soul
ann-: see an-
ans, anz, anzi: rather; on the contrary
ant: 3 pl. pres. ind. aver
anta: shame
antięir: see entier
antre: see entre
aondansa: abundance, plenty
aǫra: now
aparelhar: to prepare
aparer: to appear
apariar, vr.: to mate, pair off, associate (with)
apartener: to pertain to
apel(l)ar: to call
apellatiọn: calling
apenre, apren(d)re: to learn
apercẹbre: to perceive
apercepęt: 3 sg. pret. apercebre
apilar, vr.: to lean
aportar: to bring
apǫstol: apostle
apen(d)re: see apenre
aprẹs: 3 sg. pret. and past part. apren(d)re
apręs: after(wards), then; near; further
apresẹs: 3 sg. impf. subj. apren(d)re
aprobencar, vr.: to approach
aprǫp, aprǫb: with, near; after
apte: suitable
aq-: see aqu-
aquẹl, pl. aquil: that (one), those
aquẹst, -qest; pl. aq(u)ist: this, these
aquí: here, there
aquo: see aco
ar, aras, ęr, ęras: now; d'... enans: henceforth
arabar, arr-: to take away, snatch, pull out
arbre, albre: tree
archángel: archangel
ardẹn: burning
ardidamẹn(t): boldly, daringly
ardor: ardor
argen(t): silver
argus: a giant in Greek mythology

arma: see anima
arnẹs: equipment, raiment
arozar, arr-: to sprinkle, bedew
arpa: claw, talon
arr-: see ar-
arreüso: backward, back
art: art, science, skill
artẹl: toe; ... major: big toe
as: see a
as: 2 sg. pres. ind. aver
as-: see also ass-
ascoltar, escoltar, acoutar: to listen (to)
aseguramẹn: assurance, guarantee
asegurar: to assure, make sure
aspis: asp
asprẹza: harshness, severity
as(s)atz: enough; (very) much, many
as(s)esmar: to organize, dispose, arrange
assís: set, placed
atendre, att-: to heed, consider, fulfill; wait
atọt: all
atraire: to draw, pull
atres(s)í: see autres(s)i
atrobar: to find
aturar, vr.: to stop, dwell
att-: see at-
auc: 3 sg. pret. aver
auçar: to raise
aucẹl: see auzel
aucir, -ssir: to kill
auçọr: height
audí: 3 sg. pret. auzir
audid: past part. auzir
auja: 3 sg. pres. subj. auzir
aujatz: 2 pl. pres. subj. and impv. auzir
aur: gold
aurá: 3 sg. fut. aver
aurẹlha: ear
aurien: 3 pl. cond. A aver
aus-: see auss-
auss-: see auc-
austorgar: to grant, authorize
aut: high, tall, lofty, exalted
autar: altar
autẹza: height, loftiness
autọrc: permission, authorization
autọritat: authority

autrejameṇ: permission, authorization
autrejaṛ: to grant, permit
autressí, atres(s)í: likewise; ... com: as if, just as
autrui: of or to another, others; another's
auven(t): in the hearing of
auzar: to dare
auzẹl, -sel, -zil, pl. auzil; -zelloṇ: bird; ... de cassa: bird of prey
auzidor: hearer
auzir: to hear, listen to; past. part. f. auzida: renowned
aval: down, downward
avaricia: avarice, greed
aveṇ: 3 sg. pres. indic. avenir
avẹnc: 3 sg. pret. avenir
avenir: to happen
aventura: chance; per ... : perchance
aver: to have; quan fon agut, when it had happened; noun: goods, property
avẹs: 2 pl. pres. ind. aver
avil: mean, cheap
avineṇ: charming, attractive; suitable
avinentẹza: graciousness
ávol: bad, base, wicked
ay-: see ai-
az: see a
azaut, ad-: charm; adj: charming
azautameṇ: charm
azautar, ad-: to charm
azautẹza: nice thing
azẹ: ass
azenant, per ... : henceforth; thenceforth
azir: hatred
azirar: to hate
azondọs: (well) provided
azorar: to adore
azornat: adorned, fashioned, equipped

Baiar: to yawn, gape
bailoṇ: bailiff
bais(s)ar: to lower
baizar: to kiss
balena: whale
barbiẹr: barber
barca: boat
baroṇ: baron, lord, nobleman; man
barta: underbrush
basme: balm

bastar: to suffice
bastir: to build, compose, make
batejar: to baptize
bat(t)re: to beat, flap
bęc: beak, mouth
bęl: fair, beautiful
beṇ: well; noun: good (thing)
benarat, -aürat: blessed
benezẹcte: blessed
benigne: benign
benignitat: benignity
bęstia: beast, animal
bẹure: to drink; noun: drinking
beutat: beauty
blanc: white
blasmar: to blame, criticize
blasme: blame
blavairǫl: bruise, wound, scar
blọs: lacking, without, deficient
bọca: mouth
bolhent: boiling
boṇ: good
bonauzat: blessed
bonẹza: goodness
bonfaitor: benefactor
bontat: goodness, virtue
bọrc: town
borguẹs: bourgeois, town-dweller
bras, bratz, pl. brasses: arm
bręu, adj.: short, brief, little, small; en ... de temps: shortly after
bręu, noun: letter
breumen(s): briefly, shortly
breviari: breviary
brizar: to break, crush, torture

Ca: see caṇ
cabal: proper, rightful (place)
cabẹl: hair
cabussar: to immerse
cadegut: past. part. cazer
cadęl: little one, cub
cadena: chain
Caersiṇ: Quercy (area of Cahors)
caia: 3 sg. pres. subj. cazer
caire: see cazer
cais: almost, as if
caisoṇ: reproach, accusation, reason

caitięu: wicked
cal, q(u)al: which, what, who
calandri: large lark
calar: to lower; be silent
caler, qual-: to concern, matter
calque: some
cambra: chamber, bedroom
camiṇ: road, way; dreg ... : straightway, at once
camp: field
caṇ, nom. sg. cas: dog
cansoṇ, canczoṇ: song, ode, poem
can(t): song
can(t), quant, conj. and adv.: when, whenever
cant, quand, quant, adv. and pron.: as much, how much, pl. as many, how many; as; however; ... a: with regard to, for
cantar: to sing; noun: singing, song
cantǫst: as soon as, when, whenever
cantre: singer
cap: head, end; a ... de pessa: after a while, soon after
capdęl: lord, leader
capęlla: chapel
capioṇ: hood
capítol: chapter
capitǫli: Capitoline hill (in Rome)
captenemẹn: behavior, conduct
car: dear, precious
car, quar, qar: because, since; why; therefore
cara: face
caramẹn: sweetly, warmly
cárcer, cha-: prison
carceral, cha-: pertaining to prison
caritat: charity
carn: flesh
carronhada: carrion
carta: page, chart
cas: case (grammatical)
cas: see caṇ
casa-: see cas(s)a-
cascuṇ, quascuṇ: each (one)
cas(s)a: hunt, prey
cas(s)ador: hunter
cas(s)ar: to hunt
castęl: castle
castiar: to chastise, castigate
castitat: chastity
castor: beaver
catre, quatre: four

causa: thing, cause
caus(s)ar: to shoe, put on shoes
cauza: see causa
cauzir, ch-: to distinguish, discern, choose
caval: horse
cavalier, cavayer: knight, gentleman
cavar: to extract, take out; albre cavat: hollow tree
cay-: see cai-
cazer, caire: to fall
cẹl, sel(h), f. celha, sella, m. pl. cil, silh, sill: that (one), those
cȩl, sel: sky, heaven
celar, selar: to hide, conceal
cẹlcle: girdle
celebrar: to celebrate
celestial: heavenly, celestial
celici, cilici, selici: hair shirt
celui, selui: that (one)
cen(t): hundred
cẹnher, sẹnher: to girdle, bind
cȩr, cerv: stag
cercar, ser-: to seek, look for
cẹrt: sure, certain
certẹza, sert-: assurance; testimony, veracity; per ... : assuredly
cerv: see cer
cervȩl, serv-: brain
cha-: see also ca-
chaia: 3 sg. pres. subj. cazer
Cherubus: Cerberus
cieutadaṇ, ciu-: citizen
cieutat, ciu-, ciptat: city
cigne, cinhe, si-: swan
cil: see cel
cinq: five
ciu-: see cieu-
clam: outcry, protest; dar ... ni cosselh: to heed, help
clamar: to call, cry, protest, appeal, ask for; vr.: to complain
clar: clear, bright; loud
claritat: brightness, splendor
clau: key
claure: to close
clauza: past part. claure
clavȩl: nail
clavelar: to nail
clẹrc, clerg(u)e: cleric
clusa: jail

coː see com
cọa: tail
coar: to hatch
cọbe: greedy, avid
cobeetar: to covet, lust for
cobeetat, cobeẹza: greed, cupidity
cọbla: stanza
cobrir, cu-: to cover
cocodrilha, -lla: crocodile
cofondre: see confondre
cǫl: neck
cǫl: 3 sg. pres. ind. colhir
colcar: to lay, put to rest; vr.: to lie down
colhir, culh-: to pluck, take (up)
colom: dove
color: color; sort, kind
colpable: guilty
com, coma, con, quo, qon, cuma: as, how, like; tant ...: as long as
Com: Como
comaire: French commère
comandamen(t): commandment
comandar: to command, commend, recommend
comenegar, comergar, comonegar, comorgar, comenegar: to take communion
comensamen(t): beginning
comensar: to begin, commence
comonegar, comorgar: see comenegar
companhia: company
companhiẹira, companhona: companion, mate (f.)
comprar: to buy
comptar, comtar: to reckon, account; relate, tell
compte: account; ses ... : past reckoning
com(p)s: see comte
comtar: see comptar
comte, nom. sg. com(p)s: count
comtẹssa: countess
comunalmẹn: commonly, generally
con: see com
concẹbre, cossebre: to conceive
conciẹncia: conscience
conegut: past part. conois(s)er
confes(s)ar: to confess
confizar: to confide (in), have confidence in
cọnfondre: to overwhelm, destroy, ruin, kill
confortar: to comfort, encourage
conjurar: to conjure, beg
conmorgar: see comenegar
conọc: 3 sg. pret. conois(s)er

conoguẹs: 3 sg. imp. subj. conois(s)er
conọis(s)er: to know, recognize, perceive
conǫrt: comfort
conọsc: 1 sg. pres. ind. conois(s)er
conossẹn: expert, conoisseur
conquerer, -ir, -re: to vanquish, conquer, win
conquẹs, conquis: 3 sg. pret. conquerer
coṇsẹlh, coss-, -el: advice, counsel, comfort
coṇsentir: to consent
coṇsir, coss-: thought, concern, worry
coṇsirar, coss-, sometimes vr.: to bethink, consider, ponder
contẹ: 3 sg. pres. ind. contener
conte: see coms
contemplacioṇ: contemplation
contemplar: to contemplate, meditate
contençọ: combat, strife, battle
contẹner: to contain
contínu: continuous
continuamen(s): continuously
continuar: to continue
contor: knight, baronet
contra: against, toward
contrafar: to imitate
contrast: dispute; ten a ... : keeps up with
coṇvenir: to be suitable, advantageous
conversioṇ, -cion: conversion
cǫr: heart
cọr, a pas de: see pas
coralmẹn: intensely
corbatoṇ: young crow, raven
cǫrda: cord
cordoan: Cordovan
coreçar: see corrossar
corn: horn
coronar: to crown
cǫrp: crow, raven
cǫr(p)s: body, person, self
cǫrre: to run, flow
corrẹga: strap
corrọssar, corẹçar: to trouble, vex, become annoyed
corruptioṇ: cǫrruption
cọrs: period of time
cǫrs: see cor(p)s
cọrt: court
cortal: courtyard
cortes, f. corteza: courtly, gracious
cosdụmna: see costum
cossẹbre: see concebre

cosselh: see conselh
cosseup: 3 sg. pret. cossebre
cossir, cossirar: see consir, consirar
costa, costat: rib, flank, side
costrech, costreit: compelled, forced, obliged
costum, cosdumna: custom, usage
coutivador: follower, worshiper
coutivament: cult
cove: 3 sg. pres. ind. convenir
covenir: see convenir
cozer: to cook, bake; burn, cause pain
cre: 1 and 3 sg. pres. ind. creire
crear: to create
creator: creator
creatura: creature
crec: 3 sg. pret. creisser
credet: 3 sg. pret. creire
creire: to believe
creiron: 3 pl. pret. creire
creisser: to grow, increase
cremar: to burn
cremor: glow, blaze, ardor
crestian, cris-: Christian
crestiandat: Christianity
crezás, crezatz: 2 pl. pres. subj. creire
crezensa: faith, obedience
crezes: 2 sg. pres. ind. creire
crezet: 3 sg. pret. creire
crezia: 3 sg. impf. ind. creire
crezon: 3 pl. pres. ind. creire
crezut: past part. creire
cridar: to cry, shout
crit: cry, shout
cruciamen: torment
cruciar: to torment
crucificar: to crucify
cubert: past part. cobrir
cubertamens: covertly
cubrir: see cobrir
cudar, cuidar, cujar, sometimes vr.: to think, believe
cuer: hide, skin, leather
cuig: 1 sg. pres. ind. cudar
culhir: see colhir
cuma: see com
cumenegar: see comenegar
czo: see so

Dan: harm, injury, ill; pity
dar: to give
davan(s), davant, devant: before, in front of; earlier
decazer: to cast down, ruin
decẹbre: to deceive, mock
decẹp, deceup: 3 sg. pret. decebre
decepciọ: deception
deceubut: past part. decebre
dechẹs: 3 sg. impf. subj. dire
defendre: to defend, resist; forbid
deges: see deg(u)es
degrá: step (of a ladder, stair)
dẹgra: 3 sg. cond. B dever
deg(u)ẹs: 3 sg. impf. subj. dever
deg(u)ẹssọn: 3 pl. impf. subj. dever
degun: see negun
deignar : see denhar
deitatz: deity
dẹja: 3 sg. pres. subj. dever
dejatz: 2 pl. pres. subj. dever
dejuni: fast, fasting
delechable, delich- : enjoyable, delicious
delechar, vr.: to delight (in), enjoy
delechọs: delightful, in delight
delicadamens: delicately, nicely
delich, delięg: delight, enjoyment
delichable: see delechable
demanda: question
demandador ẹs: it is to be asked
demandar, dọ-: to ask
demanẹs: at once
demorar: to dwell
demostrar: to show
den: tooth
denan(t): before, in front of; previously
denfra: within
denhar, deignar: to deign
depent: painted
depęrdre: to lose, ruin
derẹire: behind
derramar: to mistreat
derrięr: last; tot en ... : last of all
derrocar: to tear down, destroy
desazautar: to displease; past part.: displeasing, unpleasing
descaus: unshod
desdeng: scorn, disdain
desfach: past part. desfar
desfar, desfaire: to undo, destroy
desfẹs: 3 sg. pret. desfar

de(s)liurar: to deliver
desmembramen, desmembranza: forgetfulness
desnembrar, dis-: to forget
desọbre: above, over, on top of
desọtz: below, under, underneath
despendre: to spend, expend
desperar, vr.: to despair
despereisser: to wake; vr.: to wake up
desplazer: to displease; noun: displeasing act; offense; displeasure
despullar: to dislodge, pull out, pluck
destrẹch, destreit: pressed, harried; ...amens: tightly
destruire: to destroy
desús: above, upon, over
dẹtz: ten
dẹu: see dieu
dẹu: 3 sg. pres. ind. dever
deuria: 3 sg. cond. A dever
deus: since, from
dẹus: 2 sg. pres. ind. dever
devan: see davan(s)
devedar: to forbid
dever: to owe, be obliged to
devin, devina: soothsayer, witch
devocion: devotion
dẹvon: 3 pl. pres. ind. dever
devorar: to devour
devọt: devout
dez-: see also under des-
dezacọrdi: discord, strife
dezagradable: disagreeable
dezamparar, desam-, dezan-, dezem-: to abandon
dezazaut: displeasure, disgust
dezẹrt: desert, wasteland
dezirar: to desire, long for
dezirier: desire
dezonor: dishonor, disgrace
di, dia: day; de longs dis: old, ancient
diable: devil
diablẹssa: she-devil
dic, dig: 1 sg. pres. ind. dire
dich, dig, dit(z): past part. dire; noun: saying, word, precept
dieis: 3 sg. pret. dire
dies, enanz en ... : of old (see dia)
diẹu, deu: god
dig: see dich
diga, -gua: 3 sg. pres. subj. dire

digas, -guas: 2 sg. pres. subj. dire
digne: worthy
digu-: see dig-
dilexcioṇ: pure love
dilús: Monday
dimenge, dimorge, dimẹrgue: Sunday
dins: within
dir, dire, dízer: to say, tell, call
dis: 3 sg. pres. ind. and pret. dir
disẹn: pres. part. dir
dises: see dis(s)es
disia, -zia: 1 and 3 sg. impf. ind. dir
disnembrar: see des-
dispereisser: see des-
dissapte: Saturday
dissendre: to descend
dissẹron: 3 pl. pret. dir
dis(s)ẹs: 3 sg. impf. subj. dir
dit: see dich
ditar: to speak, write, discourse
dit(z): see dich
ditz: 3 sg. pres. ind. dir
divers: different, various, sundry
diviṇ: divine
diz: see dich, ditz
dizent: pres. part. dir
dizẹssan: 3 pl. impf. subj. dir
doas: see dos
doblar: to double
doctor: scholar, master
dọl, doll: grief, pain
dolen: unhappy, sad, wretched
doll: see dol
dolor: grief, pain, sorrow
dolz: see dous
dolzamen: see dousamen(t)
domens que, domentre que: while, as long as
domesteguẹza, -ghessa: familiarity, intimacy
Domine pater: Lord Father (Latin)
dompna, don(n)a, dọpna: lady
dom(p)nẹi: cult of ladies, courtship of ladies
don: lord, sir
doṇ: gift
don, dont, dunt: of whom, of which; whence
dona: see dompna
donar: to give
doncs: see adoncs

dọnna: see dompna
dont: see don
donzęlla: maiden, young lady
donzellẹt: youth
dopna: see dompna
doptar, dubtar, duptar: to fear, doubt
dọpte: fear, doubt
dormir: to sleep
dǫs, dǫrs: back (noun)
dọs f. doas: two; ... en ... two at a time
dossament: see dousamen(t)
dǫus, doutz, dolz: sweet
dousamen(t), dossamen(t): sweetly, gently
dous(s)or: sweetness
dragọn: dragon
drap: cloth, article of clothing
dreçar, vr.: to stand upright
drẹch, dreich, dreg, dreit: right, proper, straight; noun: law, right; per ... : dutifully; en ... d'amor: in the way of love
drechurięr: righteous, straightforward, proper
dubtar, duptar: see doptar
duc: duke
dunt: see don
dur: hard
durable: lasting, enduring
durabletat: endurance, permanence
durar: to last, endure

E, es, et, ez: and
e: see ẹn
ecoutar: see escoltar
ecvọs: behold
edificar: to build
ef-, eff-: see enf-
egal: equal
egalmen(t): equally, likewise
eiciz: past part. issir, to leave, go out, depart from
ẹis, eps: self, same; themselves, etc.; even
ẹisamen(t), iss-: likewise, also
el: for en + lo, et + lo
els: for en + los
elegut: chosen, special
elemǫsina, eli-: alms
em: 1 pl. pres. ind. es(s)er
em: see en
emblar: to take away, steal

emborigol: navel
emendamen(t): amends
empenat: feathered
emperador: emperor
empęri: empire
emperǫ: however
en: lord, sir
en, ent: partitive pronoun
eṇ, em: in
enais(s)í: thus, so
enamorar: to enamor; vr.: to fall in love; past part. enamorat: in love
enans, -z, -t: forward, ahead, before; d'aquí ... : thenceforth
enansar: to advance, forward, promote, exalt
enbẹure: to become imbued
encar, encaras: still, yet; ... que: provided that, although
encarnar: to sink into flesh
encontra: toward, against
encontrada: country, region
encontrar: to meet
endemaṇ: (the) next day
endormir: to put to sleep
endrẹg: place, situation
enemic: enemy
eṇfan, eff- (nom. sg. eṇfas): infant, child
eṇfansa: infancy
eṇfantar, eff-: to bear young, give birth
eṇfanteza: infancy
eṇfẹrm: sick
eṇfermetat: sickness, infirmity
eṇfęrn, if(f)ern: Hell, lower regions
engan(n)ar: to deceive
engenrar: to engender, arouse, procreate
engǫissa: anguish
engroissar, engrueissar: to deepen, thicken
enjoglarir, vr.: to become a jongleur
enpauzar: to place, bestow
enquęiras: 2 sg. pres. subj. enquerre
enquęrre: to seek, woo
eṇseignament, eṇsenh-: good manners, education, propriety
eṇsems, essems: together; tot ... : all at once, suddenly
eṇsenhar -nnar, -eignar: to teach, show; past part.: educated, well-bred
ent: see en (pronoun)
entendedor: suitor, admirer
entendemen(t), -imen(t): intention, dedication, aim, goal; effort, understanding, intelligence, love request, courtship

entendẹn: expert, connoisseur
entendre: to hear, understand, mean, recognize; vr. with en:
 woo, court; past part. entendut: bent on, intent on
entendudamens: closely, appreciatively
entent: 1 sg. pres. ind. entendre
entięr: entire, complete, whole
entọrn: around
entrar, intrar, to enter
entre, antre: among, between
entrels: entre or entro + los
entró: up to, until, as far as
enuęg, enueit: care, worry, trouble, annoyance; verse form
envanezir, vr.: to fade away, vanish
envẹia, evea: envy, desire, longing
envẹiọs: envious, desirous, jealous, ardent
enverinar: to poison
envęrs: overturned, prostrate
envidar: to inspire
envídia: envy
envolar: to steal, abduct
ęps: see eis
epslọr: the very same
epsamẹn: just the same
er: 3 sg. fut. es(s)er
er, eras: see ar
ęra: 3 sg. impf. ind. es(s)er
eranh: heron
ęran(t): 3 pl. impf. ind. es(s)er
ęras: 2 sg. impf. ind. es(s)er
ęrba: grass; mala ... : weed
ergolhos, -gulhos: see orgolhos
erissoṇ: hedgehog
ermitaṇ: hermit
errar: to err; past. part. erratz: wrong, in error
error: error, misbelief, mistake
ẹs, est: 3 sg. pres. ind. es(s)er
escala, -chala: ladder, stairway
escaloṇ, -chaloṇ: step, stair
escapar: to escape
escarnięr: mocker
esclau: trace, track
escoltar, escoutar: see ascoltar
escondre, escondir: to hide; vr.: to flee from
escrich, -ipt, -it: past part. escriure
escriptura: Scripture
escriure: to write
esdevenc: 3 sg. pret. esdevenir

esdevenir, sometimes vr.: to happen, come about; become
esemple: see es(s)emple
eser: see es(s)er
esforsar: to strive, exert oneself
esgardar: to look at, heed
esgart, -ard: glance, look; 3 sg. pres. subj. esgardar
eslevar: to raise (up), elevate
esmendar: to make up for, atone, compensate
ęsmes: 1 pl. pres. ind. es(s)er
ȩspaventable: frightful
espazi: space
especial: special
espcirar: to inspire, breathe into
espelir: to hatch out
esperansa: hope
esperar: to hope, expect, await
esperit: spirit, soul
esperital: spiritual
espina: thorn
esquęrn: mockery, jest
esquina: back, spine
esquintar: to tear, mangle
esquivar: to shun
es(s)emple: example
essems: see ensems
ęs(s)er: to be
ȩst/a: this
establir: to establish, provide
estacar: to attach
estaitz: 2 pl. impv. estar
estalvar, sometimes vr.: to occur, happen
estamen(t): condition, (well-)being
estampida, stam-: verse form
estaqua: stake, pillar
estar, star: to stand, be, stay
estęia: 3 sg. pres. subj. estar
estendre, vr.: to extend
estięrs: otherwise; except
estǫrtz: saved, delivered
estraign, -stranh: strange, distant, reserved; ...as paraulas: words of discord; noun: stranger
estranhar: to keep from, send away
estręnher: to envelop, embrace, press, bind
estrolomia: astrology
estrolomiayre: astrologer
estrús: ostrich
estudi: study, zeal

estudiozamen(t): zealously
esturmẹn: instrument
esvanuir: to dazzle
et: see e
etat: age; state
ę(t)z: 2 pl. pres. ind. es(s)er
ẹu (for el): he
evea, eveia: see enveia
eveios: see enveios
exceptat: except
excusaciọn: excuse disculpation
excusar: to excuse
exercici: exercise
exterior: outer
ez: see e(t)z
ezura: usury

Fa: 3 sg. pres. ind. faire
fablazọn: wild tale, nonsense
fach, fag, fait: past part. faire; noun: deed, act
facta: f. past part. faire
fada: see fat
fag: 1 sg. pres. ind. faire; see also under fach
fai: 3 sg. pres. ind. faire
faia: beech
fail, falh, failhis, faillis: 3 sg. pres. ind. falhir
faire, far, fer: to make, do, act, perform; ... semblan(t), se ...: pretend; fai a; is meant (worthy) to be
fait: see fach
fal: far + lo
falh: see fail
falhimẹn, falimẹn, failliment: failing, sin, mistake
falhir, falir: to fail, be lacking, miss; abandon
falhizọn: failing, mistake
fals: false
falsia: falsehood, deception
fam: hunger
familiarmen(s): closely, intimately
fan: 3 pl. pres. ind. faire
far: see faire
fat, f. fada: silly, foolish
fauda: lap
fasia, -zia, 3 sg. impf. ind. faire
fasiọn: 3 pl. impf. ind. faire
fassa, faza: 1 and 3 sg. pres. subj. faire
faz, 1 sg. pres. ind. faire
fẹ: faith
feeltat: fidelity, loyalty

feigner: see fenher
fe̩(i)ron̩: 3 pl. pret. faire
fe̩l: gall
fel(l)on̩: villain, adj. evil, wicked
fel(l)on̩ia, felnia: wickedness, crime, evil, treason
fem, feme: see femina
feme̩la: female
fe̩mina, fe̩mena, femna, fem, feme: woman, female
fe̩nher: to pretend, dissemble, imitate
fe̩r, ferre: iron
fer: fierce, wild, rash, cruel
ferir: to strike, wound
fe̩rm: firm, steady, secure, fixed, still
ferme̩za: firmness
feron: fe(i)ron
ferre: see fer
ferven(t): fervent
fervor: fervor
fe̩s, fez, fetz: 3 sg. pret. faire
fesse̩s, feze̩s: 3 sg. impf. subj. faire
fe̩sta: feast, celebration
festola: fistula, abscess
fetz: see fes
fez: see fes
fezes: see fesses
feze̩ssan: 3 pl. impf. subj. faire
feze̩z: 2 pl. pret. faire
fezist: 2 sg. pret. faire
fiar: to trust
fie̩l: faithful
figura: figure
figurar: to figure, prefigure
fil: thread
filh, fil(l): son, child
filha, filla: daughter
fin̩: end, death
fin̩: sincere, fine, faithful, true; delicate
flairar: to smell (of), give forth a scent; noun: sense of smell
flairor: odor, fragrance
flama: flame
flo̩r: flower
flum: river
fo̩, fon̩: 3 sg. pret. es(s)er
fo̩c, fuoc, nom. sg. fox: fire
foil: fo + lo
foison̩: harvest
fo̩l: fool, foolish

fǫlh, foll, folha, fuęlha: leaf
folia, follia, folledat, folor: madness, folly
foṇ: see fo
fons: bottom, depth
for: see fort
fọra: 3 sg. impf. subj. es(s)er
fǫra(s): out, outside
fọras: 2 pl. cond. B es(s)er
fọren: 3 pl. pret. es(s)er
forfaire: to sin, transgress
forfait: sin, transgression
forfẹs: 3 sg. pret. forfaire
fọrma: form
formar: to form, shape
fornicador: wrong-doer
fọroṇ: 3 pl. pret. es(s)er
fǫrsa: force, violence
forsar: to force
forssenat: mad, insane
fǫrt, for: strong; adv.: strongly, loudly, very (much)
fortment: greatly
fọs: 3 sg. impf. subj. es(s)er
fọssoṇ: 3 pl. impf. subj. es(s)er
fọuzer: lightning
fradiṇ: wretch
fraire: brother
francẹs, f. franceza, francesca: French
franchẹssa, -queza; frankness, loyalty, honesty; freedom
fremna: fringe
fretar: to rub
fruch, frug: fruit
fruchan: fruit-bearing
fuelha: see folh
fugir: to flee
fuoc: see foc
fust: 2 sg. pret. es(s)er

Gai: gay, lively, merry, blithe
gaire, gaigre, with negative: scarcely, barely, little; en a-banz de ...: before long, in a little while; pro non es ...: it's not much use
galiamẹn: guile, deceit
galiar: to deceive, trick
gallardia: mirth, gaiety, gallantry
gandida: evasion, subterfuge, refuge
gandir: to flee, escape; protect
ganreṇ: much, many, a good deal, a lot
ganta: stork, wild goose

ganton: young stork
garar: see gardar
garda: guard; care, concern; far la ...: to keep watch; prendre ... : to take care
gardar, garar: to look at, watch; guard, keep, observe; take care; vr.: to avoid
garir, guerir: to heal, recover
garnir: to arm, supply, equip, adorn
gasanhar: see gazanhar
gauch, gaug: joy
gauzen(t): rejoicing, happy
gazanhar, gas-, -agnar, -aignar: to earn, win, gain
gelos, gilos: jealous
gememen: groaning, gnashing (of teeth)
gen, jen: well, nicely, finely; see also gen(s)
generalmen(s): generally, in general
genre: gender
gen(s), gent: people
gens, no ... : not at all
genser: see genzor
gentil: noble, well-bred, courteous
gentileza: nobility, courtesy
genzor, nom. sg. genser: fairer, finer; fairest, finest
gerra: see guerra
ges: see gens
getar, gettar, gitar, gietar, iettar, jettar: to throw, throw out, throw up; put out
gi-: see also gui-, ge-
gietar: see getar
ginhol: knee
giquir: to leave, abandon
girar: to turn
gitar: see getar
gitec: 3 sg. pret. getar
glaia: sword lily
glatz: ice
glazi: sword
gleiza, gleyza, glieza, glieyza: church
glòria: glory
glorios: glorious, in glory
grácia, grázia: favor, privilege; grace, pl.: thanks
grafi: stylus
gramadi: scholar
gramática: grammar
gran(t), grand: great, big
grat: pleasure
grazia: see gracia
grazir: to welcome

Gręc, obl. pl. Grex: Greek
gręu: hard, ill; adv.: with difficulty, scarcely
grevẹza: heaviness, gravity, weight
grezẹsc: Greek
grilh: cricket
grua: crane
gua-: see ga-
guerir: see garir
guerpir: to abandon
guęrra, gerra: war
guia, guiza: way, manner, kind, style

Ho-, hu-, etc.: see o-, u- etc.

I, y: here, there
ia, ia-: see ja, ja-
idola: idol
idra, idre: hydra, monster
ięst: 2 sg. pres. ind. es(s)er
iettar: see getar
if(f)ern: see enfern
ilha: island
illi: she
ins, inz: in, within
int-: see ent-
io-: see jo-
ira: sadness, chagrin, anger
irat: sad, vexed, angry
isnęl: fleet, prompt
issamen: see eisamen(t)
issia: i + sia
issic: 3 sg. pres. issir
issir: to go out, come out, leave
istá: 3 sg. pres. ind. estar
iu-: see ju-

Ja: indeed, already; ... no: not at all, by no means
jaciąissǫ que, giass-: forasmuch as, although
jass-: see jaz-
jauzẹn: happy, joyful
jauzir: to enjoy
jaz: 3 sg., pres. ind. jazer
jazer, -ir, -ser, -sser, -sir: to lie (down)
jazoṇ: 3 pl. pres. ind. jazer
jen: see gen
jettar: see getar
joglar: jongleur, minstrel

joglaria: art or practice of being a joglar
jǫi, joy: joy
jǫia: joy; jewel, gift
joiọs: joyful
jọrn: day
jọveṇ: young, youthful
joven(t): youth, freshness
jurar: to swear
jusięu: Jewish
just: just, rightful, righteous
jutjamẹn: judgment
jutjar: to judge
jutje, jutge: judge

Kalenda Maya: Mayday
Karlle: Charles of Anjou
Ki: see qui

Lag, laig: f. laia: ugly, foul, wretched
lagẹza: ugliness
lágrema: tear
lai: there
laig: see lag
laïnz: within, therein, there
lais(s)ar: to leave, quit, cease, abandon; let; vr. with de:
  to give up
languir: to languish, lose strength
lansa: lance
larc: f. larga: ample, wide; generous
largamen(s): in width
largetat: generosity, liberality
lassús: (there) above
lat: side
latiṇ: Latin
lauzar: to praise
lauzengięr, laus-: scandal-monger, liar, traducer
lauzor: praise, encomium
lávia: lip
leal, lial: loyal true
lealtat, lial-: loyalty, good faith
lęga: league
legar: to melt (down)
legenda: legend
legir, lęger, lęire: to read
legre: see alegre
lẹi: law, fashion, rule
lemozin, -sin: see limozin

lenga, -gua: tongue, speech, language
lenga(t)ge: language, style of speech
lengua: see lenga
leọn: lion
leọnat: lion cub
leoṇessa: lioness
lepạr: to lick
letícia: happiness
letras: letters; schooling
lẹu: light, easy; adv.: easily
leumens: easily
leugierameṇ: lightly, easily
levamen(t): rising, elevation, levitation, exaltation
levar: to raise up, raise: vr.: to get up, arise
lial, lialtat: see leal, lealtat
libre: book
licẹncia: permission
liẹch, lieg: bed
Limozịn, Lem-, -os-, -ouz-, adj. l-: Limousin, of Limoges
linage, linnadge: lineage
liurar: to deliver, hand over
livra, livre: pound, livre
lo: there, then
lobẹira: wolf den
lọc, luoc, luẹch: place, site
lọi: lo + i
lonc, f. longa: long
lonh, loing, luenh: distant, remote, far (away)
lonhar, loign-, lunh-: to send away; vr.: to go away, take leave; separate
lọp: wolf
lucxúria: lust
luec(h), luoc: see loc
luegua: see luoga
luenh: see lonh
lunh: see nulh
lunhar: see lonhar
luọga, luẹgua: place

Madomna, madompne, madona, madonna: (my) lady
mai: see mais
maia: see Kalenda
maiestat: majesty
maint: see mant
maire: mother
mais, mai, mas: more, most; with negative.: never; al ... : usually, generally; but, except

maisọn: house, dwelling
maistre: master, teacher
major, nom. sg., májer: greater, greatest, bigger, older
majormẹn: mostly, principally
mal: bad, wicked, ill; noun: evil, illness; adv.: badly
malamen(s), malemen(s), mala ment: badly, unhappily, sorely, rudely, wrongly, maliciously
malanans: ill, sickly, poorly
malananza, -nnanza: sickness, poor health, misery
malastruc, malestrug: ill-starred, wretched
malaut(e): sick; noun: invalid
malautia: sickness
malaveiar: to suffer, fall ill
maldezidor: see maldizidor
maldich, maldig, past part. maldire: noun: bad word, calumny, invective
maldire: to speak ill; curse
maldizidor, maldez-: speaker of evil, blasphemer
malediction: curse
malestrug: see malastruc
malẹza, malignitat: malice, wickedness; misfortune, misery
maltrag, -trait: pain, hardship
malvais, malvat: wicked; wretched, ill, base, bad
man: hand
mandamẹn: command, order
mandar: to send; command, order
manhar, -jar, -gar: to eat; noun: eating
manięra, -ieira: manner, way
manifestar: to show
mant, maint: many
mantẹ: 3 sg. pres. ind.: mantener
mantẹl: mantle, cloak
mantenen(t): now, at once
mantener: to maintain, support
mar: sea
marca: march (borderland)
marce: see merce
marfezir: to fade, wilt
marinięr: sailor
marquẹs: marquis
martiri: torture, martyrdom
mas: house
mas: see mais, man
mascle: male
masnada: band, company
massipa: girl
mat: mad

matiṇ: morning
matiṇas: matins
medecina: medicine
medẹsme, f. medesma: self, same
meịllor, melhor, nom. sg. męler, męiller, męller: better, best
meillorar, melhorar, melhurar: to better, improve
meitat: half
męlhs, melz, mielh(s): better, best
męmbrar: to remind, recall
membrat: intelligent, sane
membre, men-: member
menar: to lead, take, plot: ... sęgle: make a sound; ... a mort: to put to death
menassa: threat
mens, menz: less, least
mensioṇ: mention
mensprẹzar, mes-: to scorn, blame, condemn, belittle
ment, mala ... : see malamen
menut: small, little
menzonga; -gna: falsehood, lie
meravilh, meravilha: marvel, wonder; a meravilhas: wondrously
meravilhar, -vellar, vr.: to marvel (at), wonder
meravilhọs: marvelous
meravilhọzamen(s): marvellously
mercẹ, marcẹ, merzẹ: grace, pardon, mercy
merir: to deserve
meriti: merit
merle: blackbird
męrmar: to lessen, diminish
merze: see merce
mẹs: messenger
mẹs: month
mẹs: 3 sg. pret. and past. part. met(t)re
mẹscabamẹn: ruin, failure
mescrezenza: lack of faith, false faith, error
mẹsdren: 3 pl. pret. met(t)re
mẹsprezar: see mensprezar
mesquiṇ: wretch; adj. wretched, poor
mẹssa: mass
mẹs(s)agięr: messenger
messongięr: liar
mestięr, aver ... : to be necessary
metęis, mez-, -ẹus, ẹsme: self, same; aisi ... : in like fashion
met ẹsma: herself, itself

met(t)re: to place, put (in), dispose; spend; grow ... mort: to kill
mezeis, mezeus, mezesme: see meteis
mezeron: 3 pl. pret. met(t)re
mezurar: to measure
midons: one's lady, mistress
mieg, f. mieia: middle, mid; noun: middle, midst
miel, mielh(s), mielz: see melhs
miga, miia: not at all, by no means
mil, pl. milia: thousand
milier: (a) thousand
ministre: minister, attendant
miralh, -aill: mirror
mirar: to look at
miria: thousands
misericordia: mercy, pity
moc: 3 sg. pret. mover
mogut, -uda: past part. mover
molher, mo(i)ller, nom. sg. molher: wife
molt, mout, mot: much, many; very
mon(t): world; tot lo ... : every one
monegue, morgue: monk
monestier: monastery
Monseinnh: lord, sir (title)
monstral: monstra + l
monstrar: see mostrar
mont: see mon
montada: ascent, rising
montagna: mountain
montar: to go up, ascend, mount, climb
monumen: monument, tomb
morcel: mouthful, morsel
mordre: to bite
morgue: see monegue
morir, murir: to die
morran: 3 pl. fut. morir
morretz: 2 pl. fut. morir
morria: 3 sg. cond. A morir
mors: bite; penre a ... : to bite
mort: death
mort: past part. morir; nom. pl.: the dead
mort: 3 sg. pres. ind. mordre
mortal: mortal
mortificacion: mortification
mostela: weasel
mostelon: little weasel
mostrar, mous-, mons-: to show, point out
mot: word

mot, mout: see molt
mǫu: 3 sg. pres. mover
moustrar: see mostrar
movemen(t): movement, motive, inspiration
mover, mǫure: to move, impel; vr.: to move, stir
mudar: to change; moult; remove, carry off
muęira: 1 and 3 sg. pres. subj. morir
multiplicar: to multiply
murý: 3 sg. pret. morir
musa: Muse
musarda, f: silly
mut, f. muda: mute

Nais: 3 sg. pres. naisser
náisser: to be born
nasquęt: 3 sg. pret. naisser
nat: past part. naisser
nativitat: birth
natura: nature
natural: natural
naturalmen(s): naturally
nat(z): past part. naisser
nau: ship
necessitat: necessity
negar: to deny, refuse
nẹgre: black
negụn: none, not any, no one, any
neienz: see nien(t)
nẹis: even, not even
ni, nis: nest
ni: neither, nor; and
nien(t): nothing; adv.: in no way
nis: see ni
noble: noble
noel: see novel
noig: see nueg
noirir: to nourish, bring up, take care of
nolh: non + li
nom: name
nombre: number
nomnar: to name, enunciate
nona: ọra ... : noon
nonqua: never
nons: non + nos
not, obl. pl. nos: knot
nǫta: note
nǫu, f. nova: new; de ... : again

nǫvas: news
novęl, noel: new, rare
noveṇ: ninth
nozar: to knot
nozer: to injure, hurt, trouble
nuallor: less precious
nuallọs: lazy, incompetent
nuęg, nuech, nuet, nuǫch, nuoit, noig: night
nul(h), lunh: none, not any; some
núpcias: nuptials, wedding, marriage
nut, f. nuda: naked

ǫ: it, him
ǫ, oz: or
o: see on
obedieṇ: obedient
obediencia: obedience
obẹrt: past part. obrir
obezir: to obey
oblidar, vr.: to forget
oblit: forgetfulness, oversight
ǫbra: work
obrar: to work
ǫbri: 3 sg. pres. ind. obrir
obrir: to open
ǫbs: see ops
odorans: fragrant
offendre: to offend, injure
ǫlh, ǫil, uǫl, uęl(h): eye; ... de vẹir: kind of bird
olifan, orifan: elephant
om(n)e, nom. sg. om: man; one (impersonal subject)
omnia; per ... secula seculorum (Latin): for ever and ever
omnipotent: omnipotent
oṇ, ou: where, whence, when
onęst: decent, modest, chaste
onestat: decency, modesty, chastity
onor: honor; title; empire
onrar: to honor
ǫps, obs: need; a ... de: on behalf of
ǫr: edge
ọra: hour; tọta ... : always; qual ... que, qu'oras que: whenever
oracioṇ, -tioṇ: prayer
orar: to pray
oratǫri: oratory, place of prayer
orb: see orp
ordenar: to order, compose, arrange
orgǫlh, -guęlh: pride

orgolhọs, er-, -gulhọs: proud, haughty
orifan: see olifan
original: original
ǫrp, orb: blind
ǫst: host, army
ostar: to take away, remove, dismiss
otracujador: trespasser, presumptuous person
otracujamen: outrage, excess, presumption
ou: see on
ovẹlha: sheep, ewe
oz: see o

Paire: father
páisser: to feed, nourish
palais, -latz: palace
palla: straw
palm: palm, hand-span
paṇ: bread
panar: to steal
pantẹra: panther
paoṇ: peacock
paọr: fear, fright
par: peer, equal; mate, companion; adj. even
par: 3 sg. pres. ind. parer
paradi(e)s: Paradise
parat: adorned, costumed, arrayed; fine
paraula, -ǫla: word
párcer: to spare
parec: 3 sg. pret. parer
parent: parent, relative
parer: to appear, seem, show
parẹt: wall
paria: fellowship, association, company
parladura: speech, style of speech
parlamẹn: parley, conversation, discussion
parlar: to speak
pars: 3 sg. pret. párcer
part: side, part, place, direction, quarter; a una ... : aside, away; de ... de: on behalf of
partida: part, portion; side; departure
partir: to leave, depart; divide, put away; vr.: to take leave
pas: see patz
pas: step, way; a ... de cọr: running
passar: to pass (over); cross
passioṇ: passion
pastor: shepherd
pastorę la, -turella: shepherdess; poetic genre

Patre nostre: Our Father (prayer, Latin)
patz, pas: peace
paubre: poor
pauc: little, a little, lowly; ... de: few
pauramen(s): poorly
pauretat: poverty
pauza, -sa: pause, rest, stop, repose
pauzar, -sar: to place, put; set (up); rest
pauzat: grave, calm
pe: foot
pęc: stupid
peccador, f. peccairitz: sinner; adj.: sinning, sinful
peccar: to sin
peccat: sin
pega: pitch
pei: Pi (Greek letter)
peirẹta: small stone
pẹis, peissọn: fish
Peitieys: Poitiers
pejor: worse, worst
pęl: skin
pel(l)icạn: pelican
pels: per + los
pena: pain, punishment; a penas: hardly, barely
penar: to grieve, suffer; take trouble, strive
pendre: to hang
penedẹncia, -denza, penidẹncia, penitẹncia: penitence; penance
penedens: penitent
penre, prendre: to take, accept; ... a: to begin; ... garda: to heed, be careful
pensa: thought
pensar, pessar: to think; noun: thought, thoughts
pensier: thought
per: through, by, for; intensifies following adj. or vb.; ... pur tan: as long as, provided that
percassar, pro-, vr.: to strive for, seek
pęrda: loss
perdemẹn: loss, ruin, damnation
perdiciọn: perdition
perdigọn: young partridge
perdis, -itz: partridge
perdọn: pardon; permission; indulgence
perdonar: to pardon
pęrdre: to lose
perfaig, -fait: expert, connoisseur
perjuri: perjury, disloyalty
permaner: to remain
perǫ: however, therefore

perpensar, also vr.: to reflect, ponder
persęgre, perseguir: to persecute
perseverar: to persevere
persona: person
pęrt: 3 sg. pres. ind. perdre
pertusar: to pierce
pesant: a ... : heavy
pesat: thought, worry, concern; venir a ... : to trouble
pęssa: piece, while: a cap de ...: after a while
pessar: see pẹnsar
petit: (a) little
pezada: footprint, track
piatat: see pietat
pic: woodpecker; pick, pike
picar: to peck
pietat, piatat: pity, piety
pieuzęla, -ssela: maiden
piga: magpie
plac: 3 sg. pret. plazer
plag: dispute
plaga, plaia: wound
plagar: to wound
plager: see plazer
plaia: 3 sg. pres. subj. plazer
plaia, noun: see plaga
plaissẹs: 3 pl. impf. subj. planher
planh, plang: lament, dirge
plánher: to mourn, weep (for); vr.: to complain
planięr: full, plenary
plantar: to plant, place, stick
plazer, plaire, plager: to please, charm; noun: pleasure, favor; lyric genre
plegar: to bend, fold
plẹn: full
plomb: lead
plọr: weeping
plorar: to weep, mourn
pluma: feather
plus, pus: more
pluvięr: plover
pǫbol: people
pǫc: 3 sg. pret. poder
poder: to be able; noun: power, military force
poderọs: powerful
poestat: power; chief magistrate
poguẹs: 3 sg. impf. subj. poder

pogut: past part. poder
poinnher: see ponher
poirá: 3 sg. fut. poder
poirás: 2 sg. fut. poder
poiria: 3 sg. cond. A poder
poirian: 3 pl. cond. A poder
pọis, pos, puẹis, pus, pueissa: then, accordingly
pọl: chicken, chick
polẹt: young bird
pọls: dust
polsar: to strike, touch
pom, poma: apple, fruit
pom(i)ẹr: apple tree, fruit tree
pon: bridge
ponchura: puncture
ponha: delay
pọnher, pọin(n)her: to prick
ponre: to lay (an egg)
porẹtz: 2 pl. fut. poder
poria: 3 sg. cond. A poder
pọrta: door, gate
portar: to carry, bring, bear, wear
portiẹr: doorman, gatekeeper, porter
pos: see pois
pọs: 3 sg. pret. ponre
possesion: possession
pọst: past part. ponre
pọt: 3 sg. pres. ind.: poder
pọtden: 3 pl. pres. ind. poder
pọtz: well
prebọst: provost, minister
prẹc: prayer, entreaty
prẹc: 1 sg. pres. ind. and 3 sg. pres. subj.: pregar
preclar: very bright
preg(u)ar: to pray, entreat, woo, ask, request
pre(i)son: prison
premieir, etc.: see primier
prendre: see penre
pren(h)s: pregnant
prepauzar: to propose
prẹ(i)ron: 3 pl. pret. penre
pres: see pretz
prẹs, adv.: near
prẹs: 3 sg. pret. and past part. penre
presentamen(s): closely; in the presence of
prẹtz, prez, pres: worth, value; prestige, status, dignity, nobility

prẹza: prey
prẹza: past part. f. penre
prẹzan: honorable
prezar: to prize, value, account; have regard for
prezent: present; a ...: now, at once; publicly
prezicar: to preach
prim: first; intelligent, clever, fine
primamens: cleverly, intelligencly
primas: at first
primiẹr, -ieir, premier, pru-: first; de ... :   at first
primiẹ(i)ramẹn: in the first place; above all
princip: prince
privadanza, -sa: intimacy, familiarity
privat, f. privada: intimate, familiar, unreserved, informal;
   isolated; well-known
pro: see proṇ, pro(s)
proamen: test, trial, experiment
proar, prohar, provar: to test, try, prove
prob: see prop
procassar: see percassar
proensal: Provençal
profẹrre: to proffer, offer
profẹtizar: to prophesy
profiẹch: profit, benefit, good
promẹs: 3 sg. pret. and past part. prometre
promẹtre: to promise
promẹzia: 3 sg. impf. ind. prometre
proṇ: profit, advantage, interest, utility; sufficiency;
   adv.: enough, much
prọp, prob (de): near, about, with
prọpri: proper, own
prọpriamen(s): properly, correctly
pro(s): honorable, strong, excellent, noble: pl. gentry,
   worthy people
provat: tried, familiar
prozom: gentleman, good citizen
pruẹsme: neighbor
prumier: see primier
pudir: to smell, stink
pudor: stench
puẹg, puet: hill
puẹis, pueissa: see pois
puẹsc: 1 sg. pres. ind. poder
puesca: 1 or 3 sg., pres. subj. poder
pujar: to climb, mount
pur: pure; adv.: only, even; see also per ... tan
pus: see plus, pois

puscam: 1 pl. pres. subj. poder
puscatz: 2 pl. pres. subj. poder

Q-: see qu-, c-
qon: see com
qu-: see also c-
qual: see cal, caler
quandí: white
quandius que: as long as
quant, quand: see cant
quar: see car
quaranta: forty
quart, qart: fourth
quascun: see cascun
quastiazon: correction
quatre: see catre
que, ques, quez, qued, relative pron. and conj.: that, who, which, etc.; que que: however; per ... : why
quei: que + i
quetz: que + i etz (definite article)
quelh: que + li
quęrre, querer, querir: to seek, long for
ques: see que
questioṇ: question, subject
quet: que + te
quetz: que + etz (definite article)
quez: see que
quezẹssan: 3 pl. impf. subj. querre
qui, ki: relative and interrogative pronoun: who, whom; whoever
quis: 3 sg. pret. querre
quo: see com
quọras que: whenever

Raison, -zon: see razon
rallegrar: to make happy; vr.: to cheer up
ram: branch
rancura: rancor, chagrin, wrath
rancurar, -gurar: to protest, recriminate; be displeased, resent
randọla: swallow
randoloṇ: little swallow
rascondre: see rescondre
rason: see razon
rasonar: see razonar
rauba: robe; booty, spoil; larceny; raubas: clothing
raubimen: rapture, ecstasy

raubir: to carry away, enrapture
razoṇ, rai-, -son: subject, theme, argument, matter; discourse; story, message; reason
razonamẹn: discussion, discourse; explanation, excuse
razonar: to reason, discourse, discuss
re: see ren
recẹbre, -ssebre: to receive
recẹup: 3 sg. pret. recebre
reclamar: to call on, appeal
recon(n)ọc: 3 sg. pret. reconoisser
reconogut: past part. reconoisser
reconọisser: to recognize; vr.: to come to; repent
recontar: to tell, relate
red: 3 sg. pres. ind. redre
redẹmer, -ir: to redeem; atone for
redemcioṇ, -encioṇ: redemption
redemptor: redeemer
redems: past part. redemer
redrá: 3 sg. fut. redre
rę̣dre: see rendre
refug: refuge
regardar: to look at
rẹge: stiff
rę̣ge: 3 sg. pres. ind. regir
regioṇ: region, province
regir: to rule, reign; vr.: to behave, comport oneself
regisme: kingdom, regime
regnar: to rule; dwell, live
rẹgne: kingdom
regularmen: regularly, normally
rẹi: king
religioṇ: religion, religious order
reluzir: to shine, glitter
remanẹn: rest, remainder
remaner: to remain
remembranza, -sa: remembrance, memory
remembrar, rennembar, to remember
remẹtre: to put back, replace
remirar: to look at
reṇ, nom. sg. rẹs: thing, creature; anything, nothing; gran ... de: much, many, a lot
renda: rent, income
rendre, rę̣dre: to return, give up, give back; ... razó: to give account
renegar: to deny, forswear
renhar: to reign; act, behave; live
rennembar: see remembrar

renoirir: to nourish again, in return
renomada: renown
renovelar: to renew
renovięr: usurer
repairar: to go to, return to, end in
repaus: rest, repose
repauzar, -sar: to rest
repentir, vr.: to repent
repetir: to repeat
reprendre: to reprove
reprẹs: past part. reprendre
reprẹs: embroidered
reproar: to reprove, reproach
reptar: to accuse
requęrre: to claim, demand, ask, seek
requ(i)ęr: 3 sg. pres. ind. requerre
res: see ren
rescondre, rascundre: to hide
rescọs: past part. rescondre
resegar: to crawl
respięg: respect, reference
resplandens: resplendent, shining
respondre: to answer
responsion: answer, response
respọs, respǫst: past part. respondre; noun: answer; refrain
respọs: 3 sg. pret. respondre
retenc: 3 sg. pret. retener
retenensa: restraint
retener: to retain, hold back
retenga: 3 sg. pres. subj. retener
retengut: past part. retener
retornar: to return; come to, revive
retraire: to report, tell
retroensa, retroncha: verse with refrain
revelatioṇ: revelation
revelar: to reveal
reverẹncia: reverence
revęrs: backward, perverse
revezer: to see again
revięu: 3 sg. pres. ind. reviure
reviure: to bring back to life, revive
riba: bank, shore, edge
ric: noble, powerful, wealthy
ricor: nobility, power, prominence; arrogance
rime: rhyme
riquẹza: wealth, riches, nobility

rire: to laugh
rǫda: wheel; clump, thicket
rọi, rog, f. roia: red
romaṇ: narrative verse
Romania: the Greek Empire
rǫt: stiff (French influence)
rugir: to roar

'S: for es, from esser
sa: see san, sai
sabata: shoe, boot
saber: to know, know how; noun: wisdom, knowledge, learning, science
sabloṇ: sand
saborọs: tasty
sacrament: sacrament; oath
sacrifizi: sacrifice
sadọl: satiated
sagęl: seal, stamp
sagelar: to seal
sa(i): here
sai: 1 sg. pres. ind. saber
sal, salf, salv: healthy, whole; saved
salamandra: salamander
sal(h)ir: to spring forth, go out, come out, rise; jump; ... en estant: jump to one's feet
saltęri, sau-: psalter
salut: health, welfare; greeting, salutation
salv: see sal
salvador: savior
salvamenṭ: salvation, safety
salvar: to save
salvatge, salvage, f. salvaga, -átia: savage, wild; shy, timid
saṇ, nom. sg. sas: healthy, sound
sanament: soundly
sanc: blood
sancnọs: bloody, blood-stained
sanct, sanh, sanṭ: holy, saintly; noun: saint
sap: 3 sg. pres. ind. saber
sapcha: 3 sg. pres. subj. saber
sapchatz: 2 pl. pres. subj. or impv. saber
sapiẹncia: wisdom
sapja: 3 sg. pres. subj. saber
sapjas: 2 sg. pres. subj. saber
saput, f. sapuda: past part. saber
Sarazịn: Saracen, Moor
sas: see san
sason: see sazon

satan: devil, imp
saubes: 3 sg. impf. subj. saber
saubia: 3 sg. impf. ind. saber
saubut, -put: past part. saber
saup: 3 sg. pret. saber
saupes: 3 sg. imp. subj. saber
sautar: to jump
sauteri: see salteri
savi: wise, learned, noun: sage, wise man
saviamen(s): wisely
saviza: wisdom
sazon, sason: season, time; a ... : opportunely
sc(h)ala: ladder, stair
sc(h)apla: shoulder
sciensa: science, doctrine
scola: school
sebellir: to bury
sec: 3 sg. pres. ind. segre
secret: secret; secretamens: secretly
seglar: secular, worldly, lay
segle: world; menar ... : to make a noise
segon: second
segon (que): according to, as (to)
segre, seguir: to follow
segurtat: security: assurance, safety
seinnhor, -er: see senhor
sel, sel- : see cel, cel-
semblant: appearance, expression, aspect; adj.: like, similar; per ... : likewise; far ... : to show, pretend
semblar: to seem, appear; resemble
semenar: to sow, seed
sempre: always
sen, nom. sens, senz: intelligence, wit, sense; wise thing; reason; meaning; purpose
sen: 3 sg. pres. ind. sentir
sench: past part. cenher
sener: see senhor
senescal: seneschal, steward
senhal: secret name, token
senher: see cenher
sen(h)or, seinnhor, nom. sg. sen(h)er, seinnher: lord
senhoril: lordly, dominating
senor: see senhor
sens: without
sentiment: feeling, sense, senses
sentir: to feel, perceive, hear
ser: evening

será: 3 sg. fut. es(s)er
serán: 3 pl. fut. es(s)er
serás: 3 sg. fut. es(s)er
sercar: see cercar
serena: siren
serẹs, serẹtz: 2 pl. fut. es(s)er
seria: 3 sg. cond. A es(s)er
sermoṇ: talk, word, conversation; sermon
serọr, nom. sg. sǫrre: sister
sęrp, serpẹn: serpent
serpentiṇ: serpentine
serra: a legendary fish
sertamen(s): certainly, assuredly
sęrtas: certainly, assuredly, certes
serteza: see certeza
servel: see cervel
servẹn, f. -venta, sir-: servant
serventes: see sirventes
servidor, nom. sg. servire: one who serves, servant; wooer
servir: to serve; vr. with de: to use, employ
ses: see sens
sęt: 3 sg. pres. ind. sezer
sezer: to sit, be situated; vr.: to sit (down)
si: if
si: and, then (often a pleonastic, untranslatable connective)
si: 3 sg. poss. adj.
sia: 1 or 3 sg. pres. subj. es(s)er
signe: see cigne
significar: to signify, mean
silh, sill: see cel
simi: monkey
símia: female monkey
simioṇ: young monkey
simple: simple
sirven: see serven
sirventẹs, ser-: lyric genre
sitọt: although, even if
sǫ, zo, czo: that (pronoun); per ... car: because
so: see son
sobeiraṇ: sovereign, supreme
sọbra, sobre: over, on, upon
sobrebęl: most beautiful
sobrefǫrt: most strong, strongest
sobrehumaṇ: superhuman
sobremontar: to rise above
sobresilh: eyebrow

sobtamen(s), sop-: suddenly
sọbte, sop-: sudden, quick; adv.: suddenly
so(b)til: fine, delicate, clever, sharp
soen: see soven
sofertar, suf-: to suffer, undergo, endure, tolerate
sofrir, suf-: to suffer, endure, permit; grant, support
soissidar: to shake
sǫl: ground, earth
sọl, solẹlh: sun
sọl: alone, lone, solitary, only; ... que: provided that; ni ... : not even;... no: not at all, by no means
sǫla: footsole
sǫlamen(t): only
solás, solatz, sollatz: amusement, jest, mirth, diversion
solazar: to joke, sport, amuse, make merry
solelh: see sol
solempnitat, -ll-: solemnity
soler: to be accustomed
solẹza: solitude
solitari: solitary
sollempnitat: see sol-
sọlpre: sulphur
som: top, end
somsir: to submerge, destroy
son, sọn: 3 pl. pres. ind. es(s)er
sọn, nom. sg. sos: sound, melody
sopt-: see sobt-
sor, sorre: see seror
sọrd: deaf
sosmogut: moved, shocked, shaken
sospendre: to suspend
sospirar: to sigh
sostẹn: 3 sg. pres. ind. sostener
soste(n)c: 3 sg. pret. sostener
sostener: to sustain, endure, permit
sotil: see sobtil
soufrir: see sofrir
so(v)ẹn: often
spina: thorn
stampida: see estampida
star: see estar
su: on, upon
suau: soft, gentle, sweet
sufęrt: past part. sofrir
sufertar: see sofertar
suffrenza: abstention
sufrir: see sofrir
sul: su + lo (article)

sun(t): 3 pl. pres. ind. es(s)cr
suor: sweat
superbia: pride
sus: up, over, above, on, upon

Taign: 3 sg. pres. ind. tanher
taill, de ... : proper, opportune, "comme il faut"
tal: such (a); per ... que: so that
talan(t), -len(t): will, desire, inclination
talhar: to cut (off)
talpa: mole
tánher: to be suitable, appropriate
tan(t): so, so much, so many; ... com, ... quan: as long as; pur ... que: if only, provided that
tantost: soon, early, at once
tapar: to block (up)
tart: late
taur: bull
te: see ten
tei: Theta (Greek letter)
Teiric, nom. sg. -ix: Theodoric
teiser: to weave
temensa: fear, modesty, respect
temer: to fear
temeros: fearful
tempesta: tempest, agitation; far ... : to harass
temple: temple
tem(p)s: time, season; tense (gram.)
temptacion: temptation
temptar: to tempt
ten: 3 sg. pres. ind. tener
tenc: 3 sg. pret. tener
tenebra: darkness, shadow
tenebros: dark
tener, tenir: to hold, keep, possess, have; ... pro: to avail, be useful; tenga se, si·s vol: let him hold on as he can
tenga: 3 sg. pres. subj. tener
tengut, f. -guda: past part. tener
tenson: dispute, contention; rhymed debate
terra: earth, ground, land
terrenal, terrestri: terrestrial, earthly
Tervisana: of Treviso (f.)
terz: third
testa: head
tiera: order, series
tirament: ecstasy, exaltation

tirar: to pull, draw, drag; displease, carry away
tọc: touch, trace
tocar: to touch, move
tọlc: 3 sg. pret. tolre
tolre, toler: to take away, deprive, rob
tolgues: 3 sg. impf. subj. toldre
tolles: 2 sg. pres. ind. tolre
tollon: 3 sg. pres. ind. tolre
ton: tune, melody
tondre: to clip, shear
tọr: tower
torbessalh: whirlwind
tormen, tur-: torment
tormentar: to torment
tornada: envoi of a poem
tornar: to turn, return; give back, replace; become; ... a: to do again
tortre: turtle-dove
tọst: soon, forthwith
tostemps: always, constantly, forever
tọt, tout, m. pl. tuit, tuig, tuich, f. tota, toda: all; each, every; del ... : entirely; de ... en ... : mightily; ... via: constantly; per ... everywhere
traazon: treason
trabucar: to pierce; fall through
trach, trait: past part. traire
traga: 1 and 3 sg. pres. subj. traire
tractar: to treat of, deal with
tradar: to betray
traes: 3 sg. impf. subj. traire
trahir: see traïr
traia: 3 sg. pres. subj. traire
traïr, trahir: to betray
traire: to pull, drag, draw (out); deprive of
trais: 3 sg. pret. traire
trames: 3 sg. pret. and past part. trametre
trametre: to send
tras: through
trasia: 3 sg. impf. ind. traire
traspassar: to trespass, sin; neglect
trassaillir: to exceed
trastut: all; adv.: thoroughly
traucar: to pierce, bore
trazia: 3 sg. impf. ind. traire
trebaill: work, toil, torture
trebalhar, vr.: to labor, toil
tres: three
trida: tigress

tridọn: tiger cub
trinitat: trinity
trist: sad
tristẹssa, tristicia: sadness; chagrin
tristor: sadness, wrath
tro: up to, as far as; ... que: until
trobador, nom. sg. trobaire: troubadour
trobar: to find: compose verses
trop: very (much), too (much)
tropẹl: flock
truẹga: sow
tug, tuich, tuit: see tot
turmen: see tormen

U: see un
ubẹrt: past part. obrir
udolar: to howl
uẹi: today
uel(h): see oil
ultra: beyond
um: see un
umaṇ: human
umilitat: humility; indulgence
uṇ, um: a, an; one
unicọrn: unicorn
uol: see oil
uọu: egg
upa: hoppoe, lapwing
upẹl: young hoopoe
us: usage, custom, use
uzar: to use; frequent

Va: 3 sg. pres. ind. anar
valc: 3 sg. pret. valer
valen: worthy, brave, noble
valensa: worth, virtue, valor
valer: to be worth, worthy; avail
vallat: valley
valor: worth, virtue, valor, merit
valvasor: see vavassor
van: 3 pl. pres. ind. anar
vanetat: vanity
vas, ves, vers: toward
vavas(s)or, valv-... : vassal (of a lord); nobleman
vay: see va
ve: 3 sg. pres. ind. of vezer, or venir
vea: 3 sg. pres. subj. vezer
vẹg, vei: 1 sg. pres. ind. vezer

vegilia: see vigilia
veion: 3 pl. pres. subj. vezer
veire: glass
veiria: 3 sg. cond. A vezer
veitz: 2 pl. pres. ind. vezer
vejatz: 2 pl. pres. subj. vezer
vejayre, -geyre, a ... : apparent, evident, seeming
vel, v(i)elh: old
velhar, -llar: to wake, watch (over); stay awake
venaire: hunter
venc, veng: 1 sg. pres. ind. and 3 sg. pret. venir
vengron: 3 pl. pret. venir
vengues: 3 sg. impf. subj. venir
venguesson: 3 pl. impf. subj. venir
vengut: past part. venir
venir: to come; s'en ... : to come away
venjar, vr.: to avenge, take vengeance
venques: 3 sg. impf. subj. venser
venser: to conquer, vanquish; win
ventre: belly, womb
ver: true
verai: true, loyal, sincere
verayamen: truly
verba: text (of a poem)
verge: virgin
verginitat: virginity
vergonha, -ogna, -oigna: shame
veritat, vertat: truth
verme: worm
vers: line of verse; lyric genre
vers, ves: see vas
vert: green
vertat: see veritat
vertut: virtue
ves: see vas, vetz
vescomte, nom. sg. -coms: viscount
vespre: evening
vestimen(t): clothing, dress
vestir: to dress, wear; noun: dress, clothing
vetz, ves: time, occasion
veya: 3 sg. pres. subj. vezer
vezer, veire, vezir: to see
vezin, viz-: neighbor; neighboring
vi: 1 or 3 sg. pret. vezer
via: away
vianda: food, nourishment, meal
vibra: viper, snake
vibron: little viper

vic: 3 sg. pret. vezer
vici: vice
vida, vita: life
viel(h): see vel(h)
vięu: 3 sg. pres. ind. viure
vieure: see viure
vieu: see viu
vigília, veg-: vigil, eve
vigorọs: vigorous, robust
vil: base, bad, vile, vulgar
vila: villa, town
vilaṇ: churl; person of low degree
vilhẹza: baseness, cowardice
viṇ: wine
viltat: vileness, baseness
vio̧la: musical instrument
violar: to play the viola
viroṇ: 3 pl. pret. vezer
vis: face
visitar: to visit
visquęra: 3 sg. cond. B viure
visquęroṇ: 3 pl. pret. viure
vissoṇ: 3 pl. impf. subj. vezer
vist: past part. vezer
vista: sight, vision
vit: 3 sg. pret. vezer
vita: see vida
viu, vięu, f. viva: alive, living, live
viure, viuri, vięure, vivir: to live; noun: living
vi(v)acięr: lively
vizin: see vezin
vọill: 1 sg. pres. ind. voler
volar: to fly; en volans: in flight
vọlc, volg: 3 sg. pret. voler
voler: to wish, want, be willing; ... ben: to love; ... mal: to hate
vọlgroṇ: 3 pl. pret. voler
volontat: will, goodwill, desire, wish
volontięr, -teir: willing, eager
volontięrs: willingly, gladly
volontọs: desirous, eager
volrás: 2 sg. fut. voler
vọlp: fox
vọls: 2 sg. pres. ind. voler
vostro: Italian for vostre
vọtz: voice
voutor: vulture

vuęlh, vuell, vueill: 1 sg. pres. ind. voler
vuęlha, vuella: 1 and 3 sg. pres. subj. voler

Yęst: 2 sg. pres. ind. es(s)er

Zo: see sǫ

BIBLIOGRAPHY

This selective bibliography indicates some of the many works which the reader may profitably consult on the OP language in general and on points corresponding to our specific chapters.

Normalized SP Spelling

Väänänen, Veikko, reporter. "Corpus des troubadours." Union Académique Internationale, *Compte rendu de la quarante-huitième session annuelle du comité*, 98-105. Brussels: UAI, 1974.

Smith, Nathaniel B. "The Normalization of Old Provençal Spelling: Criteria and Solutions." In *Studia occitanica in memoriam Paul Remy*, edited by Hans-Erich Keller et al., forthcoming.

Dictionaries

Harris, Marvyn Roy. *Index inverse du "Petit dictionnaire provençal-français."* Heidelberg: Carl Winter, 1981.

Levy, Emil. *Petit dictionnaire provençal-français* 5th ed. Heidelberg: Carl Winter, 1973.

________. *Provenzalisches Supplement-Wörterbuch.* 8 vols. Leipzig, 1894-1924. Rpt. Geneva: Slatkine, 1973.

Raynouard, François. *Lexique roman.* 6 vols. Paris, 1836-44. Rpt. Geneva: Slatkine, 1977.

Medieval Provençal Grammars

Gatien-Arnoult, Adolphe-Félix, ed. *Las flors del Gay Saber, estiers dichas Las Leys d'Amors.* Paris and Toulouse, 1841-43. Rpt. (3 vols. in 2). Geneva: Slatkine, 1977. (Treatise by Guilhem Molinier.)

Marshall, J.H., ed. *The "Donatz proensals" of Uc Faidit.* Univ. of Durham Publications. London: Oxford University Press, 1969.

________, ed. *The "Razos de trobar" of Raimon Vidal and Associated Texts.* Univ. of Durham Publications. London: Oxford Univ. Press, 1972.

Modern Grammars of OP

Anglade, Joseph. *Grammaire de l'ancien provençal.* Paris: C. Klincksieck, 1921.

Cremonesi, Carla. *Nozioni de grammatica storica provenzale.* 3d ed. Varese and Milano: Istituto Editoriale Cisalpino, 1967.

Crescini, Vicenzo. *Manuale per l'avviamento agli studi provenzali.* 3d ed. Milan: Ulrico Hoepli, 1926.

Grandgent, Charles H. *An Outline of the Phonology and Morphology of Old Provençal.* Rev. ed. Boston: D. C. Heath, 1905.

Jensen, Frede. *From Vulgar Latin to Old Provençal.* Univ. of North Carolina Studies in the Romance Languages and Literatures, no. 120. Chapel Hill: Univ. of North Carolina Press, 1972.

Mahn, Carl August Friedrich. *Grammatik und Wörterbuch der altprovenzalischen Sprache.* Vol. 1, *Lautlehre und Wortbiegungslehre* (no more published). Köthen: P. Schettler, 1885.

Mok, Q.I.M. *Manuel pratique de morphologie d'ancien occitan.* Muiderberg, Holland: Dick Coutinho, 1977.

Pellegrini, Gian Battista. *Appunti di grammatica storica del provenzale.* 3d ed. Pisa: Libreria Goliardica, 1960.

Roncaglia, Aurelio. *La lingua dei trovatori.* Rome: Edizioni dell'Ateneo, 1965.

Schultz-Gora, Oscar. *Altprovenzalisches Elementarbuch.* 6th ed. Heidelberg: Carl Winter, 1973.

Other Works Pertinent to OP Grammar in General

Appel, Carl. *Provenzalische Chrestomathie.* 6th ed. Leipzig, 1930. Rpt. Hildesheim and New York: Georg Olms, 1971. ("Abriss der Formenlehre," pp. VII-XLI.)

Bourciez, Edouard. *Eléments de linguistique romane.* 4th ed. Paris: C. Klincksieck, 1956. ("L'ancien français et le provençal," pp. 285-393.)

Grafström, Åke. *Etude sur la morphologie des plus anciennes chartes languedociennes.* Romanica Stockholmiensia, no. 4. Stockholm: Almquist & Wiksell, 1968.

Hamlin, Frank R., Peter T. Ricketts, and John Hathaway. *Introduction à l'étude de l'ancien provençal.* Geneva: Droz, 1967. (Pp. 13-36 of the Introduction deal with language.)

Lafont, Robert. *La phrase occitane*. Publications de la Faculté des Lettres et Sciences Humaines de l'Université de Montpellier, no. 28. Paris: Presses Universitaires de France, 1967. (Syntax, with some reference to the Middle Ages.)

________, ed. *Trobar*. Montpellier: Centre d'Etudes Occitanes, 1972. ("La langue du trobar," pp. 9-23).

Lewent, Kurt. "Bemerkungen zur provenzalischen Sprache und Literatur." *Neuphilologische Mitteilungen* 38 (1937): 1-69.

Mejean, Suzanne, ed. *La chanson satirique provençale au moyen-âge*. Paris: Nizet, 1971. ("Introduction grammaticale," pp. 20-74.)

Ronjat, Jules. *Grammaire istorique des parlers provençaux modernes*. 4 vols. Montpellier: Société des Langues Romanes, 1930-41.

Sutherland, Dorothy R. "Flexions and Categories in Old Provençal." *Transactions of the Philological Society*, 1959 (published 1960): 25-70.

Chapter 1

Bec, Pierre. *La langue occitane*. 2d ed. Que sais-je?, no. 1059. Paris: Presses Universitaires de France, 1967.

________. *Manual pratique de philologie romane*. 2 vols. Paris: Picard, 1970-71.

Brunel, Clovis, ed. *Les plus anciennes chartes en langue provençale*. Paris, 1926. Rpt. Geneva: Slatkine, 1973. Also *Supplément*: Paris: A. et. J. Picard, 1952.

Jeanroy, Alfred. *La poésie lyrique des troubadours.* Toulouse, 1934. Rpt. (2 vols. in 1). New York, N.Y.: AMS, 1974.

Pfister, Max. "Die Anfänge der altprovenzalischen Schriftsprache." *Zeitschrift für romanische Philologie* 86 (1970): 305-23.

Rohr, Rupprecht. "Untersuchungen über den Ausgangsdialekt der altprovenzalischen Dichtungssprache." *Estudis Romànics* 13 (1963-68, published 1970): 245-68.

Chapters 2-4: Pronunciation and Orthography; Vowels and Semivowels; Consonants

Appel, Carl. *Provenzalische Lautlehre.* Leipzig: O.R. Reisland, 1918.

Erdmannsdörffer, Ernst. *Reimwörterbuch der Trobadors.* Berlin: E. Ebering, 1897.

Grafström, Åke. *Etude sur la graphie des plus anciennes chartes languedociennes.* Uppsala: Almqvist & Wiksell, 1958.

Hengesbach, Joseph. *Beitrag zur Lehre von der Inclination im Provenzalischen.* Ausgaben und Abhandlungen, vol. 37. Diss. Marburg: N.G. Elwert, 1885.

Kutscha, Kurt. *Das sogenannte n-mobile im Alt- und Neuprovenzalischen.* Romanistische Arbeiten, 21. Halle/Saale: M. Niemeyer, 1934.

Monfrin, Jacques. "Notes sur le chansonnier provençal *C*." In *Recueil de travaux offert à M. Clovis Brunel* 2:292-311. Paris: Société de l'Ecole des Chartes, 1955.

Pfister, Max. "Beiträge zur altprovenzalischen Grammatik." *Vox Romanica* 17 (1958): 281-362. (Vowels, consonants, problems.)

Pfützner, Ferdinand. *Ueber die Aussprache des provenzalischen A.* Diss. Halle/Saale: C. Colbatzky, 1884.

Pleines, August. *Hiat und Elision im Provenzalischen.* Ausgaben und Abhandlungen, vol. 50. Diss. Marburg: N.G. Elwert, 1886.

Tavera, Antoine. "Graphies normatives et graphies casuelles de l'ancien provençal." In *Mélanges d'histoire littéraire, de linguistique et de philologie romanes offerts à Charles Rostaing* 2: 1075-94. Liège: Association des Romanistes de l'Université de Liège, 1974.

Chapters 5-7: Nouns; Articles; Adjectives

Betz, Manfred L. *Aussagegehalt und Syntax deverbaler Adjective im Altprovenzalischen.* Romanistik, no. 4. Diss. Munich: Schäuble, 1975.

Jensen, Frede. *The Old Provençal Noun and Adjective Declension.* Etudes Romanes de l'Université d'Odense, vol. 9. Odense, Denmark: Odense University Press, 1976.

Kendrick, Denise. "The Morphology and Syntax of the Articles in Old Provençal." Ph.D. diss., Univ. of Colorado, Boulder, 1976. Ann Arbor: University Microfilms, 1979.

Neunkirchen, Hans. "Zur Teilungsformel im Provenzalischen." *Zeitschrift für romanische Philologie* 42 (1922): 35-68, 158-91.

Chapters 8-9: Pronouns, Adjectives

Bohnhardt, Wilhelm. *Das Personal-Pronomen im Altprovenzalischen*. Ausgaben und Abhandlungen, vol. 74. Diss. Marburg: N.G. Elwert, 1888.

Bourciez, Jean. "Note sur le relatif analytique en vieux provençal." *Revue des Langues Romanes* 67 (1933-36), 471-87.

Elsner, Alfred von. *Ueber Form und Verwendung des Personalpronomens im Altprovenzalischen*. Diss. Kiel: H. Fiencke, 1886.

Kjellman, Hilding. *Etude sur les termes démonstratifs en provençal*. Göteborgs Högskolas Årsskrift, no. 34. Göteborg: Elander, 1928.

Lewent, Kurt. "Three Little Problems of Old Provençal Syntax." In *French and Provençal Lexicography: Essays Presented to Honor Alexander Herman Schutz*, edited by Urban T. Holmes and Kenneth R. Scholberg, 164-82. Columbus: Ohio State Univ. Press, 1964. (The first two "problems" are omission and pleonasm of relative pronouns.)

Lipton, Wallace S. "Imposed Verb Pronominalization in Medieval French and Provençal." *Romance Philology* 14 (1960-61): 111-37.

Mériz, Diana Teresa. "Observations on Object Pronoun Collocation with Finite Verb-Parts in Medieval Occitan (to 1300)." *Romania* 99 (1978), 145-82. 289-310.

Chapters 10-12: Verbs

Betz. See Bibliography, chapters 5-7. (Includes -*dor* words, 12.4.)

Dittes, Rudolf. "Ueber den Gebrauch der Participien und des Gerundiums im Altprovenzalischen." Separata from *Programm der Staatsrealschule in Budweis*. Budweis: author, 1902.

________. "Ueber den Gebrauch des Infinitivs im Altprovenzalischen." *Romanische Forschungen* 15 (1903): 1-40.

Fischer, August. *Der Infinitiv im Provenzalischen*. Ausgaben und Abhandlungen, vol. 6. Diss. Marburg: N.G. Elwert, 1883.

Harnisch, Albert. *Die altprovenzalische Praesens- und Imperfect-Bildung mit Ausschluss der A-Conjugation*. Ausgaben und Abhandlungen, vol. 40. Diss. Marburg: N.G. Elwert, 1886.

Henrichsen, Arne Johan. *Les phrases hypothêtiques en ancien occitan*. Bergen: John Grieg, 1955.

________. "Les deux conditionnels de l'ancien occitan." In *Actes du VIe Congrès International de Langue et de Littérature d'Oc* ... 2: 337-47. Montpellier: Centre d'Estudis Occitans, 1971.

Linder, Karl P. *Studien zur Verbalsyntax der ältesten provenzalischen Urkunden*. Tübinger Beiträge zur Linguistik, vol. 12. Tübingen, 1970. (Subjunctive as future; modal *dever*, *poder*, *voler*; conditional *qui*.)

Mann, Paul. *Das Participium Praeteriti im Altprovenzalischen*. Ausgaben und Abhandlungen, vol. 41. Diss. Marburg: N.G. Elwert, 1886.

Meyer, Karl Fr. Th. *Die provenzalische Gestaltung der mit dem Perfectstamm gebildeten Tempora des Lateinischen*. Ausgaben und Abhandlungen, vol. 12. Marburg: N.G. Elwert, 1884.

Meyer, Paul. "Les troisièmes personnes du pluriel en provençal." *Romania* 9 (1880): 192-215.

Moore, Clarence K. "The Use of the Subjunctive Mood in the Works of Six Mediaeval Provençal Lyric Poets." *Modern Language Notes* 23 (1908): 47-52.

Müller, Bodo. Die Herkunft der Endung -i in der 1. Person Singular Präsens Indikativ des provenzalischen Vollverbs. Diss. Erlangen, 1955.

Paden, William D., Jr., "L'emploi vicaire du présent verbal dans les plus anciens textes narratifs romans." *Atti del XIV Congresso Internazionale di Linguistica e Filologia Romanza* (1974) 4: 545-57. Naples: Macchiaroli, 1977. (Present tense with past meaning.)

Morgan, Raleigh, Jr. "Occitan Verbal Substantives in *-dor, -doira*." In *Italic and Romance Linguistic Studies in Honor of Ernst Pulgram*, edited by Herbert J. Izzo, 177-88. Amsterdam: John Benjamin, 1980.

Schmidt, Otto. *Ueber die Endungen des Praesens im Altprovenzalischen*. Diss. Strassburg. Darmstadt: C.W. Leske, 1887.

Skubić, Mitja. "Le passé simple et le passé composé dans la langue des troubadours." *Linguistica* (Ljubljana) 5 (1963): 61-70.

Wesenberg, Thor G. "The Contrary to Fact Condition in Provençal." *The Romanic Review* 22 (1931): 43-46.

________. "A Study of the Conditional and the Subjunctive in Provençal Narrative Poetry." Ph.D. diss., Harvard Univ., 1924.

________. "The Subjunctive in Provençal Narrative Poetry." *The Romanic Review* 24 (1933): 315-23.

Chapter 13: Other Parts of Speech and Syntactical Observations

Adams, Edward L. *Word-Formation in Provençal.* New York: Macmillan, 1913.

Grad, Anton. "Deux cas de l'inversion du sujet en ancien provençal." *Linguistica* 9 (1969): 3-11.

Kalepky, Theodor. "Koordinierende Verknüpfung negativer Sätze im Provenzalischen." *Zeitschrift für romanische Philologie* 32 (1908): 513-32.

Köcher, Edmund. "Beitrag zum Gebrauch der Praeposition 'de' im Provenzalischen." Diss. Marburg, 1888.

Lewent, Kurt. "A Phenomenon of Provençal Syntax: Parts of a Sentence without Reference to its Grammatical Subject." *Estudis Romànics* 8 (1961, published 1966): 219-43.

________. "A Special Use of the Preposition *a*." In "Three Little Problems ..." (see Bibliography, chapters 8-9), 171-80. ("Per lo castel a recobrar," etc.).

Linder, Karl P. "Per lo castel a recobrar": Un Problème de syntaxe provençale." In *Actes du VIe Congrès* ... (see Bibliography, chapters 10-12, Henrichsen, 2) 2:385-92.

Mériz, Diana Teresa. "Remarques sur l'ordre respectif des pronoms régimes conjoints en occitan médiéval." *Studia Neophilologica* 55 (1983):47-69.

Pape, Richard. *Die Wortstellung in der provenzalischen Prosaliteratur des XII. und XIII. Jahrhunderts.* Diss. Jena: J. Hoggfeld, 1883.

Price, Glanville. "Aspects de l'emploi des particules négatives en occitan." In *Actes du Xe Congrès International de Linguistique et de Philologie Romanes* 1:265-72. Paris: C. Klincksieck, 1965.

Schultz, Oscar. "Unvermitteltes Zusammentreten von zwei Adjektiven oder Participien im Provenzalischen." *Zeitschrift für romanische Philologie* 16 (1892): 513-17.

Shepard, William P. "Parataxis in Provençal." *PMLA* 21 (1906):519-74.

SELECTED INDEX OF TERMS AND CONCEPTS